Without books, history is silent, literature dumb, science crippled, thought and speculation at a standstill. Without books, the development of civilization would have been impossible. They are engines of change, windows on the world, and lighthouses erected in the sea of time. They are companions, teachers, magicians, bankers of the treasures of the mind. Books are humanity in print.

Barbara Tuchman

CONTENTS

Section Two   Academic Terms   205

Introduction   205

ACKNOWLEDGMENTS

I wish to thank the professional staff at Houghton Mifflin for their continued guidance and efficiency, specifically Lisa Kimball, Senior Sponsoring Editor; Peter Mooney, Development Editor, for his attention to every detail involved in this edition; Rachel Zanders, Associate Project Editor, for her expertise in bringing this edition to completion; and Sage Anderson, Editorial Assistant.

I wish to express my appreciation for all the reviewers, colleagues, students, and editors who have contributed so significantly to the previous editions of this text. For this new edition, I am specifically indebted to the following professors for their conscientious reviews of and suggestions for this book:

Rhonda Carroll of Pulaski Technical College

Dorothy D. Chase of Community College of Southern Nevada

Barbara E. Nixon of Salem Community College

Michele Renee Pajer of Gonzaga University

Stephen W. B. Rizzo of Bevill State Community College

Lois Ann Ryan of Manchester Community College

I'd like to extend a special thanks to Carolyn E. Gramling of Suffolk Community College—her corrections and suggestions were right on the mark.

Finally, I am extremely appreciative for the continued interest and encouragement I have received from colleagues, students, friends, and family.

R. Kent Smith

TO THE STUDENT

It is difficult to overemphasize the value of developing an extensive vocabulary: Not only do we use words to communicate, but we also do most of our thinking in words. Research also reveals that an extensive vocabulary is closely associated with outstanding grades. As a college student, you will discover that familiarity with the words used in your classes and textbooks will determine your ability to understand the material being discussed.

Fortunately, no one is born with a larger vocabulary than anyone else; those who possess an impressive vocabulary have made the necessary efforts to enlarge their knowledge of words. If you are willing to do likewise, the benefits of a broad vocabulary can be yours.

Although it is true that most of the words you know you learned in a natural, incidental manner as you matured, you must now make deliberate efforts to increase your stock of words if your vocabulary is to grow significantly. In fact, you will find that your college work will be easier and more meaningful if you endeavor to build your knowledge of words.

This book provides you with an excellent opportunity to increase your vocabulary in a practical, systematic, and comprehensive manner. **Section One** will deepen your understanding of common prefixes, suffixes, and roots, which, in turn, will help you to master the meanings of the numerous challenging words also presented in this section. **Section Two** is devoted to academic terms associated with many of the college subjects you are likely to elect or be required to take.

No doubt you will already be familiar with a number of the words, terms, and word parts included in this book, and others you will know vaguely. Most of them, however, will be new to you. Regardless of your present situation, your vocabulary will increase significantly with a conscientious effort on your part. As a result, your speaking, writing, reading, listening, and thinking abilities will grow, as will your ability to unlock the definitions of unknown words. These accomplishments will unquestionably enhance your chances for academic success in college—which is precisely what your instructor and I wish for you.

R. Kent Smith

BUILDING VOCABULARY FOR COLLEGE

WORD PARTS AND CHALLENGING WORDS

INTRODUCTION

WORD PARTS

Prefixes, suffixes, and roots are the major elements of words. Developing an under-standing of these elements and their meanings is an excellent first step to building a college-level vocabulary. These word parts are defined in this way:

A **prefix** is a word part added at the beginning of a word; a prefix can dramatically affect a word's meaning: correct—*in*correct; regard—*dis*regard.

A **suffix** is a word part added at the end of a word; a suffix can change a word's part of speech: jump (verb)—jump*er* (noun); poison (noun)—poison*ous* (adjective).

A **root** is the base part of a word that conveys the bulk of the word's meaning; a pre-fix and a suffix can be attached to a root to form variants of the root: *cred* (a root mean-ing "believe") + *in-* (a prefix meaning "not") + *-ible* (a suffix meaning "capable of ") = *incredible* (not capable of being believed).

Although word parts don't always reflect their usual meaning (*pre-*, for example, usually means "before," such as in *pre*view and *pre*caution, but this isn't true of *pre-* in *pre*cisely and *pre*varicate), they do consistently enough to make it worthwhile to master their common meanings. For example, you might encounter "monolithic column" in a reading assignment, with *monolithic* being an unfamiliar word to you. However, if you

Copyright © by Houghton Mifflin Company. All rights reserved.

know that the prefix *mono-* means "one," the root *lith* means "block of stone," and the suffix *-ic* means "having the characteristic of," you will be able to conclude that a "monolithic column" is a pillar made of a single block of stone.

Obviously, the ability to analyze unfamiliar words in the preceding way (referred to as **word analysis**) depends on a comprehensive understanding of prefixes, suffixes, and roots, an understanding you will have an opportunity to acquire by completing the thirty lessons in **Section One**.

DOING THE LESSONS FOR WORD PARTS

- Begin each lesson by carefully reading the sentences appearing after each word part, paying particular attention to the underlined element in the italicized word. In some instances, more than one element will be underlined to reflect what you have studied previously.

- Then select what you believe is the correct meaning for the word part by writing either **a** or **b** in the space provided.

- After you have done this for all ten word parts in each lesson, follow the directions for completing the four sets of exercises on the ensuing pages.

CHALLENGING WORDS

Mastering the meanings of the **challenging words** presented after each word parts lesson will help you comprehend material written on a college level because these words frequently appear in textbooks, newspapers, periodicals, and standardized tests. You will learn these words by applying your knowledge of word parts and by using contextual clues, that is, by studying the relationship between a challenging word and the other words surrounding it. Following are the types of contextual clues you will find particularly helpful:

- **Direct Definition**

  It's rare these days to see anyone wear a *monocle,* an eyeglass for just one eye?
  Intrinsic motivation is a desire for action coming from within an individual.
  (Both sentences provide straightforward definitions of the italicized words.)

- **Indirect Definition**

  Although the pain is not intense, it is *chronic,* having bothered me <u>for the past two months</u>.

  Her desire for financial security, she realized, was <u>not a sufficient</u> *rationale* for accepting his marriage proposal.

  (In the first sentence, "for the past two months" indicates that *chronic* describes a condition lasting a long time; in the second sentence, "not a sufficient" suggests that a *rationale* is a reason or a motive.)

Copyright © by Houghton Mifflin Company. All rights reserved.

- **Examples**

  Arthropods, such as crabs and lobsters, live in water.

  Unrestricted television viewing can have *deleterious* effects on children, including apathy and insensitivity.

  (In the first sentence, the examples of "crabs and lobsters" indicate that *arthropods* are animals with a hard outer covering and jointed legs. In the second sentence, "apathy and insensitivity" suggest that *deleterious* describes something harmful.)

- **Synonyms**

  The *arbitrator,* or judge, ruled in favor of the club owners.

  As a result, the players were *irate;* in other words, they were furious.

  (In the first sentence, "or" makes it clear that *arbitrator* and *judge* are synonyms, that is, words with similar meanings. In the second sentence, "in other words" makes it obvious that *irate* and *furious* are also synonyms.

- **Antonyms**

  Early in her career, she was careless in her public remarks, but today she is much more *discreet.*

  Although the mayor was *churlish* yesterday, he was pleasant and agreeable at today's news conference.

  (In the first sentence, "but" indicates *careless* and *discreet* are antonyms, that is, words with opposite meanings. In the second sentence, "Although" signifies *churlish* has an opposite meaning to those of *pleasant* and *agreeable.*)

- **Key Phrases Plus Knowledge of Word Parts**

  The tyrant wanted to rule all of Europe, and his attempt to *subjugate* the continent resulted in tragedy for thousands of people.

  (The phrase "wanted to rule all of Europe," when combined with the knowledge that *sub-* means "under," provides the clue for understanding *subjugate,* which means "to put under authority.")

  Infidelity is the only grounds for divorce in that country.

  (The phrase "only grounds for divorce," when combined with the knowledge that *in-* means "not" and *fid* means "faith," provides the clue for understanding that *infidelity* means "a state of not being faithful.")

Specific contextual clues like the ones in the preceding examples are not always present to help unlock the meaning of an unfamiliar word. When that is the case, a reasonable inference about the unknown word can often be made by concentrating on what is being said about the subject of the sentence and by identifying the word's part of speech. Here is an example to illustrate this approach:

Bereft of money, friends, and jobs, numerous immigrants struggled to survive in the New World.

Copyright © by Houghton Mifflin Company. All rights reserved.

(It is stated that *immigrants,* the subject of the sentence, "struggled to survive." *Bereft* is an adjective; the combination of this information suggests *bereft* is describing immigrants who *lacked* money, friends, and jobs. *Bereft,* then, means "lacking" or "deprived of.")

LIMITATIONS OF CONTEXTUAL CLUES

Although using contextual clues is generally reliable and is the most practical way of unlocking the meanings of unfamiliar words, this approach has limitations. Specifically, contextual clues

- often reveal vague rather than precise meanings;
- usually reveal a single meaning, whereas many words have several meanings;
- are sometimes absent or too obscure to be helpful;
- seldom provide certainty of definition.

It should be clear, then, that there are times when you should consult a dictionary (see **Appendix B,** pages 363–364), particularly when you need complete and precise meanings of words or when contextual clues are lacking in a sentence.

DOING THE LESSONS FOR THE CHALLENGING WORDS

Familiarize yourself with each word's pronunciation, part of speech, definition, and appropriate use in sentences by noting the following.

- A syllable is underlined because it is a word part you studied in the previous lesson, so use your understanding of this prefix, suffix, or root to deepen your understanding of the challenging word.
- When the challenging word is presented phonetically in parentheses, a space separates each syllable.
- The accented syllable is printed in capital letters.
- Vowels with long sounds have a line over them.
- The schwa sound (uh) in unaccented syllables is represented by ə, which looks like an upside-down *e:*

    EXAMPLES: <u>sub</u>terfuge (SUB tər fūj)

    trepi<u>da</u>tion (trep i DA sh ən)

    Note: The pronunciation given for each challenging word is a common one, but there may be other acceptable pronunciations as well.

- Each challenging word's part of speech is also presented; see **Appendix A,** beginning on page 357, if you need to review parts of speech.
- Two sentences are presented to illustrate the meaning of each challenging word, so be alert to the types of contextual clues that have been discussed in addition to applying your knowledge of the underlined word part.

Copyright © by Houghton Mifflin Company. All rights reserved.

- Select your definition for each challenging word by writing either **a** or **b** in the space provided.
- Follow the directions for completing the four sets of exercises on the ensuing pages.
- *Note:* **Exercise III** of each challenging word lesson ends with three **analogy** questions. **Analogies are pairs of words with a similar relationship.** Analogy exercises require you to study a pair of words to discover the relationship between the two words. Then, choosing from several suggested pairs of words, you must select the pair having the same relationship as the first pair of words. Consider the example that follows.

failure : ridicule :: success : praise

Analogies are read and understood in this manner: **failure** *is to* **ridicule** *as* **success** *is to* **praise.** Now think about the relationship between the first pair of words; that is, if you fail, people may ridicule you. Notice that the same type of relationship exists between success and praise; that is, if you succeed, people may praise you.

The relationship of the second pair of words must *always* be the *same* as it is in the first pair, as in these examples (**:** represents *is to* and **::** represents *as*):

similar meaning	similar meaning
cafe : restaurant :: clothes : garments	

opposite meaning	opposite meaning
cloudy : clear :: straight : crooked	

part to whole	part to whole
toe : foot :: finger : hand	

worker to product	worker to product
painter : picture :: poet : poem	

place and activity	place and activity
mall : shopping :: highway : driving	

general to specific	general to specific
car : Pontiac :: sport : basketball	

cause to effect	cause to effect
carelessness : accident :: disobedience : punishment	

noun and its association	noun and its association
clown : silly :: winter : cold	

adjective and its association	adjective and its association
generous : good :: tricky : unfair	

As the preceding examples demonstrate, the key to doing well on the analogy questions (8, 9, and 10 in **Exercise III** of each challenging words lesson) is to discover the relationship between the two words given, then to select the pairs of words (either **a, b, c,** or **d**) having a similar relationship.

Copyright © by Houghton Mifflin Company. All rights reserved.

Word Parts

1. sta

    a. My aunt's _station_ in life seems to be taking care of her elderly parents.
    b. The _statue_ in the park is in honor of all military veterans from this community.

sta is closest in meaning to (a) position (b) fame _____ _a_ _____ .

2. co, col, com, con, cor

    a. In an impressive display of civic pride, the downtown merchants _cooperated_ when they remodeled their storefronts in the same style.
    b. This summer, three of my friends and I have decided to _collaborate_ in painting houses.
    c. Ted Phillips, my _companion_ in college, is now a dentist in Minnesota.
    d. George Washington and Benjamin Franklin were _contemporaries_.
    e. Coughing is positively _correlated_ to smoking.

co, col, com, con, and **cor** mean to (a) separate (b) combine _____ _b_ _____ .

3. il, im, in, ir

    a. Did you know it's _illegal_ for businesses to open on Sundays in my community?
    b. The day after playing softball for the first time this spring, I was practically _immobile_ from soreness.
    c. I think it's _incredible_ that your grandparents want a balloon ride for an anniversary present!
    d. The judge dismissed the evidence as _irrelevant_.

il, im, in, and **ir** change a word to its (a) original (b) opposite meaning _____ _b_ _____ .

4. de

    a. A specialist was called in to _deactivate_ the bomb.
    b. The trees that had been toppled by storms through the years were in various stages of _decomposition_.

de means move (a) toward (b) away from _____ _b_ _____ .

Copyright © by Houghton Mifflin Company. All rights reserved.

5. er, or, ist

    a. My cousin is a *rancher* in Montana.

    b. Adele would like to become a high school *counselor.*

    c. Vic is fun to be around because he's such a *humorist.*

er, or, and **ist** refer to a person who (a) does (b) doesn't do what the base word indicates _____ *a* _____ .

6. pre

    a. After the *previews* were shown, the feature movie began.

    b. The staff had *prearranged* the room for the banquet, so the guests were able to be seated immediately.

pre means (a) before (b) after _____ *a* _____ .

7. re

    a. Mr. Lucas had to *revarnish* the table after it was stained by candle drippings.

    b. The Warrens had such a good vacation in British Columbia that they are planning to *revisit* this Canadian province next year.

re means to (a) avoid (b) repeat _____ *b* _____ .

8. ex

    a. The dentist reluctantly decided he would have to *extract* the patient's tooth.

    b. Oranges, which are shipped in abundance from Florida and California, are a major *export* of the United States.

ex means (a) in (b) out_____ *b* _____ .

9. mono

    a. The term *monogamy* means having only one wife or husband.

    b. Working on the assembly line was *monotonous* work because I did the same thing hour after hour.

mono refers to (a) one (b) many _____ *a* _____ .

10. un

    a. The defense lawyer contended the accident was caused by the waiter, so he feels it would be *unjust* to make his client pay damages.

    b. The cows wandered out of the pasture when the gate was left *unlatched.*

un means (a) with (b) not _____ *b* _____ .

Copyright © by Houghton Mifflin Company. All rights reserved.

EXERCISES FOR LESSON 1
Word Parts

I. *Directions:* Match each definition to the word part it defines; some definitions are used more than once.

_____ f	**1.** sta	**a.** one
_____ b	**2.** co, col, com, con, cor	**h.** person who does something
_____	**3.** il, im, in, ir	**c.** not; opposite
_____	**4.** de	**d.** do the opposite of; away from
_____ b	**5.** er, or, ist	**e.** before
_____ e	**6.** pre	**f.** stand; position
_____ i	**7.** re	**g.** out
_____ g	**8.** ex	**h.** with; together
_____ a	**9.** mono	**i.** again
_____ c	**10.** un	

II. *Directions:* Select the appropriate word part so the proper word is formed in each sentence.

sta	in	ist	re	mono
con	de	pre	ex	un

1. The belief in only one God is known as _____ mono theism.

2. The doctor _____ con curred with his colleague's diagnosis.

3. I hope Frank and Teresa will _____ re tell their hilarious story about their first camping experience.

4. An _____ un competent mechanic attempted to fix my car, much to my regret.

5. Did the optometr ist _____ say you needed glasses?

6. The judge ordered the government official to _____ de classify the document labeled "Top Secret."

7. People are guilty of _____ judice when they make judgments before they know all of the facts.

8. Vickie rides a _____ sta tionary bike for exercise.

9. Fortunately, the window was still _____ broken after it suddenly slammed shut.

Copyright © by Houghton Mifflin Company. All rights reserved.

10. After the baseball struck Jake in the chest, breathing was painful for him when he _____ haled.

III. *Directions:* Use your knowledge of the underlined word parts to match the definitions and words.

_____ **1.** <u>re</u>juvenate	**a.** to free from blame
_____ **2.** <u>un</u>chaste	**b.** person's standing or condition
_____ **3.** <u>de</u>fection	**c.** not able to read or write
_____ **4.** suffra<u>gist</u>	**d.** not pure; corrupted
_____ **5.** <u>ex</u>culpate	**e.** railway system using a single rail
_____ **6.** <u>com</u>municable	**f.** abandonment of one's duty or loyalty
_____ **7.** <u>status</u>	**g.** capable of being transmitted, such as a disease, when people come together
_____ **8.** <u>mono</u>rail	**h.** make fresh again; breathe new life into
_____ **9.** <u>il</u>literate	**i.** an introduction appearing before the main message
_____ **10.** <u>pre</u>amble	**j.** person concerned with voting rights

IV. *Directions:* Write the definitions of the words after noting the underlined word parts and studying the context of the sentences; if you are still uncertain, feel free to consult a dictionary.

1. A <u>*stabilizer*</u> was installed to prevent the machine from rolling about.

   stabilizer _____

2. A number of supervisors were asked to accept <u>*demotions*</u> as a cost-saving step.

   demotions _____

3. Our long-awaited trip had an <u>*inauspicious*</u> start because it started to sleet just as we drove out of our driveway.

   inauspicious _____

4. According to the game warden, trout, bass, and perch can <u>*cohabit*</u> in the same body of water.

   cohabit _____

5. Most drive-in movies became <u>*defunct*</u> in the 1970s.

   defunct _____

Copyright © by Houghton Mifflin Company. All rights reserved.

6. *Narcissists* never miss an opportunity to gaze fondly at themselves when they come across a mirror or a reflecting store window.

narcissists _____

7. My *predecessor* won three league championships in five years, so I knew I would be under a lot of pressure when I accepted this coaching position.

predecessor _____

8. Some homeowners were so upset that they threatened legal action if their homes were not *reappraised*.

reappraised _____

9. The lawyer was asked whether she thought the new evidence would *exonerate* her client.

exonerate _____

10. The game was canceled because the rain had been *unremitting*.

unremitting _____

Copyright © by Houghton Mifflin Company. All rights reserved.

Challenging Words

1. <u>sta</u>ture (STACH ə r)—noun

   a. My brother's *stature* as an outstanding athlete accounts for much of his popularity in our small community.
   b. Her *stature* in the community rose even higher when she was appointed principal of the new high school.

   stature has to do with (a) regard (b) health _____ *a* _____ .

2. <u>com</u>pliance (kə m PLĪə ns)—noun

   a. Because the restaurant was not in *compliance* with the state's fire code, it was closed while the necessary changes were made.
   b. The judge's decision was that the defendant was in *compliance* with the terms of the contract.

   compliance has to do with (a) praise (b) obedience _____ *b* _____ .

3. <u>incon</u>gruous (in KONG GROO əs)—adjective

   a. Reggie's friends think it's *incongruous* that he can't stand the sight of blood even though he's planning to become a doctor.
   b. It's *incongruous* to me that Lois, who never goes out of her way to make friends, is often the person others turn to for advice.

   incongruous is related to (a) inconsistency (b) intelligence _____ .

4. <u>de</u>bilitate (də BIL ə tāt)—verb

   a. Fad diets not only don't work, but they may also *debilitate* one's health.
   b. Glenn's hard life as a cross-country trucker began to *debilitate* his health when he was in his early forties.

   debilitate means (a) weakening (b) strengthening _____ .

Copyright © by Houghton Mifflin Company. All rights reserved.

13

5. hedonist (HĒ don ist)—noun

    a. When Jake first went to college, he became such a *hedonist* he almost flunked out after his first semester as his endless partying gave him little time for studying.

    b. The movie star has the reputation of being a *hedonist* because she is often pictured in newspapers and magazines in nightclubs and gambling casinos with other celebrities.

A **hedonist** is best known for seeking (a) support (b) fun _____ .

6. precocious (prə KŌ shəs)—adjective

    a. Mozart was a *precocious* child as he was giving piano concerts and composing classical music before he was ten years old.

    b. My grandfather thinks his three-year-old granddaughter is *precocious* because she can count to twenty, but I don't think such ability is unusual for a child her age.

precocious has to do with demonstrating ability at an (a) early stage of life (b) unusual place _____ .

7. replicate (REP lə kāt)—verb

    a. The researchers *replicated* the experiment many times before they were sure the same results would occur.

    b. Is it legal to *replicate* a couple of my favorite audiotapes so I could give copies to my friends?

replicate is associated with (a) starting (b) copying _____ .

8. extricate (EK strə kāt)—verb

    a. Lloyd says the only way he can *extricate* his car from the ditch is by calling a tow truck.

    b. Justin *extricated* himself from the embarrassing situation by pretending he had to make a telephone call.

extricate is associated with (a) separating (b) repairing_____ .

9. monomania (MON ə MĀ nē ə)—noun

    a. My cousin is suffering from *monomania* as he spends all of his time trying to avoid germs.

    b. I decided to limit myself to no more than one hour per day on my computer as I was starting to have a *monomania* about playing computer games.

monomania is similar to an (a) obsession (b) obligation _____ .

Copyright © by Houghton Mifflin Company. All rights reserved.

10. <u>un</u>seemly (un SĒM lē)—adjective

    a. Didn't you think it was *unseemly* of her to ask why he and his wife were divorcing?

    b. Using vulgar language is particularly *unseemly* when children are present.

unseemly means being (a) bold (b) discourteous _____ .

Copyright © by Houghton Mifflin Company. All rights reserved.

EXERCISES FOR LESSON 2
Challenging Words

I. *Directions:* Write each word before its definition.

| stature | incongruous | hedonist | replicate | monomania |
| compliance | debilitate | precocious | extricate | unseemly |

_____ **1.** advanced in mind or skills at an early age

_____ **2.** having an intense preoccupation with one subject

_____ **3.** free from a difficult situation

_____ **4.** to make weak or feeble

_____ **5.** unbecoming, impolite, inappropriate

_____ **6.** one who seeks pleasure above all else

_____ **7.** copy, duplicate

_____ **8.** out of step with one another, not in agreement

_____ **9.** act of cooperating or obeying

_____ **10.** rank, standing, position

II. *Directions:* In each space, write the appropriate word from those listed below.

| stature | incongruous | hedonist | replicate | monomania |
| compliance | debilitate | precocious | extricate | unseemly |

1. At the age of seven, Jim displayed _____ ability to handle many of the chores associated with operating his grandfather's farm.

2. Ancient Romans seldom bathed because they believed frequent baths would _____ their strength.

3. I hope I'm not being _____ by asking, but how much do you pay per month for renting this dump?

4. Gretchen is constantly checking to see whether she left her stove on; she's showing all the signs of _____ when it comes to this concern.

5. Austin, Texas, enjoys the _____ of being a wonderful city in which to live.

6. The golfer had difficulty trying to _____ his ball from the sand trap.

7. After extensive renovations, the majestic old inn was finally in _____ with the state's new safety code.

Copyright © by Houghton Mifflin Company. All rights reserved.

8. Ron was quite a _____ in his younger days, but he's given up his wild ways since he got married.

9. Ashley finds it _____ that her roommate complains all the time about her boyfriend, yet she continues to go steady with him.

10. The investigators were attempting to _____ the conditions existing before the accident to see if they could discover the cause of the tragedy.

III. *Directions:* After selecting your response, put the letter before it in the space provided.

_____ **1.** The *opposite* of **compliance** is
- **a.** obedience
- **b.** defiance
- **c.** acceptance
- **d.** submission

_____ **2.** The *opposite* of **debilitate** is
- **a.** improve
- **b.** ruin
- **c.** inspect
- **d.** deceive

_____ **3.** The *opposite* of **extricate** is
- **a.** trust
- **b.** explain
- **c.** hold
- **d.** free

_____ **4.** **Incongruous** suggests
- **a.** smoothness
- **b.** stubbornness
- **c.** dishonesty
- **d.** disharmony

_____ **5.** **Replicate** suggests
- **a.** exhaustion
- **b.** duplication
- **c.** destruction
- **d.** exception

_____ **6.** At what age is someone most likely to be **precocious?**
- **a.** eight
- **b.** eighteen
- **c.** forty-eight
- **d.** seventy-eight

Copyright © by Houghton Mifflin Company. All rights reserved.

_____ 7. If people behave in an **unseemly** manner, they act
      a. inappropriately
      b. humorously
      c. intelligently
      d. politely

_____ 8. **hedonist : pleasure ::** **a.** teacher : school
      b. athlete : joy
      c. comedian : crying
      d. judge : seriousness

_____ 9. **stature : prominence ::** **a.** fame : wealth
      b. reputation : importance
      c. size : height
      d. desire : acquire

_____ 10. **monomania : sensible ::** **a.** fad : popularity
      b. foolishness : reasonable
      c. distrubance : unpleasantness
      d. nonsense : ridiculous

IV. _Directions:_ Write an original sentence for each word that clearly demonstrates your mastery of its meaning.

1. **stature** _____

   _____

2. **compliance** _____

   _____

3. **incongruous** _____

   _____

4. **debilitate** _____

   _____

5. **hedonist** _____

   _____

6. **precocious** _____

   _____

7. **replicate** _____

   _____

8. **extricate** _____

   _____

Copyright © by Houghton Mifflin Company. All rights reserved.

9. monomania _____

_____

10. unseemly _____

_____

Copyright © by Houghton Mifflin Company. All rights reserved.

Word Parts

1. sub

    a. Although I live near an airport, I'm not bothered by sonic booms because all planes in the vicinity must travel at _subsonic_ speeds.

    b. You will have to _submerge_ the shirt in some water and bleach to remove the stain.

sub means (a) above (b) below _____ .

2. pro

    a. My folks have always been _pro-music,_ so they are delighted I'm taking guitar lessons.

    b. The Luthers, who often complain about the property taxes they have to pay, surprised me when they became leading _proponents_ for a new community swimming pool.

pro means (a) for (b) against_____ .

3. uni

    a. Everyone said in _unison,_ "Let's go!"

    b. This clock is _unique_ because it is the only one ever made of bamboo.

uni means (a) one (b) many_____ .

4. inter

    a. Our team plays a number of _intercollegiate_ basketball games with California teams.

    b. A network of _interstate_ highways links all sections of our country.

inter means (a) huge (b) between _____ .

Copyright © by Houghton Mifflin Company. All rights reserved.

5. mis

    a. A run was scored when the shortstop *misplayed* the ball.

    b. The cylinders in my car are *misfiring*.

mis is closest in meaning to (a) action (b) inefficiency _____ .

6. dis

    a. Logan has been working long hours, but that is no excuse for him to be *discourteous* to customers.

    b. The Mustangs will be at a *disadvantage* in the game because two of their best players are injured.

dis means (a) reverses (b) emphasizes a word's meaning _____ .

7. ob, op

    a. The lawyer's *objection* to the police officer's testimony was overruled by the judge.

    b. The Hawkeyes should be a tough *opponent* for the Buckeyes.

ob and **op** mean (a) support (b) against _____ .

8. ten

    a. The owners of an auto parts store are the *tenants* of the new building on the corner of Oak and Main Streets.

    b. Students held in *detention* at the high school I attended had to sit quietly for an hour and do homework.

ten relates to (a) keeping (b) rejecting _____ .

9. tion

    a. Ann is embarrassed about the ticket she received for a speeding *violation.*

    b. Rodney can't play golf or tennis until the *inflammation* in his right elbow clears up.

tion relates to the (a) condition of (b) improvement of _____ .

10. logy

    a. *Sociology* is concerned with the systematic study of society.

    b. *Zoology* is the branch of biology concerned with the animal kingdom.

logy relates to (a) people (b) study _____ .

Copyright © by Houghton Mifflin Company. All rights reserved.

EXERCISES FOR LESSON 3
Word Parts

I. *Directions:* Match each definition to the word part it defines.

_____	**1.** sub	**a.** one
_____	**2.** pro	**b.** not; opposite of
_____	**3.** uni	**c.** to hold
_____	**4.** inter	**d.** for; in favor of
_____	**5.** mis	**e.** study of
_____	**6.** dis	**f.** between; among
_____	**7.** ob, op	**g.** against
_____	**8.** ten	**h.** under
_____	**9.** tion	**i.** state of; act of; result of
_____	**10.** logy	**j.** wrong

II. *Directions:* Select the appropriate word part so the proper word is formed in each sentence.

sub	uni	mis	ob	ten	logy
pro	inter	dis	op	tion	

1. Mr. Martin presented a moving recita _____ of Shakespeare's "Sonnet 29."

2. The scuba divers discovered a(n) _____ terranean tunnel on the south side of the isolated island.

3. Psycho _____ is the most interesting subject I've studied so far in college.

4. It was difficult to find Rick because everyone was wearing _____ forms.

5. The rain _____ literated the white lines on the football field.

6. The movie star claims he was _____ quoted in the newspaper.

7. Mr. Bryan's _____ ure as mayor was twelve years, the longest anyone in our community has held that position.

8. The audience was served refreshments during the _____ lude between the first and second acts.

9. Allen had a(n) _____ agreement with his parents about his desire to get a job and continue college at night.

10. The candidate's record indicates he's _____ -labor on most issues, so he should get the support of the industrial states.

Copyright © by Houghton Mifflin Company. All rights reserved.

III. *Directions:* Use your knowledge of the underlined word parts to match the definitions and words.

_____	**1.** <u>uni</u>lateral	**a.**	wrong name
_____	**2.** etymo<u>logy</u>	**b.**	something taken for granted
_____	**3.** <u>ob</u>durate	**c.**	under the control of another
_____	**4.** assump<u>tion</u>	**d.**	spokesperson in favor of a cause; leading character in a play
_____	**5.** <u>dis</u>array	**e.**	relating to one side; performed by only one side
_____	**6.** <u>sub</u>servient	**f.**	study of the history of words
_____	**7.** <u>mis</u>nomer	**g.**	not firm; weak
_____	**8.** <u>inter</u>val	**h.**	stubborn; unyielding
_____	**9.** <u>pro</u>tagon<u>ist</u>	**i.**	period between two events
_____	**10.** <u>ten</u>uous	**j.**	not in good order; messy

IV. *Directions:* Write the definitions of the words after noting the underlined word parts and studying the context of the sentences; if you are still uncertain, feel free to consult a dictionary.

1. The coroner's clear *articula<u>tion</u>* of the technical terms, as well as her precise explanation of what they meant, helped the jury understand what had happened to the victim.

   articula<u>tion</u> _____

2. The team owners and player representatives finally agreed to have an *<u>inter</u>mediary* appointed to settle their dispute.

   <u>inter</u>mediary _____

3. The career counselor said that *audio<u>logy</u>* is a profession worth considering because numerous studies indicate that hearing loss is becoming an ever-growing problem for many people in our society.

   audio<u>logy</u> _____

4. The military commander insisted the island was *<u>ten</u>able* against any type of attack the enemy might launch.

   <u>ten</u>able _____

5. Despite pleas, coaxing, and threats, the *<u>ob</u>durate* youngster refused to open his mouth for the dentist.

   <u>ob</u>durate _____

Copyright © by Houghton Mifflin Company. All rights reserved.

6. The _miscreant_ was given an additional year in prison for contempt of court.

miscreant _____

7. Instead of having two legislative branches of government, a few states have a _unicameral_ legislature.

unicameral _____

8. Our daughter was _submissive_ throughout her elementary school years, but once she was in middle school, she gradually became rebellious.

submissive _____

9. The clerk remained _dispassionate_ while the angry customer ranted and raved at him.

dispassionate _____

10. Because she was unable to attend the meeting, Jim officially authorized Miguel to serve as his _proxy_.

proxy _____

Copyright © by Houghton Mifflin Company. All rights reserved.

Challenging Words

1. <u>subterfuge</u> (SUB tər fūj)—noun

    a. The athletic director made it clear to the coaches and members of the booster club that no *subterfuge,* such as money or cars, should be used in the recruitment of athletes.
    b. Alexandra and her brother used lies and other types of *subterfuge* to surprise their parents on their twenty-fifth wedding anniversary.

subterfuge has to do with (a) generosity (b) deceit _____ .

2. <u>proclivity</u> (prō KLIV ə tē)—noun

    a. A *proclivity* for desserts of all kinds makes it hard for me to stay on my diet.
    b. Jason's driving license was suspended because of his *proclivity* for driving too fast.

proclivity means (a) likeness for (b) suspicion of _____ .

3. <u>universally</u> (ū nə VUR sə lē)—adverb

    a. The psychologist said acceptance and love are *universally* longed for by all people everywhere.
    b. The assassination of President John F. Kennedy in 1963 was *universally* mourned throughout the world.

universally means (a) widely (b) sadly _____ .

4. <u>interim</u> (in tə r im)—noun

    a. In the *interim* between graduating from high school and serving in the marines, Rick worked in a plastics factory.
    b. Nicole plans to own a restaurant of her own someday, but in the *interim* she will continue working as the chief chef at the Green Lantern Cafe.

interim is associated with (a) consequently (b) meanwhile _____ .

Copyright © by Houghton Mifflin Company. All rights reserved.

27

5. misconstrue (MIS kən STROO)—verb

    a. Please don't *misconstrue* what I'm saying; I would like to help you, but I simply don't have time.

    b. Because the elderly clerk was somewhat hard of hearing, he will sometimes *misconstrue* what items customers ask for.

misconstrue indicates a person has (a) gotten the wrong idea (b) been foolish   _____ .

6. dissipate (DIS ə pāt)—verb

    a. Warmer temperatures caused the snow to *dissipate* by the end of the week.

    b. The tension that had filled the room began to *dissipate* after the instructor told a few jokes.

dissipate means to gradually (a) increase (b) vanish _____ .

7. obstreperous (ob STREP ər əs)—adjective

    a. My son had been *obstreperous* all day, so I sent him to bed immediately after supper.

    b. This horse should be ridden by only experienced riders because he can be extremely *obstreperous* at times.

obstreperous means (a) disobedient (b) sickly _____ .

8. tentative (TENT ə tive)—adjective

    a. Rachel wasn't *tentative* when Brent asked her for a date as she immediately said "yes!"

    b. Mr. Bryson made a *tentative* offer to buy our house; the final decision depends upon whether the bank approves his loan application.

tentative indicates (a) uncertainty (b) confidence _____ .

9. correlation (kor ə LĀ shə n)—noun

    a. A study conducted by a researcher at our college indicates a positive *correlation* between students' grades and their extracurricular activities.

    b. My math teacher said there is a *correlation* between mathematics skills and computer ability, but this relationship isn't as strong as many people seem to think it is.

correlation is about (a) connections (b) truths _____ .

10. anthropology (AN thr ə POL ə jē)—noun

    a. In my *anthropology* class we are studying the beginnings of civilization in North Africa.

    b. You will learn about many cultures in *anthropology*.

anthropology involves the study of (a) the solar system (b) human beings _____ .

Copyright © by Houghton Mifflin Company. All rights reserved.

EXERCISES FOR LESSON 4
Challenging Words

I. *Directions:* Write each word before its definition.

subterfuge	universally	misconstrue	obstreperous	correlation
proclivity	interim	dissipate	tentative	anthropology

_____ **1.** hesitant, uncertain, not final

_____ **2.** intermission, temporary period

_____ **3.** to fade slowly or disappear

_____ **4.** study of the origin, culture, and development of human beings

_____ **5.** deception, secret evasion of the rules

_____ **6.** without exception, everywhere, widespread

_____ **7.** a mutual relationship between two or more things, an orderly connection

_____ **8.** tendency, inclination, fondness for

_____ **9.** disorderly, rowdy, unruly

_____ **10.** misunderstand, misinterpret, misjudge

II. *Directions:* In each space, write the appropriate word from those listed below.

subterfuge	universally	misconstrue	obstreperous	correlation
proclivity	interim	dissipate	tentative	anthropology

1. During the _____ between semesters, Don worked at a small hardware store in his hometown.

2. The accountant's _____ was discovered by the bank's auditors, and he was eventually convicted of embezzlement.

3. A strong _____ exists between mathematical and navigational skills.

4. We thought the fog would eventually _____ during the morning hours, but it didn't, so we decided not to drive into town.

5. Tom has decided to major in _____ because of his fascination with early civilizations.

6. The teacher was understandably tense and tired after dealing with a number of _____ students throughout the day.

Copyright © by Houghton Mifflin Company. All rights reserved.

7. He may _____ your failure to return his call as an indication you are no longer interested in the job, so I would get in touch with him right away.

8. Our college is _____ admired throughout the state for its outstanding music department.

9. Because of Louis's _____ for drawing, his high school counselor suggested he might want to consider majoring in art when he enrolled in college.

10. Leigh is unsure what she's going to do this summer, but she's made _____ plans to visit some friends in Minnesota if she earns enough money.

III. *Directions:* After selecting your response, put the letter before it in the space provided.

_____ **1.** The *opposite* of **tentative** is
    a. uncertain
    b. hesitant
    c. doubtful
    d. positive

_____ **2.** The *opposite* of **misconstrue** is
    a. understand
    b. disagree
    c. cheat
    d. help

_____ **3.** The *opposite* of **proclivity** is
    a. fondness for
    b. desire for
    c. distaste for
    d. talent for

_____ **4.** The word closest in meaning to **interim** is
    a. maturity
    b. pause
    c. pity
    d. interference

_____ **5** Which of the following is most closely related to **anthropology?**
    a. astronomy
    b. history
    c. psychology
    d. chemistry

Copyright © by Houghton Mifflin Company. All rights reserved.

_____ **6.** Which of the following is most likely to be **universally** desired?
  a. acceptance
  b. solitude
  c. simplicity
  d. thriftiness

_____ **7.** The word _not_ associated with **dissipate** is
  a. diminish
  b. magnify
  c. evaporate
  d. vanish

_____ **8. subterfuge : deception :: a.** abbreviation : shortening
  b. reduction : increasing
  c. expectation : surprise
  d. confession : denial

_____ **9. obstreperous : behavior :: a.** thoughtful : kind
  b. critical : helpful
  c. wealthy : desirable
  d. disobedient : conduct

_____ **10. correlation : disharmony :: a.** spoil : ruin
  b. shame : disgrace
  c. honesty : dishonesty
  d. agreement : cooperation

IV. _Directions:_ Write an original sentence for each word that clearly demonstrates your mastery of its meaning.

1. subterfuge _____

_____

2. proclivity _____

_____

3. universally _____

_____

4. interim _____

_____

5. misconstrue _____

_____

6. dissipate _____

_____

Copyright © by Houghton Mifflin Company. All rights reserved.

7. obstreperous _____

_____

8. tentative _____

_____

9. correlation _____

_____

10. anthropology _____

_____

Copyright © by Houghton Mifflin Company. All rights reserved.

Word Parts

1. able, ible

   a. My folks believe the most *enjoyable* way of traveling is by train.
   b. The fiddlehead is an *edible*, fernlike plant.

able and **ible** mean (a) capable of (b) incapable of_____ .

2. a, an

   a. Doug is certainly *atypical* from his brothers; he doesn't enjoy hunting and fishing as they do.
   b. When the central government was overthrown, no one was able to rule or to enforce the laws, so *anarchy* reigned.

a and **an** give words (a) extra (b) opposite meanings_____ .

3. super

   a. Tyrone is a respected *supervisor* at the auto plant.
   b. The new regulations *supersede* the previous zoning restrictions.

super means (a) over (b) below _____ .

4. trans

   a. Melanie plans to *transfer* to a college in Texas.
   b. Trucks were used to *transport* the potatoes to market.

trans refers to (a) power (b) change _____ .

5. poly

   a. Are there any religions that still permit *polygamy?* I would think one husband or wife would be enough!
   b. Christie is a *polyglot* because she can speak English, French, Spanish, and Italian.

poly refers to (a) foolishness (b) many _____ .

Copyright © by Houghton Mifflin Company. All rights reserved.

6. ver

    a. Can you _verify_ that this wallet is yours?

    b. Evidence later confirmed that the young children had given _ver_acious testimony at the informal hearing.

ver relates to (a) truth (b) fiction_____ .

7. log

    a. Before Mr. Wilkinson showed his slides of China, he gave a _prologue_ explaining why he had traveled to that country.

    b. The movie has English subtitles for those who can't understand the French _dialogue_.

log is related to (a) words (b) travel _____ .

8. ism

    a. Novels featuring _romanticism_ have always been popular.

    b. The belief that there is no god is called _atheism._

ism refers to (a) realities (b) beliefs _____ .

9. chron

    a. Mike has had a _chronic_ backache since he fell rollerblading two weeks ago.

    b. Generally, history texts present material in a _chronological_ order.

chron means (a) time (b) changeless _____ .

10. post

    a. At the conclusion of the wedding ceremony, Laura played an original _postlude_ on the organ.

    b. Larry added a _postscript_ to his letter because he had forgotten to include the exact time when his plane would be arriving.

post means (a) before (b) after _____ .

Copyright © by Houghton Mifflin Company. All rights reserved.

EXERCISES FOR LESSON 5
Word Parts

I. *Directions:* Match each definition to the word part it defines.

_____	**1.** able, ible	**a.**	word; talk
_____	**2.** a, an	**b.**	many
_____	**3.** super	**c.**	above; over; beyond
_____	**4.** trans	**d.**	not; without
_____	**5.** poly	**e.**	across; change to
_____	**6.** ver	**f.**	time
_____	**7.** log	**g.**	capable of; condition of
_____	**8.** ism	**h.**	true
_____	**9.** chron	**i.**	belief or doctrine
_____	**10.** post	**j.**	after

II. *Directions:* Select the appropriate word part so the proper word is formed in each sentence.

able	ism	trans	ver	a	chron
ible	super	poly	log	an	post

1. The belief that things will improve is called optim _____ , whereas the belief that things will get worse is called pessim _____ .

2. Have you ever flown at _____ sonic speeds?

3. Martha is cap _____ of helping you with your problems, so why don't you ask her to?

4. Mr. Weston _____ planted a maple tree from his backyard to his front yard.

5. The teller said I would have to have two forms of _____ ification before she could cash the check.

6. My uncle's mono _____ ue about his operation went on for almost an hour.

7. A popular singer who had been killed in a car accident was given the prize _____ humously.

8. In geometry class, I learned to construct and measure _____ gons, which are figures having many angles.

Copyright © by Houghton Mifflin Company. All rights reserved.

9. An _____ onymous person telephoned my parents to complain about the way I drive my car.

10. My grandparents' old diary provides a(n) _____ icle of the events leading to their immigration to the United States.

III. *Directions:* Use your knowledge of the underlined word parts to match the definitions and words.

_____ **1.** habit<u>able</u>   **a.** a chain of many South Pacific islands
_____ **2.** stoic<u>ism</u>   **b.** not caring about right or wrong
_____ **3.** <u>super</u>cilious   **c.** can be lived in
_____ **4.** <u>t</u>ransit   **d.** future generations; those coming after
_____ **5.** <u>Poly</u>nesia   **e.** overly critical; conceited
_____ **6.** <u>ver</u>itable   **f.** words of praise
_____ **7.** <u>chrono</u>meter   **g.** passing across or through; a vehicle for transportation
_____ **8.** <u>a</u>moral   **h.** belief that one should be indifferent to feelings, whether pleasurable or painful
_____ **9.** eu<u>log</u>y   **i.** true; authentic; genuine
_____ **10.** <u>post</u>erity   **j.** instrument for measuring time

IV. *Directions:* Write the definitions of the words after noting the underlined word parts and studying the context of the sentences; If you are still uncertain, feel free to consult a dictionary.

1. A colorful picture of the school's mascot was <u>*super*imposed</u> on the yearbook cover.

superimposed _____

2. In this computer age, using a typewriter is considered *ana<u>chron</u>istic* by many people.

ana<u>chron</u>istic _____

3. The tinted window was still sufficiently <u>*trans*lucent</u> that I could see figures of people walking by on the sidewalk.

<u>trans</u>lucent _____

4. After the peace was finally won and the soldiers came home, the <u>*post*war</u> economy boomed.

<u>post</u>war _____

Copyright © by Houghton Mifflin Company. All rights reserved.

5. Snow was such an *anomaly* in this section of the state that many people had seldom if ever seen it before.

anomaly _____

6. People with fair skin are especially *susceptible* to sunburn.

susceptible _____

7. Though his story was hard to believe, it proved to be *veracious* in every detail.

veracious _____

8. The board of directors' actions made it clear that male *chauvinism* would not be tolerated.

chauvinism _____

9. Apparently, the *doxology* that began the service was a familiar one to most of the worshipers, but I had never heard it before.

doxology _____

10. My uncle is a *polymath* as a result of his unending curiosity, extensive education, wide traveling, and constant reading.

polymath _____

Copyright © by Houghton Mifflin Company. All rights reserved.

Challenging Words

1. <u>culpable</u> (KUL pə bəl) adjective

   a. Ted actually broke the CD player, but Ron felt *culpable* because it was his teasing that had caused the accident.
   b. Donovan felt *culpable* for his team's bowling loss because if he had made either a strike or a spare, his team would have won.

culpable means (a) interested in (b) responsible for_____ .

2. <u>apathy</u> (AP ə thē)—noun

   a. A teacher who delights in what he or she teaches is deeply disappointed when students display *apathy* for the subject.
   b. I thought Meredith would be eager to talk about her new job, but she showed complete *apathy* when I asked her to tell me about it.

apathy indicates (a) indifference (b) ignorance _____ .

3. <u>superfluous</u> (soo PUR floo ə s)—adjective

   a. Buying Helen a sweater would be *superfluous* as she must already have at least a dozen.
   b. Please don't ask him what happened because he goes into such *superfluous* detail.

superfluous means (a) too much (b) too little _____ .

4. <u>transition</u> (tran ZISH ə n)—noun

   a. Going to school for the first time is sometimes a troubling *transition* in a child's life.
   b. Electricity ushered in a major *transition* in American life.

transition has to do with (a) emotion (b) change_____ .

Copyright © by Houghton Mifflin Company. All rights reserved.

5. polychromatic (POL ē krō MAT ik)—adjective

    a. Las Vegas is noted for its flashy, *polychromatic* neon signs advertising its many hotels and gambling casinos.

    b. The evening sky was *polychromatic,* with brilliant shades of red, orange, pink, blue, and gray covering the horizon.

polychromatic has to do with many (a) noises (b) colors _____ .

6. veracity (və RAS i tē)—noun

    a. Chad's reputation was such that no one doubted the *veracity* of his story.

    b. An early biographer of George Washington claimed that Washington once threw a silver dollar across the Potomac River, but most historians question the *veracity* of that story.

veracity means (a) truthfulness (b) anger _____ .

7. epilogue (EP ə log)—noun

    a. At the end of the book, the author added a short *epilogue* to explain what eventually happened to the young boy featured in the story.

    b. A speaker gave an *epilogue* after the final act to explain what events had motivated the writing of the play.

epilogue refers to added (a) responsibility (b) information _____ .

8. nepotism (NEP ə tiz əm)—noun

    a. Many people accused the mayor of *nepotism* after he appointed his brother-in-law chief of the fire department.

    b. Mr. Healey was obviously guilty of *nepotism* when he appointed his twenty-two-year-old son district manager because there were many other employees who were much better qualified for the position.

nepotism is associated with showing (a) favoritism (b) ignorance _____ .

9. chronic (KRON ik)—adjective

    a. Jamie reluctantly gave up basketball because of *chronic* knee problems that had plagued her since her sophomore year.

    b. The doctor said the *chronic* headache Andrew had suffered from all winter was caused by a sinus infection.

chronic means (a) mysterious (b) long-lasting _____ .

10. posthumously (POS chə məs lē)—adverb

    a. Shortly after her death, she was *posthumously* honored by the college when the new science building was named after her.

    b. *Posthumously,* Van Gogh is recognized as one of the world's greatest artists, but this certainly was not the case during his lifetime.

posthumously means (a) while living (b) after death_____ .

Copyright © by Houghton Mifflin Company. All rights reserved.

EXERCISES FOR LESSON 6
Challenging Words

I. *Directions:* Write each word before its definition.

culpable	superfluous	polychromatic	epilogue	chronic
apathy	transition	veracity	nepotism	posthumously

_____ **1.** unnecessary, excessive, too much

_____ **2.** lack of interest, absence of emotion

_____ **3.** many colored, having a variety of colors

_____ **4.** after death

_____ **5.** preference given to relatives

_____ **6.** concluding information added at the end of a book, poem, play, or other literary work; postscript; supplement

_____ **7.** at fault, deserving blame, responsible for

_____ **8.** continuous, of long duration

_____ **9.** truth; something that is true

_____ **10.** movement from one place to another; changeover; passage from one stage to another

II. *Directions:* In each space, write the appropriate word from those listed below.

culpable	superfluous	polychromatic	epilogue	chronic
apathy	transition	veracity	nepotism	posthumously

1. Most people don't enjoy being around a _____ complainer because hearing constant complaining soon becomes tiresome and depressing.

2. Old photos and letters added _____ to his claim that he had once served in the Navy.

3. The judge found the defendants _____ for the accident, so they had to pay for all the damages in addition to a large fine.

4. Hannah's _____ was obvious during class as she often sighed and yawned during the teacher's lecture, and she wasn't interested in participating in any of the small group discussions.

5. My mother works at a florist shop, so I guess it would be rather _____ to send her flowers for her birthday, don't you think?

Copyright © by Houghton Mifflin Company. All rights reserved.

6. Though the actor died shortly after finishing the movie, he was nominated _____ for an Academy Award.

7. The author of this latest biography about Benjamin Franklin includes an interesting _____ after the last chapter detailing what became of many of Franklin's descendants.

8. The _____ from an urban to a rural life was a surprisingly easy one for Manuel to make.

9. Some fans believe the coach is guilty of _____ because he recently inserted his daughter into the starting lineup, but I don't agree with them because I think she is clearly one of the better players on the team.

10. When did it become possible to take _____ snapshots rather than black-and-white ones?

III. *Directions:* After selecting your response, put the letter before it in the space provided.

_____ **1.** The *opposite* of **epilogue** is
  a. index
  b. chapter
  c. preface
  d. graph

_____ **2.** The *opposite* of **posthumously** is something done
  a. In anger
  b. while living
  c. before thinking
  d. for revenge

_____ **3.** The *opposite* of **culpable** is
  a. sober
  b. humorous
  c. guilty
  d. innocent

_____ **4.** **Transition** suggests
  a. change
  b. extravagance
  c. indifference
  d. duplication

_____ **5.** **Superfluous** suggests
  a. power
  b. surplus
  c. dishonesty
  d. weakness

Copyright © by Houghton Mifflin Company. All rights reserved.

_____ **6. Veracity** suggests
- **a.** adventure
- **b.** tenderness
- **c.** popularity
- **d.** honesty

_____ **7.** If a person exhibits **apathy,** he or she displays
- **a.** confidence
- **b.** fear
- **c.** joy
- **d.** unconcern

_____ **8. polychromatic : dull :: a.** flat : dismal
- **b.** colorful : flashy
- **c.** colorful : dreary
- **d.** many : a lot

_____ **9. nepotism : resentment :: a.** optimism : hatred
- **b.** cooperation : appreciation
- **c.** bitterness : admiration
- **d.** abolish : boldness

_____ **10. chronic : persistent :: a.** anger : frequently
- **b.** happiness : temporary
- **c.** humor : permanently
- **d.** ceaseless : continuous

IV. _Directions:_ Write an original sentence for each word that clearly demonstrates your mastery of its meaning.

1. culpable _____

_____

2. apathy _____

_____

3. superfluous _____

_____

4. transition _____

_____

5. polychromatic _____

_____

6. veracity _____

_____

Copyright © by Houghton Mifflin Company. All rights reserved.

7. epilogue _____

_____

8. nepotism _____

_____

9. chronic _____

_____

10. posthumously _____

_____

Copyright © by Houghton Mifflin Company. All rights reserved.

Word Parts

1. bio

    a. More _biographies_ have been published about Abraham Lincoln than about any other American.

    b. Faye is doing extremely well in _biochemistry,_ a course concerned with the chemistry of living matter.

bio means (a) science (b) life _____ .

2. tele

    a. Our college needs a more powerful _telescope_ to see the most distant planets in our solar system.

    b. People are more likely to send an e-mail today to distant friends than a _telegram_ unless the message is particularly urgent.

tele means (a) far away (b) close by _____ .

3. auto

    a. In contrast to a carriage pulled by a horse, a car seems to move by its own power; that's why a car is called an _automobile._

    b. Our furnace will _automatically_ turn on if the temperature in the house falls below sixty-two degrees.

auto means (a) modern (b) self _____ .

4. eu

    a. Mr. Henderson gave a _eulogy_ at the memorial service for his popular neighbor.

    b. The seniors expressed their _euphoria_ on graduation night by tossing their mortarboards high in the air.

eu means (a) sorrowful (b) praiseworthy _____ .

Copyright © by Houghton Mifflin Company. All rights reserved.

5. ante

a. Harry Truman's presidency *antedates* John Kennedy's by eight years. Between their terms in office, Dwight Eisenhower was president.

b. A pronoun must refer to a previous noun. For example, in the sentence "The package will be expensive to mail because it weighs more than eight pounds," *package* is the *antecedent* of the pronoun *it*.

ante means (a) before (b) after _____ .

6. rect

a. A *rectangle* consists of four right angles.

b. He has always been a person of high principles and moral *rectitude,* so no one was surprised he entered the ministry.

rect means (a) slanted, intelligent (b) straight, correct _____ .

7. fid

a. Marjorie *confided* her secret to Brian because she knew he wouldn't tell anyone else.

b. My sound system has such good *fidelity* you would swear the musicians were in my room.

fid is related to (a) secrets (b) dependability _____ .

8. equ

a. Most people *equate* expensive cars with wealth.

b. Needless to say, tightrope walkers must have good *equilibrium.*

equ is related to (a) equality (b) equipment _____ .

9. pan

a. Athletes from North, Central, and South America participate in the *Pan-American* games.

b. Barbara's dream is to have a house on the coast with a *panoramic* view of the ocean.

pan means (a) all, wide (b) few, narrow _____ .

10. sym, syn

a. Charles appreciated his friends' expressions of *sympathy* after his grandfather died.

b. By *synthesizing* the information and clues revealed by the extensive investigation, the detectives were able to solve the baffling crime.

sym and **syn** mean (a) against (b) with _____ .

Copyright © by Houghton Mifflin Company. All rights reserved.

Name .... Section .... Date ....

EXERCISES FOR LESSON 7
Word Parts

I. *Directions:* Match each definition to the word part it defines.

_____	**1.** bio	**a.** far; distant
_____	**2.** tele	**b.** all
_____	**3.** auto	**c.** good, well
_____	**4.** eu	**d.** together with
_____	**5.** ante	**e.** equal
_____	**6.** rect	**f.** life
_____	**7.** fid	**g.** faith
_____	**8.** equ	**h.** before
_____	**9.** pan	**i.** straight, correct
_____	**10.** sym, syn	**j.** self

II. *Directions:* Select the appropriate word part so the proper word is formed in each sentence.

bio	auto	ante	fid	pan
tele	eu	rect	equ	syn

1. The earth is divided into two hemispheres at the _____ ator.

2. The police were afraid the large crowd would break into _____ demonium when the concert was canceled.

3. By making it possible to send voices from distant places, the _____ phone revolutionized communications.

4. It's important to have con _____ ence in your doctor.

5. College students have more _____ nomony than high school students, so they must learn to be responsible for themselves.

6. Dr. Morton's _____ room was filled with patients.

7. After our teacher cor _____ ed our essays, we rewrote them one more time.

8. The _____ sphere is the part of the earth's crust, waters, and atmosphere that supports living organisms.

9. *Sanitary engineer* is a _____ phemism for *garbage collector.*

10. Mr. Nickerson formed a _____ dicate with other business people to buy the trucking firm.

Copyright © by Houghton Mifflin Company. All rights reserved.

III. *Directions:* Use your knowledge of the underlined word parts to match the definitions and words.

_____ **1.** <u>rect</u>ify

_____ **2.** <u>synchron</u>ize

_____ **3.** <u>eu</u>phonic

_____ **4.** <u>equi</u>nox

_____ **5.** <u>ante</u>diluvian

_____ **6.** <u>bio</u>mass

_____ **7.** <u>pan</u>acea

_____ **8.** <u>autobio</u>graphy

_____ **9.** <u>tele</u>pathy

_____ **10.** af<u>fid</u>avit

a. time of year when day and night are equal in length

b. life of a person written by that person

c. a cure-all; an answer to all problems

d. to set right; to correct

e. written statement made under oath

f. communication through distance by thoughts only

g. make to occur at the same time

h. belonging to the period before the biblical Flood; extremely old

i. the total quantity of living matter within a specific area

j. pleasant sounding

IV. *Directions:* Write the definitions of the words after noting the underlined word parts and studying the context of the sentences; if you are still uncertain, feel free to consult a dictionary.

1. Being accountable to no one, the *<u>auto</u>crat* ruled the country with absolute authority.

autocrat _____

2. The weekend *<u>tele</u>thon* raised millions of dollars from people and corporations throughout the country.

telethon _____

3. A small band of rebels attempted to incite an *in<u>sur</u><u>rect</u>ion* to topple the newly established government.

insurrection _____

4. Some people believe *<u>eu</u>thanasia* should be permitted if the patient is suffering terribly from an incurable disease.

euthanasia _____

5. Some religious people in the community considered my grandfather an *in<u>fid</u>el* because he never went to church.

infidel _____

Copyright © by Houghton Mifflin Company. All rights reserved.

6. A _synthesis_ of durable metals revolutionized the making of golf clubs in the latter part of the 20th century.

synthesis _____

7. Most ancient people practiced _pantheism_ rather than _monotheism_, which is the belief in one god.

pantheism _____

8. The federal government and our state government are _equivalent_ in their makeup as they both contain legislative, executive, and judicial branches.

equivalent _____

9. The science of _bionics,_ based upon the study of how the human body works, has led to much-improved artificial limbs.

bionics _____

10. After World War II, only a few of the beautiful _antebellum_ buildings were still standing in this historic city.

antebellum _____

Copyright © by Houghton Mifflin Company. All rights reserved.

Challenging Words

1. **bio**psy (BĪ op sē)—noun

   a. Pathologists are specialists in studying samples of patients' tissues obtained through *biopsies.*
   b. Fortunately, the *biopsy* revealed the mole on the patient's arm was harmless.

biopsy is an examination of (a) living tissues (b) medical procedures _____ .

2. **tele**pathy (tə LEP pə thē)—noun

   a. Though the twin sisters are often separated by many miles, they claim to know what each other is thinking at all times; they obviously believe in *telepathy.*
   b. Many scientists are skeptical about *telepathy,* but there are some who believe it is possible to communicate to those far away by thoughts only.

telepathy is communicating by using (a) the sense of touch
(b) minds only _____ .

3. **auto**nomy (ə TON ə mē)—noun

   a. India received its *autonomy* from Great Britain in 1947.
   b. The parents permitted their fifteen-year-old daughter a great deal of *autonomy* on most matters, but they did not allow her to babysit on school nights.

autonomy is associated with (a) independence (b) dependence _____ .

4. **euhe**mism (U f ə miz əm)—noun

   a. "Senior citizen" is a *euphemism* for "old person."
   b. The words "false teeth" are not featured in the ad; instead, the *euphemism* "dentures" is used.

euphemism is a word that is thought to be more (a) refined (b) descriptive than a word that is more commonly used _____ .

Copyright © by Houghton Mifflin Company. All rights reserved.

5. <u>antediluvian</u> (AN ti di LOO vē ə n)—adjective

   a. The *antediluvian* period is the time before the Flood mentioned in the book of Genesis in the Old Testament.
   b. When I was younger, I thought my parents' philosophy for raising children was so old-fashioned that it was *antediluvian,* but now I've changed my mind since I've become a parent.

antediluvian is related to (a) complicated times (b) ancient times _____ .

6. <u>rectify</u> (REK tə f ī)—verb

   a. Pat attempted to *rectify* his clumsiness by slowing down and treading carefully.
   b. I must try to *rectify* this dangerous situation before someone else gets hurt.

rectify means to make (a) right (b) excuses _____ .

7. <u>infidelity</u> (in fi DEL ə tē)—noun

   a. The diplomat's *infidelity* to his country led to his arrest for treason.
   b. *Infidelity* is a leading cause of divorce because it is devastating to be betrayed.

infidelity is (a) foolishness (b) disloyalty _____ .

8. <u>equivocal</u> (ē KWIV ə k ə l)—adjective

   a. Apparently, Beth hasn't decided what to do about the matter because she gave me an *equivocal* answer when I asked her.
   b. I hate to be so *equivocal,* but both jobs appeal to me, so I don't know what to do.

equivocal means (a) indefinite (b) ashamed _____ .

9. <u>panacea</u> (PAN ə SĒ ə)—noun

   a. Unfortunately, there seems to be no *panacea* for ending all poverty in every country.
   b. One of the candidates for the school board said the *panacea* for improving the community's public schools was simple: Hire excellent teachers.

panacea is a (a) lie (b) cure-all _____ .

10. <u>syndrome</u> (SIN drom)—noun

   a. The *syndrome* for diabetes includes fatigue, loss of weight, and thirstiness.
   b. The economist warned that the *syndrome* of a recession includes a high rate of unemployment and an unstable stock market.

syndrome is a set of (a) agreements (b) symptoms _____ .

Copyright © by Houghton Mifflin Company. All rights reserved.

EXERCISES FOR LESSON 8
Challenging Words

I. *Directions:* Write each word before its definition.

| biopsy | autonomy | antediluvian | infidelity | panacea |
| telepathy | euphemism | rectify | equivocal | syndrome |

_____ **1.** cure for all ills, a universal remedy

_____ **2.** self-direction, independence

_____ **3.** unfaithfulness, treason

_____ **4.** set of symptoms

_____ **5.** examination of tissue from a living subject

_____ **6.** before the Flood, ancient

_____ **7.** wavering, uncertain, indefinite

_____ **8.** mind reading, extrasensory perception (ESP)

_____ **9.** make right, correct

_____ **10.** the substitution of a mild word for one thought to be harsh or offensive

II. *Directions:* In each space, write the appropriate word from those listed below.

| biopsy | autonomy | antediluvian | infidelity | panacea |
| telepathy | euphemism | rectify | equivocal | syndrome |

1. We employees have _____ when it comes to choosing the hours we prefer to work, so that's a big plus, particularly for those of us who are parents.

2. Some of my older relatives believe young men with shoulder-length hair look positively _____ rather than up-to-date and sophisticated.

3. The _____ revealed the tissue was cancerous, so the doctor prepared herself to give the patient this disturbing news.

4. We were in a(n) _____ state of mind for some time because we couldn't decide whether to paint or wallpaper our apartment.

5. The doctor explained that the _____ for meningitis includes a stiff neck, headache, and fever.

6. Sometimes "antiques" seems to be a(n) _____ for "junk."

Copyright © by Houghton Mifflin Company. All rights reserved.

7. The political candidate insisted he had been faithful to his ex-wife during their marriage, strongly denying that _____ on his part had led to their divorce.

8. The _____ for ridding our city of smog is to ban all vehicles from the downtown area.

9. You may not believe in mental _____ , but I have an open mind when it comes to ESP because I've sometimes thought about getting in touch with someone when out of the blue he or she telephones me.

10. I completely botched the job when I tried to install a garbage disposal unit in our kitchen sink, so the only way I knew to _____ matters was to call a plumber.

III. *Directions:* After selecting your response, put the letter before it in the space provided.

_____ **1.** The *opposite* of **infidelity** is
    a. dedication
    b. talent
    c. crankiness
    d. loyalty

_____ **2.** The *opposite* of **antediluvian** is
    a. modern
    b. stubborn
    c. ambitious
    d. boring

_____ **3.** The *opposite* of **rectify** is
    a. blame
    b. request
    c. harm
    d. fix

_____ **4.** **Autonomy** suggests
    a. poverty
    b. self-sufficiency
    c. indecency
    d. delicacy

_____ **5.** **Biopsy** is most closely associated with
    a. engineering
    b. business
    c. law
    d. medicine

Copyright © by Houghton Mifflin Company. All rights reserved.

6. Telepathy is most closely associated with
    a. communication
    b. charity
    c. illness
    d. freedom

7. If a person acts in an **equivocal** manner, he or she is acting
    a. uncertainly
    b. confidently
    c. arrogantly
    d. maturely

8. panacea : rare :: a. beautiful : desirable
    b. view : occasionally
    c. cure : unusual
    d. noise : frequently

9. syndrome : related :: a. cluster : similar
    b. group : unlike
    c. symptoms : unreliable
    d. collection : dependable

10. euphemism : tactful :: a. request : impolite
    b. statement : politeness
    c. exclamation : indifference
    d. curse : rude

IV. *Directions:* Write an original sentence for each word that clearly demonstrates your mastery of its meaning.

1. biopsy _____

_____

2. telepathy _____

_____

3. autonomy _____

_____

4. euphemism _____

_____

5. antediluvian _____

_____

6. rectify _____

_____

Copyright © by Houghton Mifflin Company. All rights reserved.

7. infidelity _____

_____

8. equivocal _____

_____

9. panacea _____

_____

10. syndrome _____

_____

Copyright © by Houghton Mifflin Company. All rights reserved.

Word Parts

1. phil

    a. *Philosophy* is an excellent major for students who love to study wisdom and reasoning.

    b. People who admire England and revere anything English are known as *anglophiles.*

phil means (a) intelligence (b) love _____ .

2. mal

    a. *Malicious* gossip has harmed his reputation in the community.

    b. Thomas Jefferson suffered from migraine headaches, a *malady* that would disable him for days.

mal is associated with (a) harmful (b) mysterious _____ .

3. spec

    a. I always *inspect* my car before I take a long trip.

    b. At our college baseball games, the *spectators* are knowledgeable and well mannered.

spec has to do with (a) viewing (b) assisting _____ .

4. omni

    a. Young children often believe their parents are *omniscient,* but as they grow older, they realize their parents don't know everything after all.

    b. Dogs seem to be *omnipresent* at any picnic.

omni means (a) large (b) limitless _____ .

Copyright © by Houghton Mifflin Company. All rights reserved.

5. hyper

    a. Gail is *hyperactive,* so she enjoys jogging four miles every evening.

    b. Alex is *hypersensitive,* so be tactful when you offer your suggestions.

hyper means (a) excessive (b) lacking _____ .

6. anti

    a. The scientist's watch is *antimagnetic,* so its accuracy is unaffected by experiments involving magnets.

    b. The development of *antibiotics,* because of their effectiveness against harmful bacteria, has contributed significantly to the average life span.

anti means (a) increasing (b) opposing _____ .

7. voc, vok

    a. A *convocation* was called by the college dean to discuss the new graduation requirements.

    b. The unexpected letter *evoked* memories of her old friend.

voc and **vok** relate to (a) a calling (b) an arrival _____ .

8. bi

    a. The United States *bicentennial* in 1976 celebrated the country's two-hundredth anniversary.

    b. One of my neighbors has been accused of *bigamy;* apparently, his divorce was not finalized before he remarried.

bi means (a) two (b) luxury _____ .

9. path

    a. The newspaper's picture of the *pathetic* puppy brought many offers for adoption.

    b. The movie was full of *pathos,* and a number of people in the audience cried.

path has to do with (a) imagination (b) feelings _____ .

10. ben

    a. As the result of a generous contribution from an unannounced *benefactor,* our college will be able to complete its building plans.

    b. Hazel was the *beneficiary* of her aunt's insurance policy, so she can now afford to open a florist shop of her own.

ben means (a) disagreeable (b) favorable _____ .

Copyright © by Houghton Mifflin Company. All rights reserved.

EXERCISES FOR LESSON 9
Word Parts

I. *Directions:* Match each definition to the word part it defines.

_____ **1.** phil	**a.** to call; voice
_____ **2.** mal	**b.** good; well
_____ **3.** spec	**c.** to love
_____ **4.** omni	**d.** two
_____ **5.** hyper	**e.** to look
_____ **6.** anti	**f.** feelings
_____ **7.** voc, vok	**g.** over; excessive; beyond what is normal
_____ **8.** bi	**h.** all
_____ **9.** path	**i.** opposite; against
_____ **10.** ben	**j.** bad

II. *Directions:* Select the appropriate word part so the proper word is formed in each sentence.

phil	spec	hyper	voc	path
mal	omni	anti	bi	ben

1. I felt no sym _____ y for the rude young man when he was expelled from the restaurant.

2. Lately, my husband has been _____ social—he refuses to go anyplace where he might have to mingle with other people.

3. Gordon is pleased with the physical and emotional _____ efits regular exercise has brought him.

4. The airport is equipped with a(n) _____ directional device capable of transmitting or receiving signals in all directions.

5. The _____ anthropist's concern and generosity were deeply appreciated by those left homeless by the fire.

6. Coach Page admits she was _____ critical when she first began coaching, but now she offers suggestions in a positive, encouraging way.

7. Louise is unsure what _____ ation she should pursue.

8. Unfortunately, a great amount of _____ ice exists between the couple filing for divorce.

Copyright © by Houghton Mifflin Company. All rights reserved.

9. Pat brought _____ noculars to the game as our seats were high in the grandstand.

10. Ralph says that in retro _____ t, his high school years were some of the happiest years of his life.

III. *Directions:* Use your knowledge of the underlined word parts to match the definitions and words.

_____ 1. <u>bi</u>partisan

_____ 2. <u>bene</u>diction

_____ 3. biblio<u>phile</u>

_____ 4. <u>hyper</u>ventilate

_____ 5. <u>omni</u>bus

_____ 6. psycho<u>path</u>

_____ 7. <u>anti</u>dote

_____ 8. <u>mal</u>ign

_____ 9. <u>re</u>voke

_____ 10. <u>spec</u>ter

a. to breathe abnormally fast

b. both parties cooperating to achieve a common goal

c. a serious personality disorder in which a person expresses no normal feelings toward others

d. a haunting, disturbing image; a ghost

e. to speak badly about; to slander

f. substance that acts against poison

g. a prayer requesting God's blessing

h. to call back or to cancel what once was given or said

i. person who loves books

j. all-encompassing; comprehensive

IV. *Directions:* Write the definitions of the words after noting the underlined word parts and studying the context of the sentences; if you are still uncertain, feel free to consult a dictionary.

1. Cats and dogs are four-footed, but humans are *bipeds*.

   bipeds _____

2. The doctor diagnosed her injury as a *hyperextension* of her right knee.

   hyperextension _____

3. Did you get rid of your contact lenses so you could wear those groovy *spectacles?*

   spectacles _____

4. We were baffled by his *apathetic* response after we told him our exciting news.

   apathetic _____

Copyright © by Houghton Mifflin Company. All rights reserved.

5. The player glared *malevolently* at the referee after he was charged with a technical foul.

malevolently _____

6. As a result of the <u>bene</u>volent acts of many people in the community, a new house was built for the family who had lost their home due to lightning.

<u>bene</u>volent _____

7. When it was discovered that the young woman did not actually have a master's degree, the *revocation* of her recent appointment swiftly followed.

revocation _____

8. My neighbors are devoted to *philharmonic* music, so they never miss an opportunity to attend a symphony concert.

philharmonic _____

9. The *antiphonal* composition was performed by having the sopranos and altos singing at the front of the church and the tenors and basses responding at the back of the sanctuary.

antiphonal _____

10. The park's *omnifarious* garden contained every type of flower and bush that can grow in this state.

omnifarious _____

Copyright © by Houghton Mifflin Company. All rights reserved.

Challenging Words

1. philanthropy (fə LAN thrə pē)   noun

    a. As a result of the Webbs' *philanthropy,* the college was able to build a new Student Union.

    b. The famous athlete's *philanthropy* included generous financial contributions to the Salvation Army, the YWCA, and the United Way.

philanthropy has to do with a love of (a) publicity (b) humankind _____ .

2. malicious (mə LISH əs)—adjective

    a. A *malicious* rumor began circulating that the defendant had been found innocent because he had bribed a witness to lie for him.

    b. The police have just arrested the people responsible for the *malicious* attack on the elderly couple.

malicious is related to (a) wicked (b) bold _____ .

3. specter (SPEK tə r)—noun

    a. The swiftly moving fog was like some sort of *specter* one would see in a horror movie.

    b. A shimmering, blinding figure burst into view, a *specter* that filled us with dread.

specter is similar to a (a) storm (b) ghost _____ .

4. omnipotent (om NIP ə tent)—adjective

    a. The arrogant supervisor felt she was *omnipotent,* so she was shocked when the company's president took away much of her authority.

    b. Although the Supreme Court justices may appear to be *omnipotent*, their power is limited by the Constitution.

omnipotent means (a) all-powerful (b) everywhere _____ .

Copyright © by Houghton Mifflin Company. All rights reserved.

5. hypertension (HĪ pə r TEN shə n)—noun

    a. After checking the patient's blood pressure a number of times, the doctor gave the middle-aged man a prescription for his *hypertension.*

    b. My neighbor is watching her diet and exercising more in an effort to reduce her *hypertension.*

hypertension is (a) lack of muscular strength (b) high blood pressure _____ .

6. antithesis (an TITH ə sis)—noun

    a. She, fortunately, was the *antithesis* of a spoiled celebrity as she graciously signed autographs, posed for pictures with the children, and stayed to answer the reporters' questions.

    b. The sales representative first showed me a four-door blue sedan, which was the *antithesis* of what I was looking for, so I told him I wasn't interested in giving the car a test drive.

antithesis means (a) model of (b) opposite of _____ .

7. vociferous (vō SIF ər ə s)—adjective

    a. Our team's hockey fans have the reputation for being rowdy and *vociferous.*

    b. City council members have heard *vociferous* complaints about the rise in property taxes.

vociferous means (a) adventurous (b) loud _____ .

8. bilingual (bı LING gwəl)—adjective

    a. Sandra's *bilingual* ability was helpful to us all as she was able to speak to the waiter in French and then translate into English what he said.

    b. One of the requirements for that particular position with the Border Patrol is to be *bilingual* or, to be more specific, to have the ability to speak Spanish and English.

bilingual is the ability to (a) speak two languages (b) offer sound advice _____ .

9. empathy (EM pə thē)—noun

    a. My *empathy* for my young nephew was genuine because I can distinctly remember how upset I felt when my dog died during my childhood.

    b. I can generate no *empathy* for the striking ballplayers because they make so much more money than I do.

empathy is most closely related to (a) impatience (b) sympathy _____ .

Copyright © by Houghton Mifflin Company. All rights reserved.

10. <u>benign</u> (bə NĪN)—adjective

   a. My ferocious-looking dog actually has a *benign* disposition, so you have nothing to fear from him.

   b. I thought the food might be too spicy for my tastes, but it actually had a *benign* flavor.

benign means (a) mild (b) interesting _____ .

Copyright © by Houghton Mifflin Company. All rights reserved.

EXERCISES FOR LESSON 10
Challenging Words

I. *Directions:* Write each word before its definition.

philanthropy	specter	hypertension	vociferous	empathy
malicious	omnipotent	antithesis	bilingual	benign

_____ **1.** noisy, blaring, disruptive

_____ **2.** harmless, mild, inoffensive

_____ **3.** brutal, cruel

_____ **4.** opposite, other extreme

_____ **5.** helpfulness, generosity, charity

_____ **6.** identification with the feelings of another person

_____ **7.** almighty, all-powerful

_____ **8.** able to speak and/or write two languages

_____ **9.** high blood pressure

_____ **10.** ghost, spook

II. *Directions:* In each space, write the appropriate word from those listed below.

philanthropy	specter	hypertension	vociferous	empathy
malicious	omnipotent	antithesis	bilingual	benign

1. What started out as a friendly snowball fight between members of the two fraternities escalated into a(n) _____ brawl, resulting in a number of injuries and arrests.

2. Vincent's high-strung personality is the _____ of that of his older brother, who is much more laid-back.

3. The proceeds from the exhibition game were given to a charity; this _____ on the part of the promoters and players was wildly applauded by those in attendance.

4. The television ad stressed that untreated high blood pressure can lead to heart attacks and strokes, that everyone should be checked for _____ .

5. My boss usually has a calm, _____ personality, but she becomes extremely upset with her employees if they are late to work or ignore or are indifferent to customers in the store.

Copyright © by Houghton Mifflin Company. All rights reserved.

6. The _____ complaints of the coach, which could be heard throughout the gym, led to his dismissal from the game.

7. The man quietly responded, "Only God is immortal and _____ ."

8. I didn't know Julie was _____ until I heard her carry on a long conversation in Italian with her grandparents.

9. Steve has always enjoyed studying history, so he has no _____ for those who complain that it is a dry, uninteresting subject.

10. I never believed in ghosts until I saw some type of eerie _____ late one night when I drove by a graveyard.

III. *Directions:* After selecting your responses, put the letter before it in the space provided.

_____ **1.** The *opposite* of **benign** is
    a. nonthreatening
    b. deadly
    c. costly
    d. inexpensive

_____ **2.** The *opposite* of **philanthropy** is
    a. good health
    b. sickness
    c. generosity
    d. stinginess

_____ **3.** The *opposite* of **hypertension** is
    a. low blood pressure
    b. high blood pressure
    c. uncaring
    d. uptight

_____ **4. Empathy** suggests
    a. misunderstanding of
    b. anger within
    c. identification with
    d. nervousness about

_____ **5.** The word most closely associated with **vociferous** is
    a. infection
    b. insecurity
    c. intensity
    d. information

Copyright © by Houghton Mifflin Company. All rights reserved.

6. Bilingual is most closely associated with
a. mathematics
b. social sciences
c. biological sciences
d. languages

7. If a person thinks he or she sees a **specter,** he or she likely feels
a. frightened
b. delighted
c. unconcerned
d. confident

8. malicious : vicious :: a. laughing : crying
b. rebelling : obeying
c. kindliness : compassion
d. loss : tragedy

9. antithesis : identical :: a. captivating : interesting
b. opposite : same
c. alter : change
d. seek : search

10. omnipotent : weak :: a. weak : feeble
b. feeble : powerful
c. powerful : strong
d. strong : mighty

IV. *Directions:* Write an original sentence for each word that clearly demonstrates your mastery of its meaning.

1. philanthropy _____

_____

2. malicious _____

_____

3. specter _____

_____

4. omnipotent _____

_____

5. hypertension _____

_____

6. antithesis _____

_____

Copyright © by Houghton Mifflin Company. All rights reserved.

7. **vociferous** _____

_____

8. **bilingual** _____

_____

9. **empathy** _____

_____

10. **benign** _____

_____

Copyright © by Houghton Mifflin Company. All rights reserved.

Word Parts

1. fin

   a. The project should be *finished* by the first of October.
   b. What was the *final* score?

fin is associated with (a) completion (b) assignment _____ .

2. geo

   a. *Geography* involves the study of the earth's surface, climate, population, and natural resources.
   b. *Geochemistry* is the study of the earth's composition and chemical changes.

geo has to do with the (a) universe (b) earth _____ .

3. bell

   a. A *rebellion* erupted in the capital city.
   b. My enjoyment of the hockey game was undermined by the *bellicose* behavior of some of the players; their fighting spoiled an otherwise good contest.

bell means (a) war (b) noise _____ .

4. hydro, hydr

   a. The first automatic transmissions in cars were called *hydromatics* because fluids were the key to their operation.
   b. A *hydraulic* lift operates by fluid pressure.

hydro and **hydr** are associated with (a) power (b) liquids _____ .

5. ambi, amphi

   a. Shawn demonstrated his *ambidexterity* by writing first with his right hand and then with his left.
   b. An *amphibian,* such as a frog, can live on land or in water.

ambi and **amphi** mean (a) highly developed (b) both _____ .

Copyright © by Houghton Mifflin Company. All rights reserved.

6. less

    a. Holly is a *fearless* skier.
    b. It was another beautiful, *cloudless* day in New Mexico.

less means (a) without (b) until _____ .

7. hem

    a. *Hemoglobin* is the protein matter contained in red blood cells.
    b. *Hematology* is the medical study of the blood and blood producing organs.

hem means (a) small (b) blood _____ .

8. intra, intro

    a. *Intrastate* commerce refers to business transactions within a state.
    b. *Introverts* are people primarily concerned with their own thoughts and feelings.

intra and **intro** mean (a) modern (b) within _____ .

9. man

    a. Jess did *manual* work all summer, so he felt fit and strong when he reported for football practice in the fall.
    b. His hands and fingernails needed a *manicure*.

man has to do with (a) hands (b) skills _____ .

10. derm, dermis

    a. The rash only affected the outer layer of skin and was therefore *epidermal*.
    b. The *ectodermis* is the outer tissue of the embryo, which is the early developmental state of an organism.

derm and **dermis** have to do with (a) growth (b) skin _____ .

Copyright © by Houghton Mifflin Company. All rights reserved.

EXERCISES FOR LESSON 11
Word Parts

I. *Directions:* Match each definition to the word part it defines.

_____ **1.** fin	**a.** blood
_____ **2.** geo	**b.** water; fluids
3. bell	**c.** skin
_____ **4.** hydro, hydr	**d.** without
_____ **5.** ambi, amphi	**e.** hand
_____ **6.** less	**f.** war
_____ **7.** hem	**g.** end; limit
_____ **8.** intra, intro	**h.** earth
_____ **9.** man	**i.** both
_____ **10.** derm, dermis	**j.** inside; within

II. *Directions:* Select the appropriate word part so the proper word is formed in each sentence.

fin	bell	amphi	hem	man
geo	hydro	less	intra	derm

1. Athletic contests among students attending the same institution are referred to as _____ mural sports.

2. _____ bious planes can land on land or water.

3. All living things are _____ ite; their days are numbered.

4. The patient began to feel immediate relief after the doctor administered a hypo- _____ ic injection.

5. _____ electric power is generated by water.

6. A heavy discharge of blood is called a _____ orrhage.

7. Citizens are re _____ ing because of the dictator's repression.

8. _____ logy is concerned with the study of rocks and other aspects of the earth's physical history.

9. He was accused of _____ ipulating the records to cover his fraud.

10. Although it was a gray, cheer _____ day, Monica was in good spirits.

Copyright © by Houghton Mifflin Company. All rights reserved.

III. *Directions:* Use your knowledge of the underlined word parts to match the definitions and words.

_____ **1.** peer<u>less</u>   **a.** the stoppage of bleeding

_____ **2.** <u>geo</u>thermal   **b.** existing before the U.S. Civil War

_____ **3.** <u>hydro</u>foil   **c.** handcuffs

_____ **4.** <u>hemo</u>stasis   **d.** relating to earth's internal heat

_____ **5.** <u>in</u>finite   **e.** skin inflammation

_____ **6.** <u>intro</u>spection   **f.** having no equals; can't be matched

_____ **7.** <u>ante</u>bellum   **g.** having more than one possible

_____ **8.** <u>ambi</u>guous   meaning; uncertain

_____ **9.** <u>derm</u>atitis   **h.** without ending

_____ **10.** <u>man</u>acles   **i.** winglike boat

j. observation of one's own mental processes

IV. *Directions:* Write the definitions of the words after noting the underlined word parts and studying the context of the sentences; if you are still unsure, feel free to consult a dictionary.

1. The director recommended that the rare bird that had just died be taken to the local *taxi<u>derm</u>ist* so museum visitors would still be able to see what the bird had looked like in real life.

taxi<u>derm</u>ist _____

2. The beautiful old *manu<u>script</u>,* written in the 17th century, was in remarkably good condition.

manu<u>script</u> _____

3. The *<u>intra</u>venous* injection soon relieved the patient's discomfort.

<u>intra</u>venous _____

4. Do you have any other fears besides *<u>hemo</u>phobia?*

<u>hemo</u>phobia _____

5. He remained *heed<u>less</u>* of the advice offered him by his fellow employees, so, as a consequence, he was soon out of a job.

heed<u>less</u> _____

Copyright © by Houghton Mifflin Company. All rights reserved.

6. After being in the scorching sun much of the day, she felt _dehydrated,_ so she drank plenty of water when she got home.

dehydrated _____

7. The child attempted to count the raindrops running down his bedroom window, but they proved to be _infinitesimal,_ so he eventually turned his attention to the toys scattered about his room.

infinitesimal _____

8. After the _rebellious_ crowd was finally quieted, a police officer told the people to disperse or they would be arrested for disturbing the peace.

rebellious _____

9. His responses were characteristic of a person who displays both an inward and an outward personality, so he was classified as an _ambivert._

ambivert _____

10. Most astronomical measurements are _geocentric_ because objects in space are usually related to their distance from earth.

geocentric _____

Copyright © by Houghton Mifflin Company. All rights reserved.

Challenging Words

1. **finale** (fə NAL ē)—noun

   a. When the orchestra finished the *finale* of Beethoven's Ninth Symphony, the audience stood and applauded.

   b. The Fourth of July celebration's *finale* was highlighted by a spectacular fireworks display.

finale means (a) conclusion (b) prominence _____ .

2. **geopolitics** (JĒ ō POL i tiks)—noun

   a. *Geopolitics* is a major determiner as to how countries relate to each other economically.

   b. An understanding of a nation's *geopolitics* is important because a country's natural resources and location in the world significantly contribute to the living conditions of its people, including the type of government under which they live.

geopolitics involves the study of how (a) biology (b) geography influences international relationships _____ .

3. **belligerent** (bə LIJ ər ənt)—adjective

   a. Police officers arrested some members of the *belligerent* crowd after they tried to block the entrance to the park.

   b. The teacher sent the sassy, *belligerent* pupil to the principal's office.

belligerent means (a) argumentative (b) independent _____ .

4. **hydrology** (hī DROL ə jē)—noun

   a. As a civil engineer specializing in the construction and maintenance of dams, Mr. O'Neil is an expert in *hydrology*.

   b. Irrigation and landscape specialists must be knowledgeable in *hydrology* since water plays such an important part in their work.

hydrology is a science concerned with the study of (a) water (b) plants _____ .

Copyright © by Houghton Mifflin Company. All rights reserved.

5. ambivalence (am BIV ə lə ns)—noun

    a. Ed is experiencing *ambivalence* because he can't decide whether to go to college or to join the Navy.

    b. Helen's *ambivalence* about whether to audition for the repertory theater is understandable because of her already demanding college schedule.

ambivalence is associated with (a) sorrow (b) indecision _____ .

6. dauntless (DANT lis)—adjective

    a. The *dauntless* eight-year-old girl jumped off the high diving board.

    b. The firefighters were recognized for their *dauntless* courage in rescuing the terrified family from their burning home.

dauntless means without (a) planning (b) fear _____ .

7. hemostat (H$\overline{E}$ mə STAT)—noun

    a. The surgeon clamped a *hemostat* on the vein to stop the bleeding.

    b. The bleeding was slight, so no *hemostat* was needed.

hemostat is a medical instrument used to stop (a) bleeding (b) pain _____ .

8. introvert (IN trə VURT)—noun

    a. Reena was an *introvert* during her early teenage years, but now she is much more sociable and outgoing.

    b. The young man became so much of an *introvert* over the years that he seldom visited or even inquired about his friends and relatives.

introvert refers to a person concerned mainly with (a) becoming well known (b) his or her own thoughts and feelings _____ .

9. manhandle (MAN han d ə l)—verb

    a. Our young son soon learned not to *manhandle* the kitten after she scratched him on the arm.

    b. If you continue to *manhandle* the ladder in that way, you're either going to hurt yourself or break a window.

manhandle means to do something in a (a) rough (b) complex manner _____ .

10. dermatology (DUR mə TOL ə jē)—noun

    a. Teenagers sometimes suffer so much from acne that they have to consult a specialist in *dermatology*.

    b. According to this article about *dermatology* matters, sun-tanning booths are unsafe.

dermatology is concerned with (a) psychological problems (b) the skin _____ .

Copyright © by Houghton Mifflin Company. All rights reserved.

Name .... Section .... Date ....

EXERCISES FOR LESSON 12
Challenging Words

I. *Directions:* Write each word before its definition.

finale	belligerent	ambivalence	hemostat	manhandle
geopolitics	hydrology	dauntless	introvert	dermatology

_____ **1.** the final section, end, climax, final event

_____ **2.** without fear, bold, daring

_____ **3.** science dealing with the skin and its diseases

_____ **4.** person concerned primarily with his or her own thoughts and feelings

_____ **5.** to do something in a gruff or abusive way

_____ **6.** disagreeable, combative, aggressively disobedient

_____ **7.** uncertainty, hesitation, doubt, conflicting feelings

_____ **8.** instrument used to compress bleeding vessels

_____ **9.** science concerned with the occurrence, circulation, distribution, and properties of water

_____ **10.** study of how geography affects relationships among countries

II. *Directions:* In each space, write the appropriate word from those listed below.

finale	belligerent	ambivalence	hemostat	manhandle
geopolitics	hydrology	dauntless	introvert	dermatology

1. Despite the driver's rude and _____ behavior, the state trooper remained calm and respectful.

2. Roger is certainly not a(n) _____ as he loves to be around people and know what their opinions are about every subject imaginable.

3. Brooke has finished her basic medical training, and now she plans to specialize in _____ as she is interested in helping patients with skin cancer and other serious skin diseases.

4. Although Jim weighs only 130 pounds, he is a(n) _____ hockey player as he's not afraid to slam into much bigger opponents to get to the puck.

5. For the _____ , the rock band played a medley of its hits, then left the stage to thunderous applause and cheers.

Copyright © by Houghton Mifflin Company. All rights reserved.

6. Phil is enrolled in a two-year program having to do with golf courses, and one of the classes he's presently taking is _____ since water plays such a crucial role in the proper care of a course's fairways and greens.

7. "Geographical factors," the instructor stressed, "must be understood if insight is to be gained on how a nation interacts with other nations, so pay particular attention to matters relating to _____ when this subject enters our discussions."

8. The basketball coach at our small but prestigious college is well known and greatly admired by everyone associated with our school, including players, students, staff, faculty, and administrators, so I can understand his _____ when it comes to whether he should accept the pressure-packed coaching offer from a large out-of-state university.

9. The instructor scolded the students after he saw them _____ some of the expensive laboratory equipment.

10. The nervous medical student had difficulty clamping the _____ on the patient's spurting vein.

III. *Directions:* After selecting your response, put the letter before it in the space provided.

_____ **1.** The *opposite* of **dauntless** is
a. tightness
b. fearless
c. timid
d. grouchy

_____ **2.** The *opposite* of **ambivalence** is
a. harshness
b. certainty
c. accelerate
d. inspect

_____ **3.** The *opposite* of **finale** is
a. demotion
b. promotion
c. demonstration
d. beginning

_____ **4.** **Geopolitics** is associated with
a. foreign policy
b. national scandal
c. advanced mathematics
d. dishonest elections

Copyright © by Houghton Mifflin Company. All rights reserved.

5. Manhandle suggests
    a. precision
    b. distinction
    c. weakness
    d. mistreatment

6. Hydrology is associated with
    a. language
    b. psychology
    c. fire
    d. water

7. If a person is an **introvert,** he or she is likely to be
    a. popular
    b. elderly
    c. shy
    d. extravagant

8. hemostat : medicine :: a. chalk : teaching
    b. trombone : talent
    c. radio : advertisements
    d. tire : necessity

9. belligerent : rival :: a. unfaithful : patriot
    b. courageous : coward
    c. cooperative : friend
    d. insulting : stranger

10. dermatology : peculiar :: a. biology : required
    b. psychology : average
    c. ecology : expected
    d. ophthalmology : odd

IV. *Directions:* Write an original sentence for each word that clearly demonstrates your mastery of its meaning.

1. finale _____

_____

2. geopolitics _____

_____

3. belligerent _____

_____

4. hydrology _____

_____

Copyright © by Houghton Mifflin Company. All rights reserved.

5. ambivalence _____

_____

6. dauntless _____

_____

7. hemostat _____

_____

8. introvert _____

_____

9. manhandle _____

_____

10. dermatology _____

_____

Copyright © by Houghton Mifflin Company. All rights reserved.

Word Parts

1. bon, boun

    a. Carolyn received a _bonus_ for exceeding the yearly sales quota.

    b. The winners of the contest donated their _bounty_ to a number of charities.

bon and **boun** mean (a) beneficial (b) unexpected _____ .

2. multi

    a. A _multitude_ of people were crowded in front of the courthouse.

    b. It was a _multinational_ meeting, with representatives from as far away as Finland and China.

multi means (a) many (b) noisy _____ .

3. hypo

    a. _Hypothyroidism_ is a deficient functioning of the thyroid gland.

    b. The patient has _hypotension,_ the opposite of high blood pressure.

hypo is related to (a) vagueness (b) lack _____ .

4. neo

    a. The _Neolithic_ period in history was the first time farming and certain advanced stone tools were introduced.

    b. A _neologism_ is a new word or phrase.

neo is associated with something that is (a) old-fashioned (b) recent _____ .

5. ful, ous

    a. A _frightful_ tornado carried Dorothy's house away.

    b. The well water was found to be _poisonous._

ful and **ous** mean (a) full of (b) changeable _____ .

Copyright © by Houghton Mifflin Company. All rights reserved.

6. non

   a. My cousin is a _nonconformist,_ so he has trouble with those in authority.

   b. I'm _nonpartisan,_ so I don't care which candidate wins the election.

non means (a) super (b) not _____ .

7. aud

   a. The _audio_ circuits in the television set reproduce the sound.

   b. The _auditorium_ was almost empty although the game was scheduled to begin in fifteen minutes.

aud is related to (a) technology (b) sound _____ .

8. extra, ultra

   a. It was _extraordinary_ for Miami to be so cool in March.

   b. Mr. Michaels is an _ultraconservative_—he doesn't believe in any type of federal aid for education.

extra and **ultra** mean beyond (a) normal (b) possibility _____ .

9. temp

   a. _Tempo_ refers to the speed at which a musical passage is played.

   b. Angela was appointed as a _temporary_ replacement for Brenda.

temp refers to (a) authority (b) time _____

10. ward

   a. It had been a long, tiring trip, so we were happy to be finally heading _homeward._

   b. After resting for a while, the elderly lady hobbled _forward_ to the post office.

ward means (a) toward (b) slowly _____ .

Copyright © by Houghton Mifflin Company. All rights reserved.

Name .... Section .... Date ....

EXERCISES FOR LESSON 13
Word Parts

I. *Directions:* Match each definition to the word part it defines.

_____	**1.** bon, boun	**a.**	full of
_____	**2.** multi	**b.**	good
_____	**3.** hypo	**c.**	not
_____	**4.** neo	**d.**	beyond; extreme
_____	**5.** ful, ous	**e.**	toward; in the direction of
_____	**6.** non	**f.**	time
_____	**7.** aud	**g.**	under; insufficient
_____	**8.** extra, ultra	**h.**	hear; listen
_____	**9.** temp	**i.**	many
_____	**10.** ward	**j.**	new

II. *Directions:* Select the appropriate word part so the proper word is formed in each sentence.

bon	hypo	ous	aud	temp
multi	neo	non	extra	ward

1. The wallpaper is _____ colored, including shades of blue, red, green, and brown.

2. We were able to understand her speech because she explained the basic concepts in plain, _____ technical language.

3. My son bought a hide _____ Halloween mask.

4. The Gardners are living _____ orarily in an apartment on Maple Street.

5. The patient was suffering from _____ calcemia, a deficiency of calcium in the blood.

6. I'm not fond of heights, so I never look down _____ once I climb a ladder.

7. The medical laboratory announced it had developed a(n) _____ mycin, a new antibiotic to fight a variety of infections.

8. Martha won the cash prize, which was a much-needed _____ anza for her.

9. The Olympic Games were a wonderful _____ vaganza to watch.

10. The _____ ience sat in complete silence during the children's concert.

Copyright © by Houghton Mifflin Company. All rights reserved.

III. *Directions:* Use your knowledge of the underlined word parts to match the definitions and words.

_____ **1.** <u>tempor</u>al	**a.** unwilling to take sides or commit oneself; cautious
_____ **2.** <u>extra</u>curricular	**b.** deficiency in size; underdeveloped condition
_____ **3.** <u>non</u>committal	
_____ **4.** <u>audi</u>tory	**c.** concerned with time
_____ **5.** tumultu<u>ous</u>	**d.** reflecting a new interest in or rebirth of old architectural, artistic, or musical styles
_____ **6.** <u>neo</u>classic	
_____ **7.** <u>hypo</u>plasia	**e.** abundant; generous
_____ **8.** <u>multi</u>farious	**f.** in addition to or outside of the regular academic offerings
_____ **9.** lee<u>ward</u>	
_____ **10.** bountiful	**g.** facing the direction toward which the wind is blowing

h. having to do with sound or hearing

i. full of violence or noisy commotion

j. of various kinds; having many different parts

IV. *Directions:* Write the definitions of the words after noting the underlined word parts and studying the context of the sentences; if you are still uncertain, feel free to consult a dictionary.

1. Since his retirement, my grandfather has become a *vora<u>cious</u>* reader, reading everything from newspapers to novels and from poems to periodicals.

   vora<u>cious</u> _____

2. What he said was *in<u>audible</u>* to me because of the noisy traffic passing by.

   in<u>audible</u> _____

3. The infection had spread to the *<u>hypo</u>dermal* area, so it was fortunate indeed that Bradley's friends had finally succeeded in persuading him to go to the emergency room for treatment.

   <u>hypo</u>dermal _____

4. Every time Greg asked about his promised promotion, his boss either changed the subject, pretended he didn't hear, or resorted to some other *<u>tempo</u>rizing* tactic.

   <u>tempo</u>rizing _____

Copyright © by Houghton Mifflin Company. All rights reserved.

5. The realtor told us that ours was the only _bonafide_ offer made for the property, so she was sure the owners would accept it.

bonafide _____

6. His tendency to _inwardness_ became even more noticeable to his few friends after his girlfriend broke up with him.

inwardness _____

7. The teacher often supplemented her lectures with impressive _multimedia_ presentations.

multimedia _____

8. Stan is known for being a _nonconformist_, so few people were surprised that he showed up at the banquet wearing bib overalls instead of a tuxedo.

nonconformist _____

9. Having never been around babies much before, the medical student was pleasantly surprised by how much he enjoyed working in the _neonatal_ section of the hospital.

neonatal _____

10. The machine's _ultrasonic_ frequency is well beyond a human's hearing capacity.

ultrasonic _____

Copyright © by Houghton Mifflin Company. All rights reserved.

Challenging Words

1. **bounteous** (BOUN tē əs)—adjective

   a. All the wheat farmers I've recently talked to are in a happy frame of mind because they expect a *bounteous* harvest in a couple of weeks.
   b. The flood victims expressed their gratitude for the *bounteous* gifts of food, furniture, appliances, and money from their fellow citizens throughout the country.

bounteous means (a) beautiful (b) plentiful _____ .

2. **multifaceted** (MUL tə FAS ə tid)—adjective

   a. Bradley has *multifaceted* interests, ranging from Civil War history to kayaking.
   b. Kathy's *multifaceted* acting talent enables her to play many roles.

multifaceted is related to (a) many (b) impressive _____ .

3. **hypochondria** (HĪ pə KON drē ə)—noun

   a. My uncle was usually in good physical health, but his spirits were often low because he worried constantly that he was harboring some serious illness; *hypochondria,* unfortunately, had plagued him much of his life.
   b. The doctor said a significant number of his patients had nothing wrong with them other than depression brought on by their *hypochondria,* or imaginary illnesses.

hypochondria is a preoccupation with (a) social approval (b) supposed ailments _____ .

4. **neophyte** (NĒ ə FĪT)—noun

   a. I had played golf only once before, but, fortunately, my companion was also a *neophyte.*
   b. Rick is certainly not a *neophyte* drummer as he's been playing with one band or another since he was in seventh grade.

neophyte means a (a) beginner (b) shy person _____ .

Copyright © by Houghton Mifflin Company. All rights reserved.

5. acrimonious (ak rə MŌ nē əs)—adjective

    a. I thought my friends were having an *acrimonious* discussion, but I finally realized they were just kidding one another.

    b. The *acrimonious* shouting was from one of my neighbors who was upset because my dog had made a mess on his lawn.

acrimonious means (a) unreasonable (b) angry _____ .

6. nondescript (NON də SKRIPT)—adjective

    a. Most of the guests were stylishly dressed, but a few were wearing *nondescript* jeans, khakis, and rumpled sweaters or sweatshirts.

    b. He obviously isn't interested in cars or doesn't make much money because he drives a ten-year-old *nondescript* four-door sedan.

nondescript means (a) colorful (b) dull _____ .

7. audible (Ö də bəl)—adjective

    a. Because Olivia had yelled so much at the game, her voice was barely *audible* when she got home.

    b. The instructor uses a microphone to make his voice *audible* throughout the large lecture hall.

audible means (a) hearable (b) accented _____ .

8. extraneous (ik STRĀ nē əs)—adjective

    a. One of the committee members continuously made comments having nothing to do with the topic, and his *extraneous* remarks unnecessarily prolonged the meeting.

    b. The contractor tried to add some *extraneous* charges to his bill, but when I challenged him about their fairness, he agreed to drop them.

extraneous means (a) complicated (b) irrelevant _____ .

9. contemporary (kən TEM pə rer ē)—adjective, noun

    a. My older brother, a classically trained musician, doesn't care much for *contemporary* music.

    b. Ron was a *contemporary* of mine in high school, so he must be around twenty-six years old, as I am.

contemporary refers to the (a) present, or of the same time (b) past, or of a different era _____ .

Copyright © by Houghton Mifflin Company. All rights reserved.

10. way<u>ward</u> (WĀ wərd)—adjective

    a. The kindergarten teacher at first had difficulty with the *wayward* youngster because he refused to sit down or to participate in any activity.

    b. One of my relatives' *wayward* way of life has resulted in two failed marriages and the loss of numerous jobs.

wayward means (a) secretive (b) unruly _____ .

Copyright © by Houghton Mifflin Company. All rights reserved.

EXERCISES FOR LESSON 14
Challenging Words

I. *Directions:* Write each word before its definition.

bounteous   hypochondria   acrimonious   audible   contemporary
multifaceted   neophyte   nondescript   extraneous   wayward

_____   **1.** unremarkable, lacking in distinctive qualities
_____   **2.** beside the point, irrelevant, unnecessary
_____   **3.** many-sided, wide-ranging
_____   **4.** harsh, bitter, hostile, angry
_____   **5.** capable of being heard
_____   **6.** turning away from what is right and proper; disobedient, contrary, obstinate
_____   **7.** a preoccupation with imaginary illnesses
_____   **8.** plentiful, generous, overflowing, abundant
_____   **9.** amateur, beginner
_____   **10.** of the same time or date, or of the here and now

II. *Directions:* In each space, write the appropriate word from those listed below.

bounteous   hypochondria   acrimonious   audible   contemporary
multifaceted   neophyte   nondescript   extraneous   wayward

1. We were talking about the importance of Russell getting a doctor's appointment when Wally started making _____ remarks about the great time he had had in Las Vegas.

2. I grew up in a(n) _____ housing development, the type you see in almost every city.

3. One of my grandfathers is now wearing hearing aids because normal sounds and conversations were no longer _____ to him.

4. In my opinion, _____ cars are much better designed and engineered than those of any other time.

5. The employee benefits are indeed _____ , so it's no wonder the company has no difficulty filling a position when one does become available.

6. An elderly person well known for his _____ throughout his life had engraved on his tombstone *"See, I told you I was sick!"*

Copyright © by Houghton Mifflin Company. All rights reserved.

7. Because he is a(n) _____ in the teaching profession, our instructor was obviously nervous the first couple of weeks of the semester.

8. Their _____ son, who had a previous criminal record, was recently sentenced to five years in prison.

9. Flying, I quickly learned, is a(n) _____ undertaking as there are many things to learn and many skills to master.

10. The chefs were having a(n) _____ debate over who was to be in charge of the lavish meal.

III. *Directions:* After selecting your response, put the letter before it in the space provided.

_____ **1.** The *opposite* of **acrimonious** is
    a. friendly
    b. dangerous
    c. spacious
    d. hostile

_____ **2.** The *opposite* of **bounteous** is
    a. ugly
    b. intelligent
    c. stiff
    d. scarce

_____ **3.** The *opposite* of **nondescript** is
    a. continuous
    b. interfering
    c. unique
    d. ordinary

_____ **4. Hypochondria** is associated with people who think they are
    a. foolish
    b. sick
    c. disliked
    d. religious

_____ **5.** Which of the following is likely to be the most **audible?**
    a. memo
    b. gesture
    c. whisper
    d. shout

_____ **6. Multifaceted** is associated with
    a. expense
    b. simplicity
    c. variety
    d. lying

Copyright © by Houghton Mifflin Company. All rights reserved.

_____ 7. If a person is **wayward,** he or she is likely to be
   a. popular
   b. talented
   c. defiant
   d. friendly

_____ 8. **contemporary : modern ::** **a.** modern : up-to-date
   b. up-to-date : old-fashioned
   c. old-fashioned : current
   d. current : out of style

_____ 9. **extraneous : essential ::** **a.** necessary : required
   b. character : personality
   c. happy : delighted
   d. neat : sloppy

_____ 10. **neophyte : beginner ::** **a.** neighbor : stranger
   b. rookie : trainee
   c. expert : amateur
   d. teacher : student

IV. _Directions:_ Write an original sentence for each word that clearly demonstrates your mastery of its meaning.

1. **bounteous** _____

   _____

2. **multifaceted** _____

   _____

3. **hypochondria** _____

   _____

4. **neophyte** _____

   _____

5. **acrimonious** _____

   _____

6. **nondescript** _____

   _____

7. **audible** _____

   _____

8. **extraneous** _____

   _____

Copyright © by Houghton Mifflin Company. All rights reserved.

9. contemporary _____

_____

10. wayward _____

_____

Copyright © by Houghton Mifflin Company. All rights reserved.

Word Parts

1. ann, enn

    a. Our <u>*ann*</u>*ual* family reunion will be in Ohio this year.
    b. We look forward to our *per<u>enn</u>ial* flowers blooming every spring.

ann and **enn** mean (a) beautiful (b) year _____ .

2. gram, graph

    a. We completed the project by following the steps outlined in the *dia<u>gram.</u>*
    b. The television star signed her *auto<u>graph</u>* on the restaurant's menu.

gram and **graph** mean (a) writing (b) working _____ .

3. phon

    a. A specific speech sound is known as a *<u>phon</u>eme.*
    b. Our old *<u>phon</u>ograph* still has an excellent sound.

phon is most closely associated with (a) sound (b) music _____ .

4. mor, mort

    a. After his serious illness, he realized his *<u>mort</u>ality* for the first time.
    b. Mr. Wolfe, who operates a funeral home on Sixth Street, has been a *<u>mort</u>ician* for over forty years.

mor and **mort** are most closely associated with (a) endurance (b) death _____ .

5. pos

    a. Lucas was promoted to a supervisory *<u>pos</u>ition.*
    b. During the museum's remodeling, paintings were stored in a *re<u>pos</u>itory.*

pos has to do with (a) leadership (b) location _____ .

Copyright © by Houghton Mifflin Company. All rights reserved.

6. cap

    a. Andy was elected *captain* of the team.

    b. Madison is the *capital* of Wisconsin.

cap means (a) head (b) fame   _____ .

7. dia

    a. The length of a straight line through the center of a figure is the *diameter.*

    b. The *diastolic* reading is obtained when the blood is passing through the heart's chambers.

dia means passing (a) through (b) around   _____ .

8. ness

    a. Mr. Lewis enjoys the *quietness* of the early mornings.

    b. Everybody was enjoying the child's *silliness* except his embarrassed parents.

ness relates to (a) absence of (b) condition of   _____ .

9. hetero

    a. Words having the same spelling but different pronunciations and meanings, such as *lead* (a metal) and *lead* (to conduct), are called *heteronyms.*

    b. Animals of this type are generally *heterochromatic,* that is, of mixed colors.

hetero refers to (a) difference (b) similarity   _____ .

10. homo

    a. Words having the identical spelling and pronunciation but different meanings, such as *bat* (a club) and *bat* (a flying mammal), are called *homonyms.*

    b. Animals of this type are generally *homochromatic,* that is, one color.

homo refers to (a) difference (b) similarity   _____ .

Copyright © by Houghton Mifflin Company. All rights reserved.

Name .... Section .... Date ....

EXERCISES FOR LESSON 15
Word Parts

I. *Directions:* Match each definition to the word part it defines.

_____ **1.** ann, enn	**a.** sound
_____ **2.** gram, graph	**b.** condition of; capable of
_____ **3.** phon	**c.** write
_____ **4.** mor, mort	**d.** same; like
_____ **5.** pos	**e.** head; chief
_____ **6.** cap	**f.** year
_____ **7.** dia	**g.** different
_____ **8.** ness	**h.** place; location
_____ **9.** hetero	**i.** through
_____ **10.** homo	**j.** death

II. *Directions:* Select the appropriate word part so the proper word is formed in each sentence.

enn	phon	pos	dia	hetero
graph	mort	cap	ness	homo

1. His stooped _____ ture is due to a back injury.

2. A _____ gonal path had been worn in the grass leading from the post office to the bank.

3. Our college will be celebrating its cent _____ ial this year.

4. Tragically, the injuries the young woman suffered in the accident proved _____ al; she died a few hours later.

5. The article begins with a(n) _____ tion that summarizes the major points the author discusses.

6. _____ genized milk is made by blending milk and cream.

7. _____ ics is a method of teaching reading by having students master the common sounds of letters and letter combinations.

8. Holding religious views contrary to established church doctrines is known as _____ doxy.

9. Linda eventually tired of her boyfriend's moodi _____ , so she broke up with him.

10. The term associated with correct spelling is ortho _____ y.

Copyright © by Houghton Mifflin Company. All rights reserved.

III. *Directions:* Use your knowledge of the underlined word parts to match the definitions and words.

_____ 1. pho<u>net</u>ic   **a.** to place, put, or set

_____ 2. haughti<u>ness</u>   **b.** having a common center

_____ 3. <u>graph</u>ite   **c.** muscular membrane across the

_____ 4. de<u>capit</u>ate   lower part of the chest

_____ 5. <u>homo</u>centric   **d.** funeral room

_____ 6. <u>dia</u>phragm   **e.** excessive pride and arrogance

_____ 7. <u>mort</u>uary   **f.** occurring twice a year

_____ 8. bi<u>ann</u>ual   **g.** pertaining to speech sounds

_____ 9. <u>hetero</u>sexual   **h.** pertaining to the opposite sex

_____ 10. po<u>sit</u>   **i.** mineral used for pencil leads

                                             j. to cut off the head

IV. *Directions:* Write the definitions of the words after noting the underlined word parts and studying the context of the sentences; if you are still uncertain, feel free to consult a dictionary.

1. Fred's tendency for gaudiness in clothes was very much in evidence as he was wearing orange slacks, red shirt, purple tie, green sneakers, and an old-fashioned straw hat.

   gaudi<u>ness</u> _____

2. Management refused to *<u>capit</u>ulate* to the union's demands, so a strike costly to both sides occurred.

   <u>capit</u>ulate _____

3. A small white *mono<u>gram</u>* on the upper-left side of his blue sweater read "Bluejays."

   mono<u>gram</u> _____

4. My aunt's *<u>hetero</u>dox* religious views contrasted sharply with those held by all the churches in the community, so she never became a member of any of them.

   <u>hetero</u>dox _____

Copyright © by Houghton Mifflin Company. All rights reserved.

5. A number of new file cabinets and an impressively large walnut desk were *juxtaposed* against the south wall of his spacious new office.

juxtaposed _____

6. The manager's *diatribe* against the homeplate umpire could be heard throughout the stands.

diatribe _____

7. The houses in the new subdivision were attractive, but their *homogeneity* turned me off.

homogeneity _____

8. If the Cubs, White Sox, Bears, Blackhawks, and Bulls would all win championships in the same years, it would certainly be an *annus mirabilis*!

annus mirabilis _____

9. The state trooper warned the young woman to drive slower and more carefully in such conditions; otherwise, he said, she might discover she wasn't *immortal,* as she apparently assumed she was.

immortal _____

10. Words such as *great-grate, to-two-too,* and *bare-bear* are *homophones.*

homophones _____

Copyright © by Houghton Mifflin Company. All rights reserved.

Challenging Words

1. <u>annuity</u> (ə NOO ə tē)—noun

   a. Holly is contributing to a financial plan that will pay her an *annuity* of guaranteed income every month after she retires.

   b. My grandparents' income is based upon social security payments and an *annuity* they receive four times a year.

annuity refers to financial (a) deductions (b) payments during specific times of the year _____ .

2. <u>graphology</u> (gra FOL ə jē)—noun

   a. An expert on *graphology* is studying the suspect's handwriting to see if it corresponds to that on the ransom note.

   b. A *graphology* analysis indicated my friend is a confident, optimistic person, but I'm not convinced handwriting reveals that much about a person's personality.

graphology is concerned with the study of (a) handwriting (b) health _____ .

3. <u>cacophony</u> (kə KOF ə nē)—noun

   a. The *cacophony* of music, laughter, and shouting next door made sleeping impossible.

   b. Before the concert began, members of the orchestra tuned their instruments separately, creating a *cacophony* of weird sounds.

cacophony refers to sounds that are (a) harsh (b) pleasant _____ .

4. <u>moribund</u> (MOR ə BUND)—adjective

   a. My friend's limousine business has been in a *moribund* condition for some time, so I wasn't surprised that he's started bankruptcy proceedings.

   b. The veterinarian told us she was sorry, but that our dog was in a *moribund* state and would probably die before the day was over.

moribund means near (a) danger (b) death _____ .

Copyright © by Houghton Mifflin Company. All rights reserved.

5. **composure** (kəm PŌ zhər)—noun

    a. The speaker kept his *composure* despite the heckling from some members of the audience.

    b. After a hectic day at work, Teri regains her *composure* by taking a refreshing shower, listening to some soothing music, drinking herbal tea, and stretching out in a recliner.

composure refers to (a) calmness (b) humor _____ .

6. **capricious** (kə PRISH əs)—adjective

    a. My youngest brother is so *capricious* he's likely to do anything that suddenly pops into his head.

    b. Spring can be *capricious,* with summer temperatures one day and winter ones the next.

capricious means (a) steady (b) erratic _____ .

7. **diaphanous** (dī AF ə nəs)—adjective

    a. Nylon is an example of a sheer, *diaphanous* material.

    b. The new model was obviously self-conscious in her flimsy, *diaphanous* dress.

diaphanous means (a) transparent (b) expensive _____ .

8. **blandness** (BLAND nəs)—noun

    a. Rose, known for the *blandness* of her personality in high school, surprised her old classmates at the reunion because of her charming, outgoing manner.

    b. The *blandness* of the flat, brown countryside made Logan yearn for the lush, green valleys of his home state.

blandness means lacking in (a) simplicity (b) interest _____ .

9. **heterogeneous** (HET ər ə JĒ nē əs)—adjective

    a. A *heterogeneous* group of business people, including a laundromat owner, a dog trainer, a beauty salon operator, and a pharmacist, attended the city council meeting on the proposed zoning change.

    b. Justin's *heterogeneous* talents, ranging from painting to plumbing, made him the ideal choice for the custodian's job at the summer camp.

heterogeneous means (a) related (b) unrelated _____ .

10. **homogeneous** (HO mə JĒ nē əs)—adjective

    a. One reason we cousins get along so well is because of our *homogeneous* interests as we all love to fish, hunt, hike, and camp.

    b. The houses along one side of the lake were a *homogeneous* group of A-frames.

homogeneous means (a) related (b) unrelated _____ .

Copyright © by Houghton Mifflin Company. All rights reserved.

EXERCISES FOR LESSON 16
Challenging Words

I. *Directions:* Write each word before its definition.

annuity	cacophony	composure	diaphanous	heterogeneous
graphology	moribund	capricious	blandness	homogeneous

_____ **1.** similar, alike, corresponding

_____ **2.** impulsive, changeable, flighty, unstable, acting as if one can do anything at any time

_____ **3.** money received at specific times of the year

_____ **4.** calm state of mind, tranquility, poise, self-control

_____ **5.** dullness, something boring or indistinct

_____ **6.** the study of handwriting

_____ **7.** in a dying state, near death

_____ **8.** dissimilar, various, unlike

_____ **9.** transparent, see-through, delicate

_____ **10.** disagreeable sound that is grating, harsh, or unharmonious

II. *Directions:* In each space, write the appropriate word from those listed below.

annuity	cacophony	composure	diaphanous	heterogeneous
graphology	moribund	capricious	blandness	homogeneous

1. Until the AMTRAK system was developed, passenger trains were practically _____ in most states.

2. Sue suddenly felt like doing something _____ , so instead of going to work, she turned her car around and headed for the mall.

3. The soldiers looked so _____ in their uniforms when they marched by the reviewing stand that Jennifer couldn't pick out her husband.

4. According to experts in _____ , people's handwriting reveals a great deal about their character.

5. The racetrack was a _____ of squealing tires, gunning motors, and blaring reports from the stadium's speakers.

6. Brent said his IRA (individual retirement account) will eventually provide him with a(n) _____ , guaranteeing him a certain income for life.

7. Although the Eagles trailed throughout most of the game, they kept their _____ and were able to rally and pull out a victory.

Copyright © by Houghton Mifflin Company. All rights reserved.

8. We had nothing in common, but despite our _____ backgrounds and interests, my new roommate and I became good friends by the end of the semester.

9. Even though it's a(n) _____ material, gauze is a strong cloth.

10. Some critics panned the movie for its _____ , saying the dialogue was boring and the plot predictable.

III. *Directions:* After selecting your response, put the letter before it in the space provided.

_____ 1. The *opposite* of **capricious** is
    a. capable
    b. healthy
    c. predictable
    d. stingy

_____ 2. The *opposite* of **cacophony** is
    a. genuine
    b. melodious
    c. embarrassing
    d. hilarious

_____ 3. The *opposite* of **composure** is
    a. frantic
    b. confident
    c. secretive
    d. calm

_____ 4. **Graphology** is associated with
    a. music
    b. penmanship
    c. swimming
    d. mathematics

_____ 5. Who would most likely receive an **annuity**?
    a. beginning lawyer
    b. experienced electrician
    c. retired teacher
    d. elected official

_____ 6. If a person is **heterogeneous,** he or she is likely to be interested in the
    a. stock market
    b. sports world
    c. outdoors
    d. opposite sex

Copyright © by Houghton Mifflin Company. All rights reserved.

_____ 7. If a material is **diaphanous,** then it can
    a. be seen through
    b. be purchased at a reasonable price
    c. rarely be made
    d. resist wear

_____ 8. **homogeneous : similar :: a.** large : small
    b. neighborly : unfriendly
    c. attractive : repulsive
    d. identical : same

_____ 9. **moribund : lively :: a.** winning : joyful
    b. sad : depressed
    c. inactive : energetic
    d. complex : interesting

_____ 10. **blandness : vigor :: a.** vigorous : peppy
    b. peppy : dynamic
    c. dynamic : exciting
    d. exciting : dull

IV. _Directions:_ Write an original sentence for each word that clearly demonstrates your mastery of its meaning.

1. **annuity** _____

_____

2. **graphology** _____

_____

3. **cacophony** _____

_____

4. **moribund** _____

_____

5. **composure** _____

_____

6. **capricious** _____

_____

7. **diaphanous** _____

_____

8. **blandness** _____

_____

Copyright © by Houghton Mifflin Company. All rights reserved.

9. heterogeneous _____

_____

10. homogeneous _____

_____

Copyright © by Houghton Mifflin Company. All rights reserved.

Word Parts

1. contra, contro, counter

    a. She _contradicted_ what Wanda had told me.
    b. The _controversy_ was about who was responsible for paying the bill.
    c. Our team made several successful _counterattacks,_ finally winning the game in the closing minutes of the fourth quarter.

contra, contro, and **counter** mean (a) against (b) support _____ .

2. psych

    a. _Psychosis_ is a general term to indicate a severe mental disorder or disease.
    b. A _psychosomatic_ problem is a physical disorder caused by the mind or emotions.

psych refers to the (a) body (b) mind _____ .

3. semi

    a. A _semicolon_ (;) is part colon and part comma.
    b. We arranged our chairs in a _semicircle,_ but after more people arrived, we made a complete circle.

semi means (a) complete (b) half _____ .

4. dic

    a. Norman's _diction_ was influenced by his childhood years in England.
    b. Mr. Reed's _dictation_ was concerned with the sales campaign.

dic has to do with (a) talk (b) intelligence _____ .

5. meter, metr

    a. A _barometer_ measures atmospheric pressure.
    b. _Trigonometry_ is a branch of mathematics concerned with the calculations of sides and angles of triangles.

meter and **metr** have to do with (a) measuring (b) solving _____ .

Copyright © by Houghton Mifflin Company. All rights reserved.

6. terr

    a. This area is the best farming *territory* in the entire state.

    b. Firm, solid land is sometimes referred to as *terra firma*.

terr is associated with (a) wealth (b) land _____ .

7. anthrop

    a. *Anthropology* involves the study of the origins, beliefs, and cultural developments of humankind.

    b. *Anthropomorphic* means attributing human forms and characteristics to things not human.

anthrop is associated with (a) humans (b) beliefs _____ .

8. fore

    a. The weather *forecast* indicates that snow is on its way.

    b. No one can *foretell* what the nation's economy will be like during the upcoming year.

fore refers to the (a) past (b) future _____ .

9. se

    a. Ms. Artesani's photographs were *selected* for first prize.

    b. South Carolina became the first state to *secede* from the Union.

se means (a) apart from (b) awarded to _____ .

10. therm

    a. Jason set the *thermostat* to 62 degrees.

    b. The *thermometer* indicated the temperature was below freezing, but it didn't seem that cold.

therm means (a) technical (b) heat _____ .

Copyright © by Houghton Mifflin Company. All rights reserved.

EXERCISES FOR LESSON 17
Word Parts

I. *Directions:* Match each definition to the word part it defines.

_____ **1.** contra, contro, counter	**a.** measure
_____ **2.** psych	**b.** heat
_____ **3.** semi	**c.** mind; spirit
_____ **4.** dic	**d.** human
_____ **5.** meter, metr	**e.** opposed to
_____ **6.** terr	**f.** say; tell
_____ **7.** anthrop	**g.** before
_____ **8.** fore	**h.** half of
_____ **9.** se	**i.** apart from; away
_____ **10.** therm	**j.** earth

II. *Directions:* Select the appropriate word part so the proper word is formed in each sentence.

counter	semi	meter	anthrop	se
psych	dic	terr	fore	therm

1. A _____ tator exercises absolute control; his or her word becomes the law of the land.

2. A _____ ace is a strip of land with steep sides.

3. _____ odynamics is concerned with the relationships between heat and the mechanical energy of work.

4. Andy longed for the _____ clusion of his country home after experiencing the hustle and bustle of the city.

5. _____ oanalysis is concerned with the relationship between the conscious and unconscious minds.

6. It was a _____ gone conclusion they would marry soon after graduation.

7. _____ oids are animals, such as apes, that resemble humans.

8. People included in this study were examined _____ annually, in January and July.

9. Smoking is certainly _____ productive to your otherwise good health practices.

10. A hygro _____ measures the water content in the atmosphere.

Copyright © by Houghton Mifflin Company. All rights reserved.

III. *Directions:* Use your knowledge of the underlined word parts to match the definitions and words.

_____ 1. <u>semi</u>spheric
_____ 2. <u>psych</u>ogenic
_____ 3. gravi<u>meter</u>
_____ 4. <u>terr</u>arium
_____ 5. <u>dict</u>um
_____ 6. <u>fore</u>shadow
_____ 7. <u>contra</u>ry
_____ 8. <u>therm</u>al
_____ 9. <u>se</u>gregate
_____ 10. <u>anthropomorph</u>ism

a. official pronouncement, saying
b. separate, set apart
c. stubborn, disobedient, opposite, clashing
d. pertaining to heat or temperature
e. association of human characteristics with nonhuman beings or things
f. originating in the mind
g. to show or indicate beforehand
h. a glass case containing land animals and plants
i. shaped like half of a round figure
j. instrument used to measure gravity

IV. *Directions:* Write the definitions of the words after noting the underlined word parts and studying the context of the sentences; if you are still uncertain, feel free to consult a dictionary.

1. At times, Mr. McPherson reluctantly used a computer to write short messages, but he still preferred to use his old-fashioned *<u>dict</u>aphone* for letters.

   <u>dict</u>aphone _____

2. Beth finally decided to write her term paper on *<u>anthropo</u>genesis* because she thought learning about the beginning and development of humankind would be interesting.

   <u>anthropo</u>genesis _____

3. The veteran sergeant decided to *<u>contra</u>vene* the newly commissioned lieutenant's order because he knew the order would actually result in trouble for him, the lieutenant, and the troops under their command.

   <u>contra</u>vene _____

4. Her outstanding athletic success in high school provided her with a *<u>fore</u>taste* of the fame that could await her in college.

   <u>fore</u>taste _____

Copyright © by Houghton Mifflin Company. All rights reserved.

5. Sheila Walker, M.D., has always been interested in the mental and emotional health of people, so she has decided to specialize in _psychiatry._

   psychiatry _____

6. The _secretion_ from the gland was causing the condition.

   secretion _____

7. After he got back from his week's jaunt, Todd checked his motorcycle's _odometer,_ which showed he had traveled 2,011 miles.

   odometer _____

8. On the first day of class, our professor asked, "So what do you good people think _thermochemistry_ will be about?"

   thermochemistry _____

9. The victim was found _semiconscious_ sprawled underneath a ladder.

   semiconscious _____

10. Actually, dolphins, porpoises, whales, and sharks are not considered _terrestrial_ animals because they live in water.

    terrestrial _____

Copyright © by Houghton Mifflin Company. All rights reserved.

Challenging Words

1. **contraband** (KON trə BAND)—noun

   a. The Border Patrol arrested the pair for trying to sneak *contraband,* including stolen jewelry, into the country.

   b. Among the major duties of the Coast Guard is to seize all ships carrying any type of *contraband,* such as banned drugs, near our shores.

contraband refers to trade and items that are (a) priceless (b) illegal _____ .

2. **psychedelic** (SĪ kə DEL ik)—adjective

   a. Members of the rock band were wearing *psychedelic* short-sleeve shirts containing splashes of purple, blue, yellow, red, orange, and green.

   b. The artist who painted this *psychedelic* picture must have been hallucinating as all the people and objects in it are badly distorted.

psychedelic describes perceptions that are (a) wild (b) dignified _____ .

3. **semicentennial** (SEM ē sen TEN ē əl)—noun

   a. Westlake High School will celebrate its *semicentennial* this fall, and as part of the festivities, the graduates of fifty years ago will be especially honored.

   b. In recognition of its *semicentennial* in our community, one of our local radio stations is giving away fifty dollars to each of the first fifty listeners who call the station for the next two days.

semicentennial is a (a) 50th (b) 100th anniversary _____ .

4. **malediction** (MAL ə DIK shən)—noun

   a. Suddenly, the angry politician shouted a *malediction* at the journalists; a few minutes later, he calmed down and apologized for his remark.

   b. In a number of fairy tales, a witch mutters a *malediction* to cast a spell on her unsuspecting victim.

malediction is a (a) promise or secret (b) curse or threat _____ .

Copyright © by Houghton Mifflin Company. All rights reserved.

5. altimeter (al TIM ə tər)—noun

    a. The pilot of the small plane checked the *altimeter* on the instrument panel to make sure she had sufficient altitude to clear the approaching mountain range.

    b. The weather balloon contains an *altimeter* among its instruments so the height above sea level can be checked in various parts of the country.

altimeter is an instrument used to measure (a) altitude (b) a variety of weather conditions _____ .

6. terrain (tə RĀN)—noun

    a. Much of the *terrain* of western Washington is mountainous.

    b. The scientist is convinced part of the planet's *terrain* contains water, indicating to him that some form of life may exist there.

terrain refers to (a) outer space (b) land _____ .

7. misanthrope (MIS ən THRŌP)—noun

    a. He really seems to hate everybody; has he always been a *misanthrope?*

    b. The crazed tyrant became a *misanthrope,* despising everyone, including members of his own family.

misanthrope is a person who (a) hates (b) misunderstands others _____ .

8. foreboding (fōr BŌ ding)—noun

    a. Matthew had a *foreboding* he wouldn't be happy living in the apartment he had verbally agreed to rent, so he called the apartment manager to tell him he had changed his mind.

    b. Megan's *foreboding* about going to class turned out to be justified as the instructor gave a surprise test for which she was completely unprepared.

foreboding is (a) an uneasy feeling about the future (b) an immature response _____ .

9. sedition (si DISH ən)—noun

    a. After years of turmoil, the colonists finally declared their independence from Great Britain, but the British authorities took forceful steps in a futile attempt to stop the *sedition.*

    b. The dictator, fearing *sedition,* ordered the military to arrest the rioters and to enforce an 8:00 P.M. curfew for all citizens.

sedition is a (a) strike (b) rebellion _____ .

Copyright © by Houghton Mifflin Company. All rights reserved.

10. hypothermia (HĪ pə THUR mē ə)—noun

    a. Although the crew members were rescued from the icy sea within minutes of their ship's capsize, they all suffered from *hypothermia.*

    b. After I got home from sledding one frigid day in January, I couldn't stop shivering because of *hypothermia,* so Dad wrapped me in a couple of blankets and Mom had me drink a couple of cups of hot chocolate.

hypothermia is a body temperature that is (a) above (b) below _____ normal.

Copyright © by Houghton Mifflin Company. All rights reserved.

EXERCISES FOR LESSON 18
Challenging Words

I. *Directions:* Write each word before its definition.

contraband   semicentennial   altimeter   misanthrope   sedition
psychedelic   malediction   terrain   foreboding   hypothermia

_____ **1.** curse, damning, threat, insult, slander
_____ **2.** hater of humankind
_____ **3.** smuggled goods, goods prohibited in trade
_____ **4.** incitement of public disorder against the government, rebellion, riot
_____ **5.** fiftieth anniversary
_____ **6.** plot of land with reference to its natural features
_____ **7.** below normal body temperature
_____ **8.** describes distorted images or exaggerated representations
_____ **9.** a strong inner certainty of a future misfortune, an omen
_____ **10.** instrument used to measure altitude

II. *Directions:* In each space, write the appropriate word from those listed below.

contraband   semicentennial   altimeter   misanthrope   sedition
psychedelic   malediction   terrain   foreboding   hypothermia

1. The wealthy man, considered a(n) _____ because of the nasty way he treated people throughout his life, left his entire fortune to various charitable causes.

2. After we refused to give money to the young beggar, he shouted a(n) _____ at us as we walked away.

3. When the phone rang around one in the morning, I had a(n) _____ I was about to receive some bad news, but, fortunately, I was wrong.

4. The plane's _____ indicated we had quickly reached a height of nearly 7,000 feet.

5. The _____ picture looked like the artist had simply thrown buckets of red, purple, yellow, and black paint on the canvas.

6. Iowa, one of the leading agricultural states, has some of the richest _____ in the nation.

Copyright © by Houghton Mifflin Company. All rights reserved.

7. A popular rebel leader was arrested and accused of _____ by leaders of the central government.

8. Canadian customs officials checked our car, packages, and luggage for _____ before waving us on our way.

9. When we go ice fishing, we make sure we wear sufficient winter clothes and have a source of heat as there is always a danger of _____ because of the freezing temperatures and frigid wind.

10. The _____ anniversary of the Youth Center in our small community will be celebrated by special events throughout the year.

III. *Directions:* After selecting your response, put the letter before it in the space provided.

_____ **1.** The *opposite* of a **malediction** is a
   a. blessing
   b. triumph
   c. defeat
   d. curse

_____ **2.** The *opposite* of **sedition** is
   a. laughter
   b. reward
   c. transfer
   d. loyalty

_____ **3.** The *opposite* of **psychedelic** is
   a. unhealthy
   b. colorful
   c. realistic
   d. disturbing

_____ **4.** An **altimeter** is an instrument used to measure
   a. precipitation
   b. altitude
   c. relative humidity
   d. wind velocity

_____ **5.** **Semicentennial** is associated with the number
   a. twenty-five
   b. fifty
   c. seventy-five
   d. one hundred

120   Word Parts and Challenging Words   Lesson 18

Copyright © by Houghton Mifflin Company. All rights reserved.

_____ **6. Contraband** is associated with goods obtained by
   a. illegal means
   b. trading
   c. credit
   d. cash

_____ **7.** If a person is a **misanthrope,** he or she is likely to
   a. enjoy entertaining
   b. enjoy family reunions
   c. dislike exercise
   d. dislike social gatherings

_____ **8. terrain: earth:: a.** earth : sky
   b. sky : ocean
   c. ocean : sea
   d. sea : sun

_____ **9. hypothermia : hyperthermia :: a.** low : high
   b. cold : frigid
   c. hot : torrid
   d. normal : average

_____ **10. foreboding : uneasiness :: a.** warning : relaxation
   b. announcement : indifference
   c. caution : promptness
   d. suspicion : worry

IV. _Directions:_ Write an original sentence for each word that clearly demonstrates your mastery of its meaning.

1. contraband _____

_____

2. psychedelic _____

_____

3. semicentennial _____

_____

4. malediction _____

_____

5. altimeter _____

_____

6. terrain _____

_____

Copyright © by Houghton Mifflin Company. All rights reserved.

7. misanthrope _____

_____

8. foreboding _____

_____

9. sedition _____

_____

10. hypothermia _____

_____

Copyright © by Houghton Mifflin Company. All rights reserved.

Word Parts

1. aster, astro

    a. _Asters_ are flowers having petals varying from white or pink to blue that radiate around a yellow disk.

    b. John Glenn was among the first American _astronauts_.

aster and **astro** mean (a) modern (b) star _____ .

2. peri

    a. Frank's not sure of the exact _perimeter_ of the property his family owns, but he knows it embraces nearly 250 acres.

    b. The commander ordered the _periscope_ raised so he could get a complete view of the submarine's surroundings.

peri means (a) around (b) wandering _____ .

3. cred

    a. Monique is honest, so I know she'll be a _credible_ witness.

    b. Have you ever subscribed to any particular religious _credo?_

cred is associated with (a) trust (b) deceit _____ .

4. em, en

    a. Do you have confidence in the lawyers who have been _empowered_ to negotiate a new employee's contract?

    b. The coach _encouraged_ Tiffany to try out for the team.

em and **en** mean (a) outside (b) put into _____ .

5. itis

    a. George is ill with _bronchitis_.

    b. The doctor prescribed aspirin for the patient's _arthritis_.

itis means (a) itch (b) inflammation _____ .

Copyright © by Houghton Mifflin Company. All rights reserved.

6. macro, magn

    a. The entire universe is sometimes referred to as a _macrocosm._

    b. Ellen was able to read the fine print by using a _magnifying_ glass.

macro and **magn** mean (a) big (b) special _____ .

7. the

    a. _Theology_ is concerned with the study of God and religion.

    b. An _atheist_ is a person who doesn't believe in the existence of God.

the relates to (a) discussion (b) God _____ .

8. pseud

    a. _Astrology_ is a _pseudoscience,_ so you may be foolish to believe in it.

    b. A _pseudocode_ is an unrelated or false program code for a particular computer's hardware.

pseud is (a) impressive (b) false _____ .

9. vid, vis

    a. The class was shown a _video_ about the Everglades.

    b. Although some things are _invisible,_ they nevertheless exist.

vid and **vis** are associated with (a) sight (b) play _____ .

10. gen

    a. A motel he built fifteen years ago became the _genesis_ of his financial success.

    b. The child was operated on to correct a _congenital_ problem with her spine.

gen relates to (a) honesty (b) beginning _____ .

Copyright © by Houghton Mifflin Company. All rights reserved.

EXERCISES FOR LESSON 19
Word Parts

I. *Directions:* Match each definition to the word part it defines.

_____	**1.** aster, astro	**a.** large; great
_____	**2.** peri	**b.** believe; trust
	3. cred	**c.** birth; beginning
_____	**4.** em, en	**d.** star
_____	**5.** itis	**e.** put into
_____	**6.** macro, magn	**f.** false
_____	**7.** the	**g.** to see
_____	**8.** pseud	**h.** around
_____	**9.** vid, vis	**i.** inflammation
_____	**10.** gen	**j.** God

II. *Directions:* Select the appropriate word part so the proper word is formed in each sentence.

astro	cred	itis	the	vis
peri	en	magn	pseud	gen

1. Can you en _____ ion what you'll be doing five years from now?

2. Congress _____ acted the bill into law last month.

3. _____ nomy, often called the science of the stars, also includes the study of planets, meteors, and other objects in the universe.

4. _____ ocracy is a form of government led by officials who claim to be guided by God.

5. A(n) _____ ificent cathedral covered the entire block.

6. A mineral that looks identical to another one but doesn't actually contain the same composition is called a(n) _____ omorph.

7. The _____ ibility of the applicant suffered when it was discovered he had exaggerated his scholastic achievements.

8. _____ esis is the first book of the Bible.

9. _____ phrasis is a roundabout way of speaking.

10. Sharon's headaches are caused by sinus _____ .

Copyright © by Houghton Mifflin Company. All rights reserved.

III. *Directions:* Use your knowledge of the underlined word parts to match the definitions and words.

_____ **1.** <u>peri</u>phery
_____ **2.** gast<u>ritis</u>
_____ **3.** <u>macro</u>phage
_____ **4.** <u>vis</u>ta
_____ **5.** <u>pseudo</u>intellectual
_____ **6.** in<u>cred</u>ulous
_____ **7.** <u>the</u>ism
_____ **8.** en<u>gen</u>der
_____ **9.** <u>astro</u>physics
_____ **10.** en<u>hance</u>

a. skeptical, unbelieving
b. to increase to a higher degree
c. to produce, cause, or give birth to
d. study of the physical matter of heavenly masses
e. field of view; landscape
f. large one-celled animal
g. the outer boundary
h. person who fakes being well informed about scholarly matters
i. inflammation of the stomach
j. belief in the existence of God or gods

IV. *Directions:* Write the definitions of the words after noting the underlined word parts and studying the context of the sentences; if you are still uncertain, feel free to consult a dictionary.

1. Diana put an *<u>aster</u>isk* beside the names of the people she intended to notify about the meeting.

   <u>aster</u>isk _____

2. Vincent's remarks, I thought, were interesting, but *<u>peri</u>pheral* at best to the main issue being discussed.

   <u>peri</u>pheral _____

3. Mike's young, *<u>cred</u>ulous* sister believed him when he said Spiderman was spinning a web around the entire shopping mall.

   <u>cred</u>ulous _____

4. Age and illness have *em<u>brittl</u>ed* her bones to such an extent that she has to use a walker or a wheelchair to move around in her apartment.

   em<u>brittl</u>ed _____

5. The concert is canceled because the lead singer has *laryng<u>itis</u>*.

   laryng<u>itis</u> _____

Copyright © by Houghton Mifflin Company. All rights reserved.

6. The Barton family's _magnanimity_ enabled the college to build a much needed new music building.

magnanimity _____

7. Although they are engaged in a variety of activities throughout the day, the monks' lives are unquestionably _theocentric_.

theocentric _____

8. These ancient writings, supposedly written by various biblical characters, are considered by most scholars to be _pseudepigrapha_.

pseudepigrapha _____

9. Leonardo da Vinci, who lived in the 15th century, is a noted painter, sculptor, architect, and engineer; he is also considered a _visionary_ as he foresaw the development of the airplane centuries before it actually occurred.

visionary _____

10. Marlene is finding her course in _genetics_ fascinating because of what she is learning about how hereditary factors influence human development.

genetics _____

Copyright © by Houghton Mifflin Company. All rights reserved.

Challenging Words

1. <u>astronautics</u> (AS trə NOT iks)—noun

   a. Jeff received a bachelor's degree in physics last spring, and he is beginning a master's degree in *astronautics* this fall as he's hoping to eventually get a job with NASA (National Aeronautics and Space Administration).
   b. Some of the *astronautics* courses are offered by the astronomy department.

astronautics is a science concerned with space (a) below the earth's atmosphere (b) beyond the earth's atmosphere _____ .

2. <u>peripatetic</u> (PER ə pə TET ik)—adjective

   a. The Dearborns are the most *peripatetic* people I know as they've traveled throughout the world, including Australia, New Zealand, Germany, and Brazil.
   b. Of all the military branches, the Navy probably offers the most *peripatetic* opportunities as its ships sail on all the oceans.

peripatetic has to do with being (a) well traveled (b) well off _____ .

3. <u>credence</u> (KRĒD əns)—noun

   a. The discovery of primitive tools, weapons, and pottery provides *credence* to the long-held belief that this small New Mexico town was once the home of a prehistoric people.
   b. The sportswriter asked the athletic director if there were any *credence* in the rumor that the basketball coach had been asked to resign.

credence has to do with (a) controversy (b) trust _____ .

4. <u>embroil</u> (em BROIL)—verb

   a. Amy's grandparents said they didn't want to *embroil* themselves in a family dispute when Amy asked them to help persuade her parents to buy her a car.
   b. Don't *embroil* me in the conversation if it has anything to do with money, politics, or religion.

embroil means to involve in a (a) conflict (b) surprise _____ .

Copyright © by Houghton Mifflin Company. All rights reserved.

129

5. neuritis (noo RĪ tis)—noun

    a. Murray is taking medicine for the *neuritis* he has in one of his elbows.
    b. Chantelle has *neuritis* in her neck as a result of a field hockey injury.

neuritis refers to a (a) nerve inflammation (b) muscle strain _____ .

6. magnanimous (mag NAN ə məs)—adjective

    a. A wealthy couple's *magnanimous* gift provided most of the funding for the new science building.
    b. The announcer on public television said the station's broadcasts were made possible by the *magnanimous* support of its listeners.

magnanimous means (a) mysterious (b) generous _____ .

7. monotheism (MON ə thē IZ əm)—noun

    a. The ancient Greeks believed in many gods, not in *monotheism*.
    b. Which civilizations were among the first to follow *monotheism* rather than the worship of many gods?

monotheism is the (a) belief in one God (b) belief in no God _____ .

8. pseudonym (SOOD ə nim)—noun

    a. The author Samuel Clemens used the *pseudonym* Mark Twain.
    b. The movie star used a *pseudonym* while she was a patient at the hospital so she and the hospital staff wouldn't be besieged by the media.

pseudonym refers to a (a) false name (b) hidden meaning _____ .

9. vis-à-vis (VĒ zə VĒ)—preposition, adverb

    a. Don't you realize a dog requires more care *vis-à-vis* a cat?
    b. *Vis-à-vis* your report, I found it interesting as well as comprehensive.

vis-à-vis means (a) difficult or troublesome (b) in relation to or relating to _____ .

10. generic (jə NER ik)—adjective

    a. Acetaminophen is the *generic* name for Tylenol and many other nonaspirin pain relievers.
    b. Mrs. Healy saved money by asking her doctor to prescribe a *generic* medicated skin cream rather than one with a brand name.

generic means (a) specific (b) general _____ .

Copyright © by Houghton Mifflin Company. All rights reserved.

Name .... Section .... Date ....

EXERCISES FOR LESSON 20
Challenging Words

I. *Directions:* Write each word before its definition.

astronautics	credence	neuritis	monotheism	vis-à-vis
peripatetic	embroil	magnanimous	pseudonym	generic

_____ **1.** compared with or regarding

_____ **2.** charitable, generous, merciful, liberal

_____ **3.** walking, traveling about, roving

_____ **4.** descriptive of an entire class

_____ **5.** to involve in a struggle, to bring into a conflict

_____ **6.** belief in one God

_____ **7.** inflammation of a nerve

_____ **8.** the science of travel beyond the earth's atmosphere

_____ **9.** false name, pen name, name used by someone to conceal his or her true identity

_____ **10.** belief, trust; trustworthiness

II. *Directions:* In each space, write the appropriate word from those listed below.

astronautics	credence	neuritis	monotheism	vis-à-vis
peripatetic	embroil	magnanimous	pseudonym	generic

1. My anthropology instructor stated that there are still cultures in the world today whose religion involves the worship of many gods, so _____ is not the center of all religious beliefs.

2. I wasn't going to pay that much for sneakers just because they were a brand name, so, instead, I bought a less expensive _____ pair.

3. She's told so many versions of what happened that her story lacks _____ as far as I'm concerned.

4. "George Eliot" was the _____ the author Mary Ann Evans (1819–1890) used because it was difficult for a woman to have her writings published under her own name in the 19th century.

5. The coach is worried about the inexperience of his players _____ those on the other team.

6. Fortunately, the nagging _____ I had been suffering from in my left shoulder went away after a couple of weeks of taking aspirin.

Copyright © by Houghton Mifflin Company. All rights reserved.

7. _____ became a popular field of study when the Space Age dawned in the early 1960s.

8. My _____ friend arrived from England, stayed with me for a couple of days, then took a flight to Finland.

9. Casey is a considerate and _____ young man, so I'm not surprised he's such a generous contributor to the hospital's fundraising efforts.

10. I really didn't want to _____ myself in my sister and her husband's argument, but before I knew it, I was right in the middle of their heated debate.

III. *Directions:* After selecting your response, put the letter before it in the space provided.

_____ 1. The *opposite* of **magnanimous** is
 a. simple
 b. stingy
 c. quiet
 d. bored

_____ 2. The *opposite* of **embroil** is to
 a. engage
 b. participate
 c. correct
 d. prohibit

_____ 3. The *opposite* of **generic** is
 a. special
 b. common
 c. happy
 d. sad

_____ 4. **Vis-à-vis** often suggests
 a. abundance
 b. survival
 c. comparison
 d. embarrassment

_____ 5. **Peripatetic** is associated with
 a. travel
 b. competition
 c. praise
 d. deception

Copyright © by Houghton Mifflin Company. All rights reserved.

6. Monotheism is associated with the belief in
    a. no God
    b. one God
    c. many gods
    d. evolution

7. A person interested in **astronautics** would be most likely to be interested in
    a. oceanography
    b. law
    c. architecture
    d. astronomy

8. credence : true ::
    a. disturbance : quiet
    b. send : arrive
    c. reliance : authentic
    d. dependable : unreliable

9. neuritis : inflammation ::
    a. flu : fever
    b. headache : migraine
    c. pneumonia : breathing
    d. arthritis : joints

10. pseudonym : alias ::
    a. synonym : antonym
    b. public : private
    c. courage : bravery
    d. deceive : restrict

IV. *Directions:* Write an original sentence for each word that clearly demonstrates your mastery of its meaning.

1. astronautics _____

_____

2. peripatetic _____

_____

3. credence _____

_____

4. embroil _____

_____

5. neuritis _____

_____

Copyright © by Houghton Mifflin Company. All rights reserved.

6. magnanimous _____

_____

7. monotheism _____

_____

8. pseudonym _____

_____

9. vis-à-vis _____

_____

10. generic _____

_____

Copyright © by Houghton Mifflin Company. All rights reserved.

Word Parts

1. ped, pod

a. *Pedestrians* were waiting patiently for the *Walk* sign to appear.
b. My feet have been bothering me, so I've made an appointment with a *podiatrist*.

ped and **pod** mean (a) foot (b) person _____ .

2. micro

a. After I focused the *microscope,* I could see the bacteria on the slide.
b. A *micrometer* is equal in length to one-millionth of a meter.

micro means extremely (a) small (b) complex _____ .

3. scrib, scrip

a. I *scribbled* down a list of groceries I needed to buy, then hurried to the store.
b. Aaron added a *postscript* to his letter telling me of his recent promotion.

scrib and **scrip** are associated with (a) memory (b) writing _____ .

4. port

a. Laptop computers, of course, have the advantage of being *portable*.
b. *Exports* are goods shipped out of a country.

port is associated with (a) weight (b) movement _____ .

5. arch

a. A *monarchy* is a form of government headed by one person, such as a king or queen.
b. Kathy's uncle was recently appointed *archbishop* in the Houston area, so he'll be in charge of many churches, priests, and parishioners.

arch means (a) chief (b) high _____ .

Copyright © by Houghton Mifflin Company. All rights reserved.

6. cent

 a. A *centennial* celebration takes place after one hundred years.
 b. A *centigrade* thermometer's scale ranges from zero to one hundred degrees.

cent means (a) large (b) one hundred _____ .

7. ven, vent

 a. The *convention* brought together educational specialists from throughout the nation.
 b. The *advent* of the holiday season brought ever-increasing crowds to the nearby malls.

ven and **vent** mean to (a) speak (b) come _____ .

8. cide

 a. The murder was made to look like a *suicide*.
 b. A police's *homicide* division has the responsibility of investigating murders.

cide means to (a) kill (b) seek _____ .

9. poten

 a. The doctor prescribed a *potent* medicine in an effort to cure the infection.
 b. Jessica has the *potential* of becoming the most influential person on the board of supervisors.

poten is associated with (a) price (b) power _____ .

10. leg

 a. Kirk is seeking *legal* advice in an effort to regain his former property.
 b. The state *legislature* is the branch of government having the responsibility for making laws.

leg is related to (a) law (b) expense _____ .

Copyright © by Houghton Mifflin Company. All rights reserved.

EXERCISES FOR LESSON 21
Word Parts

I. *Directions:* Match each definition to the word part it defines.

_____	**1.** ped, pod	**a.** hundred
_____	**2.** micro	**b.** carry
	3. scrib, scrip	**c.** come; go
_____	**4.** port	**d.** extremely small
_____	**5.** arch	**e.** law
_____	**6.** cent	**f.** foot
_____	**7.** ven, vent	**g.** possessing strength; powerful
_____	**8.** cide	**h.** chief; ruler
_____	**9.** poten	**i.** killing of
_____	**10.** leg	**j.** writing

II. *Directions:* Select the appropriate word part so the proper word is formed in each sentence.

ped	scrip	arch	ven	poten
micro	port	cent	cide	leg

1. In the vault, we found an old manu _____ t containing the town's history up to the early 1900s.

2. A(n) _____ ipede doesn't really have one hundred legs, does it?

3. A(n) _____ be is a very small living organism.

4. It was the most important athletic e _____ t in our school's history, so everyone came to the game.

5. When I was growing up, there were a few kids I didn't get along with, but my _____ enemy was a bully by the name of Tommy the Terrible.

6. After his supervisors stripped him of his authority, the manager felt worthless and im _____ t.

7. After Joan had a _____ icure, her feet, toes, and nails looked and felt much better.

8. It's il _____ al to park on this side of the street; didn't you know that?

9. Patri _____ is the killing of one's father.

10. During the summer, I worked as a _____ er at a summer resort; some of the suitcases and baggage I carried must have weighed a ton.

Copyright © by Houghton Mifflin Company. All rights reserved.

III. *Directions:* Use your knowledge of the underlined word parts to match the definitions and words.

_____ **1.** <u>arch</u>ives   **a.** instrument that measures walking distance

_____ **2.** pre<u>scrip</u>tion   **b.** person possessing great power and authority

_____ **3.** <u>leg</u>itimate   **c.** where chief or important documents are kept

_____ **4.** <u>micro</u>fiche   **d.** written instruction for a specific medicine

_____ **5.** <u>port</u>folio   **e.** to come together for an official or public purpose

_____ **6.** <u>cent</u>urion

_____ **7.** <u>pedo</u><u>meter</u>   **f.** killing of a brother or a relative

_____ **8.** fratri<u>cide</u>   **g.** sheet of film containing numerous pages in reduced form on one frame

_____ **9.** <u>potent</u>ate

_____ **10.** con<u>vene</u>   **h.** lawful, proper

     i. commander of a group of one hundred soldiers in ancient Rome

     j. a carrying case for holding papers and notebooks

IV. *Directions:* Write the definitions of the words after noting the underlined word parts and studying the context of the sentences; if you are still uncertain, feel free to consult a dictionary.

1. After the band played, the candidate quickly stepped up to the *<u>pod</u>ium* and addressed the cheering crowd.

podium _____

2. My boss is frustrating to work for because she tends to *<u>micro</u>manage* even the smallest details of everything I do.

micromanage _____

3. The *in<u>scrip</u>tion* on the monument included the dates 1941–1945.

inscription _____

4. The *im<u>port</u>ation* of foreign cars into the United States began in earnest in the early 1970s.

importation _____

Copyright © by Houghton Mifflin Company. All rights reserved.

5. After the central government collapsed, _anarchy_ reigned until the military restored order.

anarchy _____

6. A _centimeter_ is a unit of length equal to what part of a _meter_?

centimeter _____

7. The teacher was gratified to see two older students _intervene_ to settle the playground dispute between a number of third and fourth graders.

intervene _____

8. A powerful _germicide_ is used to keep this room in sterile condition.

germicide _____

9. The _potency_ of the police force was increased by the hiring of a dozen new officers.

potency _____

10. Our community college's _paralegal_ program has a well-deserved excellent reputation throughout this part of the state.

paralegal _____

Copyright © by Houghton Mifflin Company. All rights reserved.

Challenging Words

1. <u>podi</u>atry (pō DĪ ə trē)—noun

    a. Ralph developed some foot problems after line dancing for over three hours one evening, so he's getting an appointment with a doctor of *podiatry*.

    b. Students of *podiatry* must take a number of anatomy and physiology courses, particularly those involving the feet.

podiatry is the study and treatment of (a) foot ailments (b) muscle strains _____ .

2. <u>microbiology</u> (MĪ krō bī OL ə jē)—noun

    a. Before I took *microbiology* to study bacteria and other small organisms, I had a general biology course.

    b. Because she plans to go to medical school, Shelly is taking a course in *microbiology* to become familiar with using a microscope as well as to learn about the structure and function of microscopic life that can help or hinder health.

microbiology is a science devoted to the study of (a) plant life (b) extremely small organisms _____ .

3. pro<u>scribe</u> (prō SKRĪB)—verb

    a. As a result of the recent vandalism that has taken place in our state parks, the governor has written a directive that will *proscribe* entry to the parks after 7:00 P.M.

    b. I'll have to read the details about this diet carefully because if it does *proscribe* meat, eggs, and dairy products as you maintain, then I know it's not a diet I could stay with for very long.

proscribe means to (a) prohibit (b) prescribe _____ .

4. <u>portage</u> (POR tij)—noun, verb

    a. We had to *portage* our canoes over a mile before the river became navigable again.

    b. The climbers had to *portage* all of their supplies to the base of the mountain before nightfall.

portage means to (a) repair (b) carry _____ .

Copyright © by Houghton Mifflin Company. All rights reserved.

5. archetype (AR ki TĪP)—noun

    a. A textile factory in Lowell, Massachusetts, was the *archetype* of similar factories built throughout New England in the 1800s.

    b. Humphrey Bogart is the *archetype* of the hard-bitten detective that has been the hero in countless movies since the 1940s.

archetype refers to (a) the original model (b) a bad example _____ .

6. centenarian (SEN tə NAR ē ən)—noun

    a. This article says that life expectancy may be one hundred before too many years pass; can you imagine yourself being a *centenarian?*

    b. Although many friends and a number of relatives passed away when she was in her eighties and nineties, Mrs. Russell, now a *centenarian,* has kept her interest in life as well as her marvelous sense of humor.

centenarian is a person who is (a) an active senior citizen (b) one hundred
years old _____ .

7. convene (kən VĒN)—verb

    a. Lawyers for both parties will *convene* this morning to see if a settlement can be reached before the matter reaches the court.

    b. Those interested in auditioning for the play should *convene* at the performing arts building tomorrow evening at 7:30.

convene means to (a) discuss thoroughly (b) meet together _____ .

8. genocide (JEN ə SĪD)—noun

    a. The shocking report accuses the top leaders of that country of plotting to murder all members of an opposition party, a *genocide* that must be prevented.

    b. The old science fiction movie I saw on TV the other night was about a planet of evil people, the Puxacrotons, who attempt *genocide* against all the people living on the other planets so that they, the Puxacrotons, could rule the entire galaxy.

genocide is the (a) extermination (b) organization _____ of a particular group of people.

9. potency (PŌT ən sē)—noun

    a. According to the label on the bottle, the *potency* of these vitamins expired two months ago, so I guess I'll throw this bottle away and buy a new one.

    b. The coach cautioned his players not to underestimate the *potency* of their next opponent, that it was a team capable of beating anyone in the conference.

potency is related to (a) conduct (b) strength _____ .

Copyright © by Houghton Mifflin Company. All rights reserved.

10. legacy (LEG ə sē)—noun

    a. The wealthy widow left her entire *legacy,* which includes numerous properties and investments, to her two nieces.

    b. The *legacy* I received from my grandparents is to work hard and to value family and friends above everything else.

legacy is similar to (a) an inheritance (b) a lesson _____ .

Copyright © by Houghton Mifflin Company. All rights reserved.

EXERCISES FOR LESSON 22
Challenging Words

I. *Directions:* Write each word before its definition.

podiatry   proscribe   archetype   convene   potency
microbiology   portage   centenarian   genocide   legacy

_____ 1. a person who has reached the age of one hundred

_____ 2. money or property left legally to someone, anything handed down from the past

_____ 3. act of carrying, the carrying of boats or goods overland from one navigable water to another

_____ 4. science concerned with the study of extremely small organisms

_____ 5. systematic killing of a particular large group of people

_____ 6. study and treatment of foot ailments

_____ 7. vigor, powerfulness, strength, force

_____ 8. chief or original model after which other things are patterned

_____ 9. to prohibit, ban, or banish

_____ 10. to come together, to assemble, to meet

II. *Directions:* In each space, write the appropriate word from those listed below.

podiatry   proscribe   archetype   convene   potency
microbiology   portage   centenarian   genocide   legacy

1. Our new manager announced she will _____ the wearing of jeans to work starting next week because she thinks jeans are too informal for office apparel.

2. Many scholars agree that Hitler's prolonged _____ of the Jews in Germany and elsewhere in Europe was unquestionably the evilest act of the 20th century.

3. According to the museum guide, this 1975 computer became the _____ for the generation of computers that followed.

4. All committee members are urged to attend the meeting, which will _____ at 4:00 P.M. on Wednesday.

5. The _____ the young couple received from one of their relatives enabled them to start their own business.

Copyright © by Houghton Mifflin Company. All rights reserved.

6. Mr. Pratt recently became the fourth _____ in our community as there are three other people living here who are one hundred or more.

7. My _____ course includes a four-hour lab that meets on Thursday afternoons; that's a long time to stare through a microscope at little critters, don't you think?

8. Jim and Brook decided to canoe a different lake from us even though it meant they had to _____ their canoe, life jackets, and other materials for nearly three miles.

9. The _____ of the anesthesia soon had the patient in a deep sleep.

10. Two offices on the first floor will be assigned to doctors of _____ so patients with foot problems will not have to walk so far.

III. *Directions:* After selecting your response, put the letter before it in the space provided.

_____ **1.** The *opposite* of **potency** is
  a. energy
  b. anxiety
  c. remainder
  d. weakness

_____ **2.** Someone who would be the *opposite* of an **archetype** would be a
  a. follower
  b. leader
  c. debater
  d. peacemaker

_____ **3.** The *opposite* of a **legacy** is something that is
  a. despised
  b. adored
  c. held back
  d. passed on

_____ **4.** **Podiatry** is most closely associated with the
  a. head
  b. feet
  c. back
  d. abdomen

_____ **5.** **Genocide** is most closely associated with
  a. tragedy
  b. triumph
  c. wealth
  d. poverty

Copyright © by Houghton Mifflin Company. All rights reserved.

_____ **6.** A student majoring in **microbiology** is likely to be most interested in
  a. journalism
  b. history
  c. literature
  d. science

_____ **7.** A person who is a **centenarian** is definitely
  a. rich
  b. healthy
  c. old
  d. humorous

_____ **8. portage : carry :: a.** moist : dry
  b. grip : hold
  c. start : postpone
  d. move : drop

_____ **9. proscribe : permit :: a.** permit : allow
  b. allow : outlaw
  c. outlaw : prohibit
  d. prohibit : ban

_____ **10. convene : meet :: a.** convince : doubt
  b. generalize : specify
  c. corrupt : purify
  d. meet : gather

IV. _Directions:_ Write an original sentence for each word that clearly demonstrates your mastery of its meaning.

1. podiatry _____

_____

2. microbiology _____

_____

3. proscribe _____

_____

4. portage _____

_____

5. archetype _____

_____

Copyright © by Houghton Mifflin Company. All rights reserved.

6. centenarian _____

_____

7. convene _____

_____

8. genocide _____

_____

9. potency _____

_____

10. legacy _____

_____

Copyright © by Houghton Mifflin Company. All rights reserved.

Word Parts

1. sol

   a. There was no one else around, so after I tired of watching TV, I played a couple of games of _solitaire._

   b. For as far as I could see, the area was barren, lifeless, _de<u>sol</u>ate._

sol means (a) alone (b) challenging _____ .

2. polis, urb

   a. _Indiana<u>polis</u>_ is the largest city in Indiana.

   b. Over 4 million people live in this _<u>urb</u>an_ area.

polis and **urb** mean (a) liveliness (b) city _____ .

3. ish

   a. A _Dan<u>ish</u>_ ship was unloading cargo at one of the piers.

   b. I apologized to my girlfriend for acting so _child<u>ish</u>_ over the unimportant matter.

ish means (a) empty of (b) descriptive of _____ .

4. ly

   a. Mark is a _friend<u>ly</u>,_ considerate person.

   b. The child said _firm<u>ly</u>,_ "No! I won't go to bed!"

ly refers to how something is (a) done (b) imagined _____ .

5. age, ance, ence, ship

   a. The _foli<u>age</u>_ this fall was spectacular.

   b. Bob is a good mechanic, so he's able to do his own _mainten<u>ance</u>_ for his car.

   c. After moving into her apartment, Shirley enjoyed having more _independ<u>ence</u>._

   d. My _penman<u>ship</u>_ has never been good, so I write with a computer whenever possible.

age, ance, ence, and **ship** relate to (a) description or quality (b) nature or product _____ .

Copyright © by Houghton Mifflin Company. All rights reserved.

6. tract

    a. The telephone kept *distracting* him from his work.
    b. I was relieved when the *extraction* of my tooth was over.

tract is related to (a) attract or pull (b) noise or pain   _____ .

7. circum

    a. Do you know whether the *circumference* of a basketball is over twelve inches?
    b. *Circumlocution* is unnecessarily wordy and indirect language.

circum means (a) around (b) through   _____ .

8. onym

    a. *Antonyms* are words with opposite meanings, such as *large* and *small*.
    b. Someone slipped an *anonymous* note under my windshield wiper telling me I should "learn how to park a car."

onym refers to (a) experiences (b) words   _____ .

9. photo

    a. A camera's *photoflash* blinded me for a few moments.
    b. The *photosphere* is the visible shining surface of the sun.

photo means (a) scenic (b) light _____ .

10. dem

    a. *Democracy* is a form of government in which people elect their leaders.
    b. An *epidemic* is a disease that spreads widely and quickly among people.

dem refers to (a) people (b) vicinity   _____ .

Copyright © by Houghton Mifflin Company. All rights reserved.

Name .... Section .... Date ....

EXERCISES FOR LESSON 23
Word Parts

I. *Directions:* Match each definition to the word part it defines.

_____	**1.** sol	**a.**	done in the manner of
_____	**2.** polis, urb	**b.**	draw; pull
_____	**3.** ish	**c.**	city
_____	**4.** ly	**d.**	name; word
_____	**5.** age, ance, ence, ship	**e.**	light
_____	**6.** tract	**f.**	people
_____	**7.** circum	**g.**	alone
_____	**8.** onym	**h.**	condition, state, or quality of
_____	**9.** photo	**i.**	around
_____	**10.** dem	**j.**	descriptive of; characteristic of

II. *Directions:* Select the appropriate word part so the proper word is formed in each sentence.

sol	ish	ship	circum	photo
urb	ly	tract	onym	dem

1. My old high school friend hadn't lost any of his boy _____ charm.

2. The cold weather had caused the door's opening to con _____ , which allowed the wind to come whistling in.

3. _____ otic refers to the common people.

4. Syn _____ s are words with similar meanings, such as *scary* and *frightening*.

5. The police were absolute _____ flabbergasted by the startling developments.

6. Magellan was the first explorer to _____ navigate the world, wasn't he?

7. Keith enjoys the peace and _____ itude of fishing whenever he gets the chance.

8. At first, many Americans feared the presidency would turn into a dictator- _____ .

Copyright © by Houghton Mifflin Company. All rights reserved.

9. When I was in college, my professors would sometimes distribute _____ copies of their lectures.

10. Deborah is sophisticated and _____ ane from having such wonderful cultural experiences in New York City.

III. *Directions:* Use your knowledge of the underlined word parts to match the definitions and words.

_____ **1.** <u>urb</u>anite
_____ **2.** peev<u>ish</u>
_____ **3.** impud<u>ence</u>
_____ **4.** <u>circum</u>vent
_____ **5.** <u>sol</u>idarity
_____ **6.** <u>photo</u>metry
_____ **7.** <u>re</u>tractor
_____ **8.** demo<u>graphy</u>
_____ **9.** succinct<u>ly</u>
_____ **10.** <u>pseudonym</u>

a. surgical instrument used to draw back tissue from an incision
b. briefly and to the point; concisely
c. a city dweller
d. the measurement of the intensity of light
e. disrespect; rudeness
f. false name
g. the statistical study of human population
h. union among a group of people arising from common interests or responsibilities
i. annoyed; resentful
j. to go around or to avoid a problem

IV. *Directions:* Write the definitions of the words after noting the underlined word parts and studying the context of the sentences; if you are still uncertain, feel free to consult a dictionary.

1. Margo said she was <u>*solely*</u> responsible for the accident, so we were not to blame anybody else.

sol<u>ely</u> _____

2. Do you enjoy being an <u>*urbanite*</u>, or would you rather live in the country?

<u>urb</u>anite _____

3. Many families and friends seem rather *clann<u>ish</u>* in this small community, don't you think?

clann<u>ish</u> _____

Copyright © by Houghton Mifflin Company. All rights reserved.

4. I felt *blatantly* out of place eating in the posh restaurant because I was wearing an old pair of jeans, a sweatshirt, and sneakers.

blatantly _____

5. It was a happy day indeed when I was finally able to send the final *remittance* owed on my car.

remittance _____

6. I had never gone horseback riding before, but fortunately my horse was *tractable*, so I was able to relax and have a good time.

tractable _____

7. Do you know of an alternate route we could take to *circumvent* having to drive through the city?

circumvent _____

8. In this simple code, each letter is *synonymous* to its numerical order in the alphabet, so "A" is equal to "1," "B" is equal to "2," and so on.

synonymous _____

9. Did you know this machine was powered by *photoelectric* cells?

photoelectric _____

10. The flu was so *pandemic* during January that the schools, malls, and other places were closed for a number of days.

pandemic _____

Copyright © by Houghton Mifflin Company. All rights reserved.

Challenging Words

1. <u>sol</u>iloquy (sə LIL ə kwē)—noun

   a. While one of the actors was on the stage alone giving a *soliloquy* during the play *Our American Cousin,* John Wilkes Booth shot President Lincoln.
   b. Some of the guys were watching TV and a couple were playing a spirited game of Ping-Pong; Scott, on the other hand, was staring out the window and muttering a *soliloquy* about the beauty of falling snow.

soliloquy is the act of (a) being silly (b) speaking to oneself _____ .

2. **megalopolis** (MEG ə LOP ə lis)—noun

   a. Dallas, Fort Worth, and Denton, Texas, have become so densely populated that the area is now considered a *megalopolis.*
   b. In Minnesota, Minneapolis, St. Paul, and their nearby communities make up another *megalopolis.*

megalopolis refers to a region consisting of several (a) large adjoining cities (b) competing governments _____ .

3. <u>fet</u>ish (FET ish)—noun

   a. My roommate has such a *fetish* for getting good grades that he studies until after midnight every night, including weekends.
   b. My sister-in-law must have a *fetish* for earrings as I know she must have over one hundred pair.

fetish is (a) an extreme attraction to (b) a perplexing opposition to _____ .

4. **ostensib<u>ly</u>** (o STEN sə blē)—adverb

   a. My son *ostensibly* borrowed the car to go to the library, but I found out later he had actually gone to his girlfriend's house.
   b. *Ostensibly,* Fred wears a baseball cap all the time to look "cool," but I think the real reason is to hide his thinning hair.

ostensibly means (a) impressively (b) supposedly _____ .

Copyright © by Houghton Mifflin Company. All rights reserved.

5. abey<u>ance</u> (ə BĀY əns)—noun

    a. Title to the estate was in *abeyance* while legal authorities were consulted.
    b. According to Victor, all promotions are in *abeyance* until business improves.

abeyance is a temporary (a) problem (b) suspension _____ .

6. <u>retraction</u> (ri TRAK shən)—noun

    a. The paper admitted the information printed in yesterday's paper about one of the candidates for mayor was wrong, so the paper contained an appropriate *retraction* today.
    b. The singer threatened to sue the TV show's producer if the producer didn't issue a *retraction* about her being difficult to work with.

retraction is a (a) taking back of (b) twisting of certain information _____ .

7. <u>circumspect</u> (SUR kəm SPEKT)—adjective

    a. Be sure to be *circumspect* when you mention your complaint to him because he's sensitive to any type of criticism.
    b. She is *circumspect* in conducting her public, professional, and private life, so there's never been any type of scandal associated with her.

circumspect is being (a) quiet (b) cautious _____ .

8. <u>acronym</u> (AK rə nım)—noun

    a. The *acronym* for "self-contained underwater breathing apparatus" is SCUBA.
    b. The *acronym* for "situation normal all fouled up" is SNAFU.

acronym is a word formed from (a) the first letters in a group of words (b) using one's imagination _____ .

9. <u>photosynthesis</u> (FOH tə SIN thə sis)—noun

    a. Of course, sunlight is necessary for *photosynthesis* to occur in plants so the plants can have nourishment.
    b. Chlorophyll, carbon dioxide, and water are also necessary for *photosynthesis* to take place.

photosynthesis refers to plants (a) reproducing themselves (b) making food for themselves _____ .

Copyright © by Houghton Mifflin Company. All rights reserved.

10. <u>dem</u>agogue (DEM ə gog)—noun

    a. Many historians consider the late Senator Joseph McCarthy, who served in the Senate in the 1950s, a *demagogue* because he convinced thousands of people that the federal government was full of communists.

    b. She is a dangerous *demagogue* because many people believe her when she insists all the major television networks are controlled by people whose chief objective is to undermine the morality of our young people.

demagogue is a person who seeks power by appealing to people's (a) fears (b) generosity _____ .

Copyright © by Houghton Mifflin Company. All rights reserved.

EXERCISES FOR LESSON 24
Challenging Words

I. *Directions:* Write each word before its definition.

soliloquy   fetish   abeyance   circumspect   photosynthesis
megalopolis   ostensibly   retraction   acronym   demagogue

_____ **1.** the taking back of a statement, opinion, or promise

_____ **2.** an outsize city; a urban area consisting of several large, adjoining cities

_____ **3.** a word formed from the initial letters of a group of words

_____ **4.** a person who attempts to gain power and influence by appealing to people's fears and other emotions

_____ **5.** the act of speaking to oneself

_____ **6.** supposedly, apparently, done in a manner to deceive

_____ **7.** the process by which plants form food

_____ **8.** any object or idea abnormally adored, compulsion

_____ **9.** careful, proper, wisely cautious, using good judgment

_____ **10.** postponement, temporary suspension, waiting period, delay

II. *Directions:* In each space, write the appropriate word from those listed below.

soliloquy   fetish   abeyance   circumspect   photosynthesis
megalopolis   ostensibly   retraction   acronym   demagogue

1. Brian was _____ my pal, but it eventually became apparent he was more interested in being "friends" with my steady date than he was in being "friends" with me.

2. NATO is a(n) _____ for North Atlantic Treaty Organization.

3. Although the editor was confident the information in the article was correct, he decided to print a(n) _____ rather than risk a libel suit.

4. When he is alone, doesn't Hamlet whisper a remorseful _____ after the tragic deed is done?

5. Sheila's boss said he would hold her job in _____ while she completes her eight weeks of basic training in the Air National Guard.

Copyright © by Houghton Mifflin Company. All rights reserved.

6. Some sociologists predict that Denver, Colorado Springs, Boulder, and Fort Collins will be a(n) _____ within a couple of decades because of the continuing rapid population growth in that area of the country.

7. Mr. Williams said that although it's known that sunlight, carbon dioxide, water, and chlorophyll are involved in the process of _____ that takes place in plants, the process is still not fully understood.

8. Cindy was dying to meet the attractive young man who sat near her in class, but her _____ behavior did not give her away.

9. One of the candidates is nothing more than a(n) _____ in my opinion because he maintains the national economy, including the Social Security system, would collapse unless he and other members of his party were elected to Congress.

10. I love anything chocolate, so I'm one of the millions of people who have a(n) _____ for this delicious food; in fact, I once saw someone wearing a sweatshirt that said, "Hand over your chocolate and no one will get hurt."

III. *Directions:* After selecting your response, put the letter before it in the space provided.

_____ 1. The *opposite* of **circumspect** is
   a. quiet
   b. funny
   c. kind
   d. careless

_____ 2. The *opposite* of a **megalopolis** is a
   a. city bordered by other large cities
   b. region of sparsely populated villages
   c. metropolitan area with a population of 4 million
   d. sprawling community with high real estate taxes

_____ 3. The *opposite* of a **soliloquy** is
   a. a discussion on stage between two actors
   b. talking to oneself on stage
   c. a plea for help over television
   d. praying silently in church

_____ 4. The person who would be most likely to know the most about **photosynthesis** would be an expert on
   a. insects
   b. microbes
   c. plants
   d. animals

Copyright © by Houghton Mifflin Company. All rights reserved.

_____ 5. A **retraction** is most likely to sound
       a. apologetic
       b. angry
       c. accusing
       d. arrogant

_____ 6. Which of the following is an **acronym?**
       a. TELEVISION
       b. NASA
       c. FORD
       d. MICHIGAN

_____ 7. A **demagogue** is most likely to be
       a. wealthy
       b. poor
       c. bold
       d. shy

_____ 8. **fetish : fixation :: a.** fixation : compulsion
       b. compulsion : unthinking
       c. unthinking : habit
       d. habit : impulsive

_____ 9. **abeyance : temporary :: a.** costly : inexpensive
       b. violence : delay
       c. postponement : suspension
       d. position: permanent

_____ 10. **ostensibly : insincerity :: a.** supposedly : phoniness
       b. flashy : sincerity
       c. honesty : insensitivity
       d. importantly : foolishness

IV. _Directions:_ Write an original sentence for each word that clearly demonstrates your mastery of its meaning.

1. **soliloquy** _____

_____

2. **megalopolis** _____

_____

3. **fetish** _____

_____

4. **ostensibly** _____

_____

Copyright © by Houghton Mifflin Company. All rights reserved.

5. abeyance _____

_____

6. retraction _____

_____

7. circumspect _____

_____

8. acronym _____

_____

9. photosynthesis _____

_____

10. demagogue _____

_____

Copyright © by Houghton Mifflin Company. All rights reserved.

Word Parts

1. ac

    a. The _acrid_ smell of the fireworks lingered long after the spectacular event was over.

    b. Michelle's coolness under stress as well as her _acumen_ at determining which patients needed treatment first and what that treatment should be made her an ideal emergency room doctor.

ac means (a) attractive; appealing (b) bitterly sharp; quickly aware _____ .

2. dys

    a. Major difficulty in recognizing and comprehending written words is known as _dyslexia._

    b. Apparently, the patient's episodes of heart _dysrhythmia_ were due to the blood pressure medicine he was taking.

dys is associated with something (a) educational (b) abnormal _____ .

3. err

    a. The shortstop's throwing _error_ allowed the runner on third to score.

    b. My cousin's _errant_ behavior was becoming increasingly common, so all of us were worried about her.

err means (a) costly; rare (b) to slip up; to stray from normal _____ .

4. medi

    a. An administrator from the school system and a representative from the post office department were selected to _mediate_ the unusual dispute between the school custodians and the mail carriers.

    b. In high school, I was a _mediocre_ student, finishing 64th in a graduating class of 128.

medi relates to the (a) middle (b) situation _____ .

Copyright © by Houghton Mifflin Company. All rights reserved.

5. be

    a. All of us loved our third grade teacher because she never *belittled* us if we made a mistake or even if we misbehaved.

    b. He thought he had *bedazzled* his date with his charm and tales of his many accomplishments, but she never would go out with him again.

be is a prefix meaning (a) to be (b) to reverse _____ .

6. claim, clam

    a. When Ryder discovered someone had dented his car while it was parked in the parking lot, he *exclaimed*, "Who in the heck did this? I wish I could get my hands on that cowardly jerk!"

    b. The winning contestant's *exclamation* of delight echoed throughout the auditorium.

claim, clam means to (a) shout (b) object _____ .

7. greg

    a. The church's *congregation* had slowly declined over the years.

    b. The cattle was *segregated* based upon their breed.

greg is related to (a) groups (b) sizes _ _____ .

8. al

    a. "*Parental* advice," the young man said, "is usually good advice, don't you think?"

    b. His *denial* of any wrongdoing was not convincing.

al means (a) one who does (b) having the quality of _____ .

9. ic

    a. The movie has *fantastic* special effects.

    b. We felt *sympathetic* when we learned about all of their troubles, so we decided to help them out.

ic means (a) having the characteristic of (b) more than one _____ .

10. ize

    a. Can you *harmonize* with me on this song?

    b. To make sure you don't *plagiarize*, cite all the sources you use to write your paper.

ize means (a) to do away with (b) to bring about _____ .

Copyright © by Houghton Mifflin Company. All rights reserved.

EXERCISES FOR LESSON 25
Word Parts

I. *Directions:* Match each definition to the word part it defines.

_____	**1.** ac	**a.** middle	
_____	**2.** dys	**b.** shout; cry out	
_____	**3.** err	**c.** to bring about	
_____	**4.** medi	**d.** to be	
_____	**5.** be	**e.** bitterly sharp; insightful	
_____	**6.** claim, clam	**f.** abnormal; impaired; faulty	
_____	**7.** greg	**g.** having the characteristic of	
_____	**8.** al	**h.** crowd; groups	
_____	**9.** ic	**i.** having the quality of	
_____	**10.** ize	**j.** to blunder; to stray from normal	

II. *Directions:* Select the appropriate word part so the proper word is formed in each sentence.

ac	err	be	greg	ic
dys	medi	claim	al	ize

1. The laboratory supervisor cautioned the students to be particularly careful when working with the _____ id because of possible burns to the skin or the eyes.

2. My egocentr _____ co-worker talks constantly about himself, and it's driving me nuts.

3. We decided to _____ friend the stray little kitten after she purred softly when we held her.

4. As is true of many people in my small town, I often synchron _____ my watch with the blowing of the factory's noon whistle.

5. My roommate's refus _____ to loan me his car for a couple of hours took me by complete surprise.

6. Indigestion, or _____ pepsia, is usually not a cause for alarm.

7. Deliberately giving the police officer _____ oneous information got the speeding motorist in even more trouble.

8. Both sides have agreed to the hiring of a _____ ator in an effort to try to settle their long-standing dispute.

Copyright © by Houghton Mifflin Company. All rights reserved.

9. The principal pro————ed Friday as "Dress-Up Day."

10. Club members will con ———— ate at the hotel's banquet hall for their next meeting.

III. *Directions:* Use your knowledge of the underlined word parts to match the definitions and words.

————	1. majes<u>tic</u>	**a.** having no fixed course; wandering
————	2. <u>acri</u>mony	**b.** decorated; adorned
————	3. jeopard<u>ize</u>	**c.** one who meets with others to worship
————	4. <u>be</u>decked	**d.** insane; excessively excited or upset
————	5. <u>dys</u>pnea	**e.** located in the middle
————	6. mania<u>cal</u>	**f.** dignified; noble; kingly; magnificent
————	7. ac<u>claim</u>	**g.** difficulty breathing
————	8. <u>err</u>atic	**h.** hostility; resentment; anger
————	9. <u>medi</u>an	**i.** to put into danger
————	10. cong<u>reg</u>ant	**j.** praise; fame; applause

IV. *Directions:* Write the definitions of the words after noting the underlined word parts and studying the context of the sentences; if you are still unsure, feel free to consult a dictionary.

1. We proofread the document a number of times before sending it to the printer, so we were disappointed to discover that there is at least one *err*atum in the bound copy.

   erratum _____

2. Despite the graduation last spring of a number of key instrumentalists, the director was determined that the band would maintain its reputation for excellence and not slip into *medi*ocrity as some people seemed to think it would.

   mediocrity _____

3. The judge ruled in favor of the *claim*ant, awarding her $100,000.

   claimant _____

4. As individuals, not everyone had distinguished himself or herself, but as an *aggregate,* their accomplishments were impressive.

   aggregate _____

Copyright © by Houghton Mifflin Company. All rights reserved.

5. Don't you think the store owner would have more customers if he didn't have such an _acerbic_ personality?

acerbic _____

6. The sales staff at the antique store even used an _archaic_ cash register.

archaic _____

7. Look, I know you don't like me and hope that I don't win, so don't _patronize_ me with your expressions of "good luck" and "best wishes."

patronize _____

8. It was frustrating when my math teacher said, "Why can't you solve these problems? They shouldn't _befuddle_ you."

befuddle _____

9. According to this source, the _autumnal equinox_ always occurs during the third week in September.

autumnal equinox _____

10. From all accounts that I've either heard or read, she grew up in a _dysfunctional_ family; nevertheless, she is reported to be well adjusted and successful in everything she has undertaken.

dysfunctional _____

Copyright © by Houghton Mifflin Company. All rights reserved.

Challenging Words

1. **exacerbate** (ig ZAS ər bāt)—verb

   a. Hot, humid weather like we've been having lately tends to *exacerbate* his breathing problems, so he stays inside his air-conditioned apartment.

   b. The road construction scheduled to begin next week will no doubt *exacerbate* the traffic congestion already existing on this route.

exacerbate means to (a) worsen (b) soothe _____ .

2. **dystrophy** (DIS trə fē)—noun

   a. The annual fall telethon has raised millions of dollars to find a cure for muscular *dystrophy,* a serious disease involving the wasting away of muscles.

   b. Rescued after nine days of floating in a raft, the young pilot was pale, thin, uncoordinated, and so weak he was unable to stand; such *dystrophy,* the doctors said, was basically due to malnutrition.

dystrophy is usually associated with the (a) kidney (b) muscles _____ .

3. **aberration** (ab ə RĀ shən)—noun

   a. I assure you that my uncle's temper tantrum yesterday was an *aberration* as generally he's a pleasant person to be around.

   b. It is India's dry season, so today's heavy rainfall was an *aberration.*

aberration is always (a) bad (b) unexpected _____ .

4. **medieval** (med Ē vəl)—adjective

   a. "I mean," Roz exclaimed, "it's like *medieval* for our principal to insist that we have four chaperones for the dance and that the dance must end at 11:00 P.M.! It's like totally insane!"

   b. The *medieval* period, also known as the Middle Ages, dates from 500 to 1500.

medieval can mean (a) outdated (b) inadequacy _____ .

Copyright © by Houghton Mifflin Company. All rights reserved.

5. bereft (bə REFT)—adjective

    a. Despite arriving in the United States *bereft* of money, friends, and jobs, countless immigrants have succeeded in making important contributions to the country.

    b. Until my cousin learned to control his temper, he was almost *bereft* of friends.

bereft indicates a (a) lack (b) bias _____ .

6. clamorous (KLAM ər əs)—adjective

    a. The loud music, the shouting and dancing people, and the clanking dishes and glasses made for a wild and *clamorous* wedding reception.

    b. The magician waited patiently for the *clamorous* children to settle down before beginning his show.

clamorous is associated with (a) hubbub (b) quiet _____ .

7. gregarious (gri GAR ē əs)—adjective

    a. Initially, Richard had a difficult time adjusting to college because he's not *gregarious* among strangers.

    b. Jamie is so *gregarious* and thoughtful that everyone knows and likes her.

gregarious means (a) sociable (b) generous _____ .

8. colloquial (kə LŌ kwē əl)—adjective

    a. The disk jockey's folksy, *colloquial* speaking style had won him a loyal audience over the years.

    b. My political science professor presents her lectures in a relaxed manner using *colloquial* rather than elaborate language.

colloquial refers to language that is (a) impressive (b) commonly used _____ .

9. sophomoric (sof ə MOR ik)—adjective

    a. A few members of my dorm still enjoy short-sheeting beds, removing light bulbs from the hallways, spraying shaving cream all over the bathrooms, and other such *sophomoric* pranks; I wish they'd grow up.

    b. After gaining a smattering of knowledge and experience, there are always a few medical students who become rather *sophomoric* in attitude and behavior, convinced they now know as much or more than their professors.

sophomoric is associated with (a) immaturity (b) sorrow _____ .

Copyright © by Houghton Mifflin Company. All rights reserved.

10. ostra<u>ize</u> (OS trə sīz)—verb

    a. Unfortunately, at my high school, the "in" group would *ostracize* others simply because they didn't wear the "right" clothes.

    b. A month or two after their wedding, one influential church member wanted to *ostracize* the couple after he learned that both had previously been married and divorced.

ostracize means to (a) flatter (b) snub _____ .

Copyright © by Houghton Mifflin Company. All rights reserved.

EXERCISES FOR LESSON 26
Challenging Words

I. *Directions:* Write each word before its definition.

exacerbate	dystrophy	aberration	medieval	bereft
clamorous	gregarious	colloquial	sophomoric	ostracize

_____ **1.** seeking and enjoying the company of others
_____ **2.** to make a condition worse
_____ **3.** exhibiting immaturity; impressed with one's knowledge when, in fact, it is limited
_____ **4.** old-fashioned; belonging to the Middle Ages
_____ **5.** lacking or deprived of something
_____ **6.** wasting away of muscles and nerves
_____ **7.** characteristic of everyday language
_____ **8.** to exclude from a group
_____ **9.** deviation from what is proper or expected; irregularity
_____ **10.** continuously noisy

II. *Directions:* In each space, write the appropriate word from those listed below.

exacerbate	dystrophy	aberration	medieval	bereft
clamorous	gregarious	colloquial	sophomoric	ostracize

1. Summer's business slump proved to be a temporary _____ as sales returned to normal in early fall.

2. I may be _____ , but I still believe wedding guests should wear suits and dresses, not jeans and slacks.

3. When you speak to them, use _____ language; don't try to impress them with fancy, high-sounding words.

4. Children _____ of parental love are often insecure.

5. Rodney is a popular waiter because of his _____ nature as his customers appreciate his pleasant chatter and friendliness.

6. Those snobs _____ anyone who isn't as rich as they are.

7. Because of some type of _____ , he had a difficult time walking without some type of assistance.

Copyright © by Houghton Mifflin Company. All rights reserved.

8. You will certainly ———————————— your sprained ankle if you attempt to play basketball today.

9. As part of the initiation process, candidates used to have to sing their school songs, howl like wolves, recite the names of the presidents, and do other such ———————————— stunts, but, fortunately, those juvenile requirements were abolished over a decade ago.

10. The party became so wild and ———————————— that the police had to be called to break it up.

III. *Directions:* After selecting your response, put the letter before it in the space provided.

——————— **1.** The *opposite* of **gregarious** is
   a. polite
   b. curious
   c. shy
   d. friendly

——————— **2.** The *opposite* of **bereft** is
   a. painful
   b. panicky
   c. peppy
   d. plentiful

——————— **3.** The *opposite* of **clamorous** is
   a. quiet
   b. exciting
   c. sadly
   d. noisily

——————— **4.** **Colloquial** is associated with language that is
   a. regrettable
   b. vague
   c. necessary
   d. conversational

——————— **5.** **Dystrophy** is associated with
   a. finances
   b. security
   c. disease
   d. crime

——————— **6.** If a person is said to be **medieval,** he or she is considered
   a. old-fashioned
   b. gallant
   c. brilliant
   d. progressive

Copyright © by Houghton Mifflin Company. All rights reserved.

_____ 7. An **aberration** would certainly be
   a. expensive
   b. unexpected
   c. praiseworthy
   d. worthless

_____ 8. **sophomoric : sophisticated ::** **a.** handsome : attractive
   b. curious : inquisitive
   c. immature : knowledgeable
   d. honorable : ethical

_____ 9. **exacerbate : worsen ::** **a.** worsen : aggravate
   b. aggravate : soothe
   c. soothe : disturb
   d. disturb : worship

_____ 10. **ostracize : include ::** **a.** shun : banish
   b. outburst : eruption
   c. recognize : identify
   d. expel : embrace

IV. *Directions:* Write an original sentence for each word that clearly demonstrates your mastery of its meaning.

1. **exacerbate** _____

_____

2. **dystrophy** _____

_____

3. **aberration** _____

_____

4. **medieval** _____

_____

5. **bereft** _____

_____

6. **clamorous** _____

_____

7. **gregarious** _____

_____

8. **colloquial** _____

_____

Copyright © by Houghton Mifflin Company. All rights reserved.

9. sophomoric _____

_____

10. ostracize _____

_____

Copyright © by Houghton Mifflin Company. All rights reserved.

Challenging Words

1. alienation (āl yə NĀ shən)—noun

    a. President Woodrow Wilson's fervent hope was that the League of Nations formed after World War I would end the *alienation* that had traditionally existed among many of the European countries.

    b. After the Bergs became acquainted with more people in the community, their feelings of *alienation* began to vanish.

alienation suggests (a) affection (b) isolation _____.

2. collateral (kə LAT ə rəl)—noun

    a. To obtain financing for their purchase of the motel, the Eddicotts used their lumber business as *collateral.*

    b. Milo plans to use his pickup truck as *collateral* to secure a bank loan.

collateral refers to a (a) bonus (b) pledge _____ .

3. deleterious (del i TER ē əs)—adjective

    a. Felicia's inattention to her car's basic maintenance needs had *deleterious* consequences later on.

    b. According to this article, unrestricted television watching can have a number of *deleterious* effects on children, including social isolation and poor physical condition.

deleterious means (a) harmful (b) unknown _____ .

4. felicitous (fə LIS ə təs)—adjective

    a. The timing of the money's arrival was so *felicitous* that Jenna now believes in miracles.

    b. The veterinarian's *felicitous* word helped to comfort the little girl over the loss of her beloved dog.

felicitous means (a) well timed; well chosen (b) out of order; out of date _____ .

Copyright © by Houghton Mifflin Company. All rights reserved.

5. hypothetical (hī pə THET i kəl)—adjective

    a. Hank could give only a *hypothetical* explanation as to why the construction boss hired him for the summer, but he believes it's because he has experience driving heavy trucks.

    b. I realize this is a *hypothetical* question, but do you think if our team were to finish the season undefeated that Coach LaPointe would receive a college coaching offer?

hypothetical is associated with (a) sarcasm (b) guessing _____ .

6. immutable (i MYOO tə bəl)—adjective

    a. My uncle, a farmer, is an *immutable* pessimist when he discusses the weather. For example, if the sun is shining, he's sure a drought is beginning; if it's raining, he's sure his crops will be washed away.

    b. One of nature's *immutable* laws is that having to do with inertia, that is, an object's natural resistance to any change in its motion.

immutable means (a) changeless (b) unreasonable _____ .

7. impeccable (im PEK ə bəl)—adjective

    a. The lovely home was *impeccable* throughout—even the basement was spotlessly clean.

    b. Lyle's old Pontiac is still in *impeccable* condition, so I suspect it's worth a lot of money.

impeccable means (a) flashy (b) flawless _____ .

8. impunity (im PŪ nə tē)—noun

    a. Because his folks were such good friends with the local police chief, Rusty apparently thought he could ignore with *impunity* the town's posted speed limits. However, he learned differently when he was slapped with a $400 fine for speeding.

    b. To their regret, three of the players learned they couldn't break training rules with *impunity* as the coach dismissed them from the team.

impunity means freedom from (a) penalty (b) passion _____ .

9. gullible (GUL ə bəl)—adjective

    a. Advertisers for cold remedies must believe most people are *gullible,* given the exaggerated claims made in their television commercials.

    b. Loraine, my young children are *gullible,* so don't tell them any stories about this old house of yours being haunted, okay?

gullible means easily (a) entertained (b) fooled _____ .

Copyright © by Houghton Mifflin Company. All rights reserved.

10. trepidation (trep ə D$\overline{\text{A}}$ shən)—noun

   a. Sydney approached her first flying lesson with *trepidation*, but afterward she was so thrilled she couldn't wait for her next lesson.

   b. Most people have feelings of *trepidation* when they are told they need to undergo hospital tests.

trepidation is (a) fear (b) shyness _____ .

Copyright © by Houghton Mifflin Company. All rights reserved.

Name .... Section .... Date.....................

EXERCISES FOR LESSON 27
Challenging Words

I. *Directions:* Write each word before its definition.

alienation	deleterious	hypothetical	impeccable	gullible
collateral	felicitous	immutable	impunity	trepidation

_____ **1.** destructive, harmful

_____ **2.** forming a reasonable opinion but without sufficient evidence or proof

_____ **3.** perfect, flawless, unblemished

_____ **4.** separation due to hostility or suspicion; isolation

_____ **5.** easily deceived, trustful

_____ **6.** appropriate, timely

_____ **7.** fear, terror, alarm

_____ **8.** security pledged in return for a loan

_____ **9.** freedom from punishment; exemption

_____ **10.** permanent, changeless

II. *Directions:* In each space, write the appropriate word from those listed below.

alienation	deleterious	hypothetical	impeccable	gullible
collateral	felicitous	immutable	impunity	trepidation

1. Erin used her house as _____ for a loan to expand her jewelry store.

2. Because these old coins are in _____ condition, they are worth much more than their face value.

3. Ironically, change is one of life's _____ laws.

4. Kindergarten helps children learn they must consider the effects of their acts on others, that they can't behave with _____ .

5. Priscella eventually realized she should stop dwelling on her disappointment about not receiving the promotion because her preoccupation with this matter was having a(n) _____ effect on her emotional state as well as on her family.

6. Rob is so _____ he actually believed me when I told him I was offered a movie contract even though I've never even been in a school play.

Copyright © by Houghton Mifflin Company. All rights reserved.

7. Lauren's _____ arrival with the car saved me from being late to work.

8. My _____ reasoning as to why Imogene broke up with Clint is that she has a crush on somebody else, but I'm just guessing.

9. The _____ and suspicion initially existing between the two neighbors gradually dissolved as they became better acquainted.

10. Despite his _____ about flying, a fear that developed four years ago when he had flown during a severe thunderstorm, Eddie was determined to fly to California to visit his friend.

III. *Directions:* After selecting your response, put the letter before it in the space provided.

_____ **1. Alienation** suggests
    a. movement
    b. participation
    c. harmony
    d. division

_____ **2.** The opposite of **impeccable** is
    a. imperfect
    b. impossible
    c. impatient
    d. immovable

_____ **3.** The word most closely associated with **collateral** is
    a. pleasure
    b. pity
    c. popularity
    d. promise

_____ **4. Impunity** suggests
    a. exception
    b. hastiness
    c. weakness
    d. disapproval

_____ **5.** Who is likely to be the most **gullible?**
    a. angry parent
    b. experienced lawyer
    c. young child
    d. senior citizen

_____ **6.** A **hypothetical** conclusion is always
    a. accurate
    b. uncertain
    c. acceptable
    d. unpopular

Copyright © by Houghton Mifflin Company. All rights reserved.

_____ 7. The word most closely associated with **deleterious** is
    a. health
    b. beauty
    c. success
    d. ruin

_____ 8. **felicitous : unfortunate ::** **a.** boring : inspiring
              b. graceful : skillful
              c. impatient : restless
              d. honest: trustworthy

_____ 9. **trepidation : trembling ::** **a.** frightening : giggling
              b. fear : shaking
              c. dread : encouraging
              d foolishness · threatening

_____ 10. **immutable : changeable ::** **a.** changeable : adjustable
              b. adjustable : flexible
              c. flexible : rigid
              d. rigid : unyielding

IV. _Directions:_ Write an original sentence for each word that clearly demonstrates your mastery of its meaning.

1. **alienation** _____

 _____

2. **collateral** _____

 _____

3. **deleterious** _____

 _____

4. **felicitous** _____

 _____

5. **hypothetical** _____

 _____

6. **immutable** _____

 _____

7. **impeccable** _____

 _____

8. **impunity** _____

 _____

Copyright © by Houghton Mifflin Company. All rights reserved.

9. gullible _____

_____

10. trepidation _____

_____

Copyright © by Houghton Mifflin Company. All rights reserved.

Challenging Words

1. <u>de</u>bacle (də BA kəl)—noun

    a. Our high school class reunion turned out to be a *debacle* because someone had failed to mail all the invitations so less than thirty people showed up; the restaurant manager had reserved the banquet room for the wrong evening; and the band knew few of the popular songs of our graduation year.

    b. Gordon threw his arms up in the air and laughingly complained that his grand plan for redecorating his apartment was quickly turning into a *debacle.* He said the wallpaper started coming off after he painted over it, and the carpet store had sent over a ghastly purple rug instead of the pale blue one he had ordered.

debacle is related to a (a) crime (b) disaster _____ .

2. <u>de</u>privation (dep rə VĀ shən)—noun

    a. Warren's salary boost finally enabled him and his family to live comfortably and not suffer any basic *deprivation,* such as the inadequate housing they had once experienced.

    b. Unfortunately, when my dad lost his job, we endured one *deprivation* after another, including the loss of our home, car, and medical insurance.

deprivation is related to (a) embarrassment (b) hardship _____ .

3. garr<u>ulous</u> (GAR ə ləs)—adjective

    a. My sister is one of the most *garrulous* persons I know; she has such a gift for gab that I told her she should become a politician.

    b. Ron is seldom *garrulous,* but when he does have something to say, he's generally worth listening to.

garrulous means (a) wordy (b) intelligent _____ .

Copyright © by Houghton Mifflin Company. All rights reserved.

4. meticulous (mə TIK yə ləs)—adjective

 a. My brother takes *meticulous* care of his new Chevrolet, driving it in only good weather and constantly polishing it.
 b. A team of government accountants was conducting a *meticulous* investigation of the company's financial records.

meticulous means extremely (a) thorough (b) suspicious _____ .

5. nebulous (NEB yə ləs)—adjective

 a. My grandparents' retirement plans are still in the *nebulous* stage, but they have talked about spending the winter months in Florida.
 b. Kirk's *nebulous* ideas about how to correct the computer problem finally crystallized into a clear solution.

nebulous means (a) unclear (b) exciting _____ .

6. sagacious (sə GĀ shəs)—adjective

 a. Due to their stockbroker's *sagacious* advice over the years, my in-laws are financially comfortable today.
 b. Molly is not only well informed about the details of the project, but she's also *sagacious* when it comes to the engineering procedures that will be used.

sagacious means (a) courageous (b) wise _____ .

7. specious (SPĒ shəs)—adjective

 a. Based upon the information contained in his resume, the personnel director felt the applicant had given *specious* responses to some of her questions, so she recommended he not be hired.
 b. My tennis opponent told me he was just an average player, a *specious* statement because I knew he had been among the top finishers in several tournaments in our area.

specious means (a) modest (b) misleading _____ .

8. redundant (ri DUN dənt)—adjective

 a. Erika said the professor of her criminal law class had been *redundant* today as he had previously lectured on the rights of the accused.
 b. I know I'm being *redundant*, but if you want to buy my car, be sure to call me by 5:30 this evening.

redundant refers to unnecessary (a) abruptness (b) repetition _____ .

Copyright © by Houghton Mifflin Company. All rights reserved.

9. <u>re</u>pudiate (rē PŪ dē āt)—verb

    a. I not only disagree with you, but I'm also sure Pam will *repudiate* your claim that this is an unfriendly neighborhood in which to live.

    b. The senator is confident her voting record will *repudiate* her opponent's charge that she is no friend of the environment.

repudiate means to (a) contradict (b) confirm   _____ .

10. <u>via</u>ble (VĪ ə bəl)—adjective

    a. Because of the unexpectedly high estimates from several carpenters, the Baylors decided the only *viable* choice for them was to remodel their old house themselves.

    b. Mr. Francis's law enforcement background made him a *viable* candidate for the sheriff's position.

viable means (a) surprising (b) practical   _____ .

Copyright © by Houghton Mifflin Company. All rights reserved.

EXERCISES FOR LESSON 28
Challenging Words

I. *Directions:* Write each word before its definition.

debacle	deprivation	garrulous	meticulous	nebulous
sagacious	specious	redundant	repudiate	viable

_____ **1.** to deny, to reject as untrue or unjust

_____ **2.** practical, workable, capable of succeeding

_____ **3.** precise, particular, thorough, exacting

_____ **4.** complete failure, disaster

_____ **5.** talkative, wordy

_____ **6.** a lack of the usual comforts and necessities of life, a hardship

_____ **7.** false, misleading

_____ **8.** unnecessarily repetitious, excessive

_____ **9.** intelligent, clever, wise

_____ **10.** hazy, vague, indistinct, incomplete

II. *Directions:* In each space, write the appropriate word from those listed below.

debacle	deprivation	garrulous	meticulous	nebulous
sagacious	specious	redundant	repudiate	viable

1. Otis is often so _____ it's virtually impossible to get a word in edgewise.

2. The pharmaceutical company had to _____ its advertising claim regarding the healing power of its new arthritis medicine because research studies clearly indicate the medicine isn't effective.

3. Although my grandmother never had the opportunity to go to college, she's the most _____ person I know, so I seek her advice whenever I have a problem.

4. Engineers say the only _____ solution for preventing floods in this part of the state is to construct a series of dams.

5. Our double date turned into a(n) _____ because after our car broke down, we arrived too late to attend the concert, so the other couple ended up pouting the rest of the evening.

Copyright © by Houghton Mifflin Company. All rights reserved.

6. Alex said the major _____ he experienced as an only child was a lack of companionship.

7. Isn't it _____ to say someone is a "rich" millionaire?

8. Archaeologists have been conducting _____ excavations in the Middle East for many years in an effort not to damage anything they might uncover.

9. Some people believe car salespeople often make _____ statements when trying to make a sale, but I've found them to be honest in their conversations with me.

10. If the film had a major point, it was too _____ for me to figure out.

III. *Directions:* After selecting your response, put the letter before it in the space provided.

_____ 1. The opposite of **sagacious** is
  a. interesting
  b. foolish
  c. expensive
  d. ill

_____ 2. The *opposite* of **specious** is
  a. honest
  b. common
  c. noisy
  d. sharp

_____ 3. The *opposite* of **viable** is
  a. impatience
  b. impressive
  c. impractical
  d. impolite

_____ 4. A **meticulous** person is
  a. unfaithful
  b. colorful
  c. dull
  d. thorough

_____ 5. A **garrulous** person is certainly *not*
  a. opinionated
  b. brief
  c. weak
  d. popular

Copyright © by Houghton Mifflin Company. All rights reserved.

_____ 6. **Deprivation** suggests
   a. elegance
   b. poverty
   c. sensitivity
   d. defiance

_____ 7. If the person talking to you was being **redundant,** you would probably feel
   a. confused
   b. fascinated
   c. encouraged
   d. bored

_____ 8. **nebulous : cloudy :: a.** dark : pale
   b. vague : plain
   c. hazy : fuzzy
   d. bright : gloomy

_____ 9. **repudiate : evil :: a.** embrace : good
   b. deny : virtue
   c. commit : crime
   d. support : wickedness

_____ 10. **debacle : commotion :: a.** failure : triumph
   b. success : celebration
   c. riot : ceremony
   d. victory : disturbance

IV. *Directions:* Write an original sentence for each word that clearly demonstrates your mastery of its meaning.

1. **debacle** _____

   _____

2. **deprivation** _____

   _____

3. **garrulous** _____

   _____

4. **meticulous** _____

   _____

5. **nebulous** _____

   _____

Copyright © by Houghton Mifflin Company. All rights reserved.

6. sagacious _____

_____

7. specious _____

_____

8. redundant _____

_____

9. repudiate _____

_____

10. viable _____

_____

Copyright © by Houghton Mifflin Company. All rights reserved.

Challenging Words

1. **catharsis** (kə THAR sis)—noun

   a. Attending basketball games is a *catharsis* for Elliot because he's able to rid himself of stress by cheering for his favorite team.

   b. As a *catharsis* for her anger and disappointment, Mitzi took a long, brisk walk.

catharsis is most related to a (a) cleansing (b) saving _____ .

2. **dearth** (DURTH)—noun

   a. There was a *dearth* of applicants for the city manager's position, so the city council is going to re-advertise the position.

   b. A *dearth* of hometown fans at the important game was a disappointment to the coaches, players, and cheerleaders as many of the bleachers were empty.

dearth is associated with (a) insufficiency (b) inactivity _____ .

3. **guile** (GĪL)—noun

   a. Are you suggesting the charges against the defendant were dismissed because of her lawyer's *guile* rather than because of her innocence?

   b. The reporter's *guile* gained him entrance to the celebrities' wedding.

guile is most related to (a) logic (b) trickery _____ .

4. **lethargy** (LETH ər jē)—noun

   a. Lying around all day watching television leads to *lethargy*, not vitality.

   b. Amy's *lethargy* the past few days is due to her recent bout with the flu.

lethargy is most related to (a) outbursts of anger (b) the blahs _____ .

5. **affinity** (ə FIN ə tē)—noun

   a. Steve's lifelong *affinity* for sports led to a coaching career.

   b. Emily's *affinity* for dancing was apparent the first time she stepped onto a dance floor.

affinity refers to (a) an inclination for (b) a confusion about _____ .

Copyright © by Houghton Mifflin Company. All rights reserved.

6. affluence (AF loo əns)—noun

    a. The Donaldsons used much of their *affluence,* which they acquired through shrewd investments, in many worthwhile ways, including generous donations to numerous charities.

    b. The large, luxurious homes and spacious, well-tended lawns made it obvious that people of considerable *affluence* lived in this area.

affluence refers to (a) influence (b) wealth _____ .

7. dichotomy (dī KOT ə mē)—noun

    a. Some parents, unfortunately, seem to believe a *dichotomy* exists between love and discipline when it comes to raising their children; however, according to most child psychologists, love and discipline go together.

    b. There is often a *dichotomy* between a business's stated policies and its daily practices.

dichotomy refers to a (a) complex arrangement (b) division into two parts _____ .

8. enigma (ə NIG mə)—noun

    a. The reason Lee Harvey Oswald assassinated President John F. Kennedy is an *enigma* that will probably never be solved.

    b. It's an *enigma* to their friends as to why the couple broke up because they seem perfect for each other.

enigma is a (a) mystery (b) mistake _____ .

9. banal (bə NAL or BA nəl)—adjective

    a. The romance novel lacked originality in all respects as it contained typical characters, *banal* dialogue, and a predictable plot.

    b. Jarret often goes home on the weekends because he thinks most of the campus activities going on then are juvenile and *banal.*

banal means (a) difficult (b) boring _____ .

10. clandestine (clan DES tən)—adjective

    a. Unknown to the public and coaching staff, the team owner and general manager had a series of *clandestine* meetings before deciding to make the controversial trade.

    b. A rebellious group of leaders made a *clandestine* plan to overthrow the government.

clandestine describes something done (a) publicly (b) secretly _____ .

Copyright © by Houghton Mifflin Company. All rights reserved.

Name .... Section .... Date ....

EXERCISES FOR LESSON 29
Challenging Words

I. *Directions:* Write each word before its definition.

| catharsis | guile | affinity | dichotomy | banal |
| dearth | lethargy | affluence | enigma | clandestine |

_____ **1.** common, lacking originality, stale, boring
_____ **2.** deceit, trickery
_____ **3.** puzzle, mystery
_____ **4.** sluggishness, a lack of energy
_____ **5.** done in secrecy, hidden
_____ **6.** division into two parts, a split
_____ **7.** discharge of pent-up emotions, a cleansing
_____ **8.** a natural liking or ability for, an attraction to
_____ **9.** lack, scarcity, insufficiency
_____ **10.** wealth, riches, prosperity

II. *Directions:* In each space, write the appropriate word from those listed below.

| catharsis | guile | affinity | dichotomy | banal |
| dearth | lethargy | affluence | enigma | clandestine |

1. A punching bag in his basement serves as a _____ for Jerry, so whenever he gets tense or angry, he heads downstairs to flail away at the bag.

2. Dennis, after sprawling on the couch for a couple of weeks after school got out, eventually overcame his _____ and went looking for a job.

3. He decided to move to Omaha because of a(n) _____ of employment opportunities in his small hometown.

4. My obnoxious uncle bragged that his recent business success was due to his "exceptional cleverness," which most people, including me, would call _____ , not "exceptional cleverness."

5. The newspaper editorial accused the school board of holding _____ rather than public meetings about the proposed school budget.

6. Actually, most people in the community know there is a(n) _____ existing among the board members because six members favor the proposed budget while the other six members oppose it.

Copyright © by Houghton Mifflin Company. All rights reserved.

7. In certain social situations when people don't know each other too well, they will often talk about the weather or other _____ subjects just to make conversation.

8. Alfred Hitchcock's films, such as *Rear Window*, always contain a(n) _____ that most moviegoers find intriguing to try to unravel.

9. Despite his lifelong _____ for candy, desserts, and other sweets, Jay has never been overweight.

10. A person must be of considerable _____ to buy a Midwestern farm.

III. *Directions:* After selecting your response, put the letter before it in the space provided.

_____ 1. The *opposite* of **banal** is
   a. old-fashioned
   b. fresh
   c. common
   d. insensitive

_____ 2. The *opposite* of **guile** is
   a. cleverness
   b. frankness
   c. exaggeration
   d. anger

_____ 3. The *opposite* of **affluence** is
   a. anxiety
   b. happiness
   c. abundance
   d. poverty

_____ 4. **Lethargy** suggests
   a. snobbery
   b. brilliance
   c. maturity
   d. fatigue

_____ 5. **Enigma** is most closely associated with a(n)
   a. location
   b. obligation
   c. riddle
   d. organization

_____ 6. If people do something in a **clandestine** manner, then they do it
   a. secretly
   b. openly
   c. skillfully
   d. awkwardly

Copyright © by Houghton Mifflin Company. All rights reserved.

_____ 7. **Catharsis** is most closely associated with
   a. illness
   b. travel
   c. purification
   d. caution

_____ 8. **dearth : expensive ::** a. plenty : costly
   b. many : priceless
   c. abundant : cheap
   d. saving : free

_____ 9. **affinity : fondness ::** a. attraction : devotion
   b. expectation : surprise
   c. bitterness : love
   d. appeal : hate

_____ 10. **dichotomy : unity ::** a. abbreviation : shortening
   b. mutiny : revolt
   c. loyalty : praiseworthy
   d. division : wholeness

IV. *Directions:* Write an original sentence for each word that clearly demonstrates your mastery of its meaning.

1. **catharsis** _____

_____

2. **dearth** _____

_____

3. **guile** _____

_____

4. **lethargy** _____

_____

5. **affinity** _____

_____

6. **affluence** _____

_____

7. **dichotomy** _____

_____

8. **enigma** _____

_____

Copyright © by Houghton Mifflin Company. All rights reserved.

9. **banal** _____

_____

10. **clandestine** _____

_____

Copyright © by Houghton Mifflin Company. All rights reserved.

Challenging Words

1. cogent (KŌ jɔnt)—adjective

    a. There are many good reasons for not smoking, but those having to do with health are the most *cogent*.

    b. The newlyweds bought the insurance policy after Mr. Downey presented them with a number of *cogent* reasons for doing so.

cogent means (a) disturbing (b) persuasive _____.

2. rationalize (RASH ə nə līz)—verb

    a. Sometimes we *rationalize* our mistakes rather than taking direct steps to correct them.

    b. Megan will often *rationalize* her son's misbehavior by saying he's just high-spirited, not deliberately naughty.

rationalize means to (a) make excuses for (b) overreact _____.

3. sordid (SOR did)—adjective

    a. The *sordid* details of the mayor's private life may jeopardize his chances for reelection.

    b. Migrant workers should never have to endure *sordid* working conditions, such as being housed in abandoned railroad boxcars.

sordid means (a) hidden (b) shameful _____.

4. eclectic (ē KLEK tik)—adjective

    a. The government adopted an *eclectic* approach rather than a single one in attempting to solve the unemployment problem.

    b. Ms. Henderson's *eclectic* teaching techniques, ranging from individual instruction to class field trips, result in impressive scholastic achievements by her students.

eclectic means (a) complicated (b) various _____.

Copyright © by Houghton Mifflin Company. All rights reserved.

5. **usurp** (ū SURP)—verb

   a. My psychology professor said parents should be careful they don't *usurp* their children's rights to make certain decisions.
   b. When the principal attempted to *usurp* authority rightfully belonging to the superintendent of schools, he was warned and his salary was temporarily decreased.

usurp is related to (a) trespass (b) defend _____ .

6. **inundate** (IN ən dāt)—verb

   a. Protests began to *inundate* the TV station when it was announced that the first two rounds of the basketball tournament would not be televised.
   b. Farmers living near the swollen river feared the raging water would *inundate* their recently planted fields.

inundate is closest in meaning to (a) protest (b) swamp _____ .

7. **parochial** (pə RŌ kē əl)—adjective

   a. A counselor needs to have broad rather than *parochial* perspectives.
   b. An elderly neighbor of mine talks only about his garden and baseball, but despite his *parochial* interests, I enjoy talking with him.

parochial means (a) sophisticated (b) limited _____ .

8. **perfunctory** (pər FUNK tə rē)—adjective

   a. Rodney was disappointed with the concert because his favorite band played in a *perfunctory* manner rather than with its usual zest.
   b. The Caldwell's dog made only a *perfunctory* sniff at the trembling puppy before continuing his jaunt through the neighborhood.

perfunctory is related to (a) superficial (b) thorough _____ .

9. **acquiesce** (ak wē ES)—verb

   a. To prevent a strike, the management representative decided to *acquiesce* to the workers' terms.
   b. Her shocked boyfriend said he would *acquiesce* to breaking up if that's what she really wanted to do.

acquiesce means to (a) agree (b) disagree _____ .

10. **ephemeral** (i FEM ər əl)—adjective

   a. The popularity of men's leisure suits proved to be *ephemeral* as they are no longer sold or worn.
   b. Although many children's interest in taking piano lessons proves to be *ephemeral*, Angela continued to take lessons until she graduated from high school.

ephemeral means (a) unpopular (b) short-lived _____ .

Copyright © by Houghton Mifflin Company. All rights reserved.

Name .... Section .... Date ....

EXERCISES FOR LESSON 30
Challenging Words

I. *Directions:* Write each word before its definition.

cogent	sordid	usurp	parochial	acquiesce
rationalize	eclectic	inundate	perfunctory	ephemeral

_____ **1.** seize control of, move in on, trespass
_____ **2.** performed in an uninterested or routine manner
_____ **3.** disgraceful, shameful
_____ **4.** lasting a short time, fleeting
_____ **5.** limited or narrow in viewpoint
_____ **6.** convincing, persuasive
_____ **7.** to overwhelm, to overflow
_____ **8.** from many sources, various
_____ **9.** to agree to, to submit to
_____ **10.** to explain away, to justify

II. *Directions:* In each space, write the appropriate word from those listed below.

cogent	sordid	usurp	parochial	acquiesce
rationalize	eclectic	inundate	perfunctory	ephemeral

1. Although he had planned to spend the day working on his car, Fred reluctantly decided he had better _____ to his supervisor's request to work on Saturday.

2. I don't think there is any valid excuse for your discourtesy to Marty, so don't try to _____ your rude behavior to me.

3. After the heavy rain, the overflow from the creek began to _____ the road leading to town.

4. Vicki has _____ interests, ranging from photography to scuba diving.

5. The couple's pledge to always remain together proved to be _____ as they broke up three weeks later.

6. The Johnsons, a retired couple, are anything but _____ in their interests because they enjoy traveling, attending concerts, refinishing furniture, bowling, and canoeing.

Copyright © by Houghton Mifflin Company. All rights reserved.

7. Every soap opera seems to have at least one major character who leads a(n) _____ life—a life full of deception, infidelity, and crime.

8. The dental hygienist gave me a number of _____ reasons for flossing my teeth after every meal, including the prevention of gum disease.

9. When the student pilot did a casual check of the plane before takeoff, his instructor sternly lectured him for making such a(n) _____ inspection.

10. The new custodian was told never to _____ a teacher's authority by disciplining students.

III. *Directions:* After selecting your response, put the letter before it in the space provided.

_____ 1. The *opposite* of **acquiesce** is to
    a. agree
    b. refuse
    c. endorse
    d. prove

_____ 2. The *opposite* of **cogent** is
    a. smart
    b. forceful
    c. vague
    d. happy

_____ 3. The *opposite* of **perfunctory** is
    a. precise
    b. tardy
    c. inconsiderate
    d. calm

_____ 4. We are most likely to **rationalize** our
    a. income
    b. dreams
    c. triumphs
    d. mistakes

_____ 5. The person most likely to **usurp** authority is a(n)
    a. boss
    b. rebel
    c. police officer
    d. athlete

Copyright © by Houghton Mifflin Company. All rights reserved.

_____ **6.** A person with **eclectic** musical interests would probably
   a. like only one type of music
   b. like many types of music
   c. be unable to read music
   d. be an accomplished musician

_____ **7.** On the other hand, a person with **parochial** musical interests would probably
   a. like only one type of music
   b. like many types of music
   c. be unable to read music
   d. be an accomplished musician

_____ **8. sordid : honorable :: a.** quiet : silent
   b. sorrow : grief
   c. dirty : clean
   d. funny : dishonorable

_____ **9. inundate : overwhelm :: a.** overwhelm : challenge
   b. challenge : admit
   c. admit : invent
   d. invent : create

_____ **10. ephemeral : passing :: a.** temporary : brief
   b. momentary : enduring
   c. impulsive : thoughtful
   d. vanishing : appearing

IV. *Directions:* Write an original sentence for each word that clearly demonstrates your mastery of its meaning.

1. **cogent** _____

   _____

2. **rationalize** _____

   _____

3. **sordid** _____

   _____

4. **eclectic** _____

   _____

5. **usurp** _____

   _____

Copyright © by Houghton Mifflin Company. All rights reserved.

6. inundate _____

_____

7. parochial _____

_____

8. perfunctory _____

_____

9. acquiesce _____

_____

10. ephemeral _____

_____

Copyright © by Houghton Mifflin Company. All rights reserved.

ACADEMIC TERMS

Section Two helps you become familiar with many of the academic terms associated with subjects you probably will be required to study in college, such as literature and composition, as well as with subjects you may elect to take, such as business and economics. Learning the definitions of these terms is important because you must know them to understand the fundamental concepts presented in college courses.

The academic terms and definitions presented in the lessons are similar to those you would find in the glossary of a textbook. The prefixes, suffixes, and roots you studied in Section One have been underlined so you can use your knowledge about them to deepen your understanding of the academic terms.

DOING THE LESSONS

Begin each lesson by familiarizing yourself with each term's pronunciation, part of speech, and definition:

- Notice that a space separates each syllable of the term and that the accented syllable is printed in capital letters.
- Observe that vowels with long sounds have a line over them and that the schwa sound (uh) in unaccented syllables is represented by ə, which looks like an upside-down e:

    EXAMPLES: connotation (kon ə TĀ shən)—noun

    mutation (myo͞o TĀ shən)—noun

Copyright © by Houghton Mifflin Company. All rights reserved.

Note: The pronunciation given for each term in the lessons is a common one, but there may be other acceptable pronunciations.

- Notice the term's part of speech, for it is often a helpful contextual clue (Appendix A, beginning on page 357, reviews the parts of speech), and pay particular attention to any word parts underlined.
- Read the sample sentence that usually follows the term's definition to deepen your understanding of the word.
- Complete the lesson's exercises.
- Be prepared for a mastery test after you have completed all the lessons for each subject.
- Be prepared for a comprehensive posttest after you have completed all of the lessons in **Section Two.**

Copyright © by Houghton Mifflin Company. All rights reserved.

Literature and Composition

Literature and composition embrace all human experiences—common, unique, sad, joyful, expected, unexpected, disenchanting, and inspirational. These subjects can provide excellent opportunities to gain valuable insights into life. The following terms are commonly used in both literature and composition, so knowledge of them will be beneficial to you.

1. **bibliography** (bib lē OG rə fē)—noun

   A list of books and other readings on a particular subject.
   A research paper's *bibliography* must list all the sources used for information.

2. **connotation** (kon ə TĀ shən)—noun

   A word's suggested meanings or emotional associations, as contrasted to its strict, exact meaning.
   The denotation of *home* is "residence," but the *connotation* of *home* suggests feelings of love and security.

3. **denotation** (dē nō TĀ shən)—noun

   The strict, exact meaning of a word.
   The *denotation* of *father* is "male parent."

4. **figures of speech** (FIG yərs uv SPĒCH)—noun

   Expressions in which the words are not meant in their literal sense but are intended to be interpreted in an imaginative way.
   To present information in an original and colorful manner, writers often use *figures of speech,* such as metaphors, personification, and similes (see below).

5. **genre** (ZHAN rə)—noun

   A category or type of literature, such as novel, autobiography, or short story.
   Biography, an account of a person's life, is the most popular *genre* of literature for many readers.

6. **literal** (LIT ər əl)—adjective

   Refers to the strict meaning of a word or phrase.
   The *literal* meaning of *mother* is "female parent."

Copyright © by Houghton Mifflin Company. All rights reserved.

7. **metaphor** (MET ə for)—noun

A figure of speech in which two unlike things are compared or one thing is said to be another thing; the word *like* or *as* is not used in the comparison. (See *simile* below.)

"On Saturday evenings, Whitney's car was a panther that slinked down Main Street, daring anyone or anything to challenge it" is an example of a *metaphor.*

8. **personification** (pər son ə fa KĀ shən)—noun

A figure of speech in which a thing is given human qualities or performs human actions.

"The tulips danced and smiled when the old gardener came their way" is an example of *personification.*

9. **prose** (PRŌZ)—noun

The ordinary form of language; that is, writing or speech that is not poetry.

Novels and short stories are almost always written in *prose.*

10. **simile** (SIM ə lē)—noun

A figure of speech in which two unlike things are compared by using the word *like* or *as.*

"The frisky puppy is like an unguided missile" is an example of a *simile.*

Copyright © by Houghton Mifflin Company. All rights reserved.

Name .... Section .... Date ....

EXERCISES FOR LESSON 31
Literature and Composition

I. *Directions:* Match each definition with the word or words it defines.

_____ **1.** prose
_____ **2.** genre
_____ **3.** bibliography
_____ **4.** denotation
_____ **5.** connotation
_____ **6.** literal
_____ **7.** figures of speech
_____ **8.** simile
_____ **9.** metaphor
_____ **10.** personification

a. imaginative expressions
b. adjective referring to the exact meaning of a word or phrase
c. noun referring to the actual meaning
d. giving a thing human qualities
e. writing that is not poetry
f. suggested meaning of a word
g. list of readings or references
h. comparison using *like* or *as*
i. form of literature
j. comparison not using *like* or *as*

II. *Directions:* In each space, write the appropriate word or words from those listed below.

bibliography	figures of speech	metaphor	simile
connotation	genre	personification	
denotation	literal	prose	

1. "Grover's motorboat is like a rocket" is a _____ .

2. "Diego was a perfectly tuned machine; he ran relentlessly mile after mile" is a _____ .

3. Personification, metaphors, and similes are _____ .

4. Most magazines are written in _____ .

5. At the end of your term paper, include a _____ containing all the references you have used.

6. The _____ of the word *football* includes fall afternoons, marching bands, and roaring crowds.

7. The _____ of the word *football* includes a game with eleven players on each team.

8. Poetry is another _____ of literature.

9. "The tree stuck out its leg and tripped me" is _____ .

Copyright © by Houghton Mifflin Company. All rights reserved.

10. The _____ meaning of *morning* is the time between 12:00 A.M. and 12:00 P.M.

III. *Directions:* If the words opposite each other in Columns A and B are similar in meaning, write *Yes* in the blank; if they are unrelated, write *No.*

A		B
1. prose	_____	rhyming words
2. genre	_____	family history
3. bibliography	_____	list of readings
4. denotation	_____	word's actual meaning
5. connotation	_____	word's opposite meaning
6. literal	_____	reading ability
7. figures of speech	_____	fanciful expressions
8. simile	_____	comparison without *like* or *as*
9. metaphor	_____	comparison with *like* or *as*
10. personification	_____	sociable

IV. *Directions:* Write either an original sentence or a definition for each word or words that clearly demonstrates your mastery of their meaning as used in literature and composition.

1. bibliography _____

_____

2. connotation _____

_____

3. denotation _____

_____

4. figures of speech _____

_____

5. genre _____

_____

6. literal _____

_____

7. metaphor _____

_____

8. personification _____

_____

Copyright © by Houghton Mifflin Company. All rights reserved.

9. prose _____

_____

10. simile _____

_____

Copyright © by Houghton Mifflin Company. All rights reserved.

Literature and Composition

1. **alliteration** (ə lit ə RĀ ɒhən)   noun

   The repetition of the first sound, usually a consonant, in a series of words.
   "Francis is fair, frank, friendly, and famous" is an example of *alliteration.*

2. **hyperbole** (hī PUR bə lē)—noun

   A figure of speech in which exaggerated words are used for emphasis.
   "The closet in my room is so small that an ant wouldn't have enough room to turn around" is an example of *hyperbole.*

3. **plagiarism** (PLĀ jə riz əm)—noun

   The copying of words or ideas of another writer and then presenting them as one's original work.
   You must give credit to the author of the words you are using; otherwise, you will be guilty of *plagiarism.*

4. **satire** (SAT īr)—noun

   The use of sarcastic humor to expose injustice or stupidity.
   The sports columnist's *satire* was obvious when she wrote that the owner of the basketball team should feel guilty for not buying his star player a luxurious house because the player was making "only" 27 million dollars a year.

5. **analogy** (ə NAL ə jē)—noun

   A comparison in which similarities are found between two unlike things.
   An analogy is often expressed as a simile, as in "The football game was like a battle between gladiators."

6. **antagonist** (an TAG ə nist)—noun; **protagonist** (prō TAG ə nist)—noun

   The antagonist is the character in a story who opposes the hero or heroine, known as the protagonist.

Copyright © by Houghton Mifflin Company. All rights reserved.

In John Updike's "The Christian Roommates," Lester Spotted Elk was the antagonist of Orson, the protagonist, when Orson was in high school.

7. **canon** (KAN ən)—noun

The works of an author that are considered authentic.

Romeo and Juliet is just one of over thirty plays included in William Shakespeare's canon.

8. **flashback** (FLASH bak)—noun

An interruption in the flow of a story, play, or film to present action that occurred earlier.

A flashback in the movie showed the old man as a college student.

9. **foreshadowing** (fōr SHAD ō ing)—noun

A hint in the story or drama of some coming event, often a tragic one.

The king's nightmare was a foreshadowing of the tragic battle that would result in his death the next day.

10. **synopsis** (si NOP sis)—noun

A summary of the main points of a story or other literary work.

Our assignment was to write a synopsis of Katherine Mansfield's short story "The Garden Party."

11. **anthology** (an THOL ə jē)—noun

A book or collection of selected writings.

Our literature class is using an anthology containing short stories, poems, and plays.

Copyright © by Houghton Mifflin Company. All rights reserved.

Name .... Section .... Date ....

EXERCISES FOR LESSON 32
Literature and Composition

I. Directions: Match each definition with the word it defines.

_____ 1. hyperbole	**a.** hero or leading character in a story
_____ 2. alliteration	**b.** authentic works of an author
_____ 3. antagonist	**c.** hint in the story of a coming event
_____ 4. flashback	**d.** representing the words or ideas of
_____ 5. synopsis	another author as one's own
_____ 6. protagonist	**e.** a string of words with the same
_____ 7. foreshadowing	initial sound
_____ 8. anthology	**f.** sarcastic humor
_____ 9. analogy	**g.** summary
_____ 10. canon	**h.** exaggeration for the sake of effect
_____ 11. satire	**i.** person who opposes the hero
_____ 12. plagiarism	**j.** comparison of unlike things
	k. interruption in a story to present a
	previous scene
	l. collection of selected writings

II. *Directions:* In each space, write the appropriate word from those listed below.

alliteration	satire	protagonist	foreshadowing
hyperbole	analogy	canon	synopsis
plagiarism	antagonist	flashback	anthology

1. The _____ in this story is a young woman who eventually triumphs over her chief _____, an evil man who seeks revenge against her and her family.

2. I'm writing a(n) _____ of Robert Frost's poem "The Death of the Hired Man," which is contained in the _____ of poems, essays, plays, and short stories we're using in our American literature class.

3. As the ship slowly sinks to the bottom of the ocean, there is a(n) _____ of the captain as a young man eagerly enlisting in the Navy.

4. The author uses a comical _____, comparing the young girl's mind to a glass of fizzy root beer.

Copyright © by Houghton Mifflin Company. All rights reserved.

Academic Terms   Lesson 32   215

5. There is no question Shakespeare wrote King Lear, so that is why it is included in the Shakespearean _____ .

6. "Bruce brutally batted ball after ball" is an example of _____ .

7. "I drove a million miles during my week's vacation" is obviously _____ .

8. Max didn't want to be guilty of _____ , so he put quotation marks around the words and cited the author's name in his bibliography.

9. In his letter to the editor, Rex used bitter humor, or _____ , to voice his criticisms about the school's new parking regulations.

10. The wilted rose in the bride's wedding bouquet provided a(n) _____ that the couple's love would not endure.

III. *Directions:* If the words opposite each other in Columns A and B are similar in meaning, write *Yes* in the blank; if they are unrelated, write *No.*

A	B
1. plagiarism	_____ summarizing a play
2. alliteration	_____ series of words with the same first sound
3. satire	_____ concluding remarks
4. hyperbole	_____ overstatement
5. flashback	_____ return to a previous time
6. synopsis	_____ comparison of unlike things
7. antagonist	_____ opponent
8. analogy	_____ a summary
9. anthology	_____ study of myths and primitive religions
10. canon	_____ genuine books of an author
11. protagonist	_____ hero
12. foreshadowing	_____ indication of a coming event

IV. *Directions:* Write either an original sentence or a definition for each word that clearly demonstrates your mastery of its meaning as used in literature and composition.

1. alliteration _____

_____

2. hyperbole _____

_____

3. plagiarism _____

_____

Copyright © by Houghton Mifflin Company. All rights reserved.

4. satire _____

_____

5. analogy _____

_____

6. antagonist _____

_____

7. protagonist _____

_____

8. canon _____

_____

9. flashback _____

_____

10. foreshadowing _____

_____

11. synopsis _____

_____

12. anthology _____

_____

Copyright © by Houghton Mifflin Company. All rights reserved.

Oral Communications

Because communicating with family, friends, associates, and countless others plays such a key role in our lives, college students, regardless of their majors, are usually required to take at least one course in oral communications (speech) to enhance their ability to interact formally and informally with others, whether in a one-to-one, small-group, or large-group situation. The terms presented in this and the following lesson are among those frequently used in introductory oral communication courses. In addition, a review of the **literature** and **composition** terms preceding these lessons is advisable as many of these words are also used in oral communication courses.

1. <u>venue</u> (VEN yoo)—noun

   The place where communication, such as a speech, takes place.
   Often, *venue* refers not only to the place where communication takes place, but also to the specific occasion and purpose of the communication.

2. <u>context</u> (KON tekst)—noun

   The environment in which communication takes place.
   Context includes the physical, social, and psychological conditions existing when communication takes place.

3. <u>encoding</u> (en KŌHD ing)—noun

   The transformation of a thought into a message.
   Encoding includes all the mental processes involved in converting ideas, feelings, opinions, and so forth into messages.

4. <u>decoding</u> (dē KŌHD ing)—noun

   The transformation of a message into meaning.
   Decoding includes all the mental processes involved in converting messages into meaning.

5. **catalyst** (KAT ə list)—noun

   Anything that improves communication.
   Humor can often serve as a *catalyst* for enriching communication.

Copyright © by Houghton Mifflin Company. All rights reserved.

219

6. noise (noiz)—noun

Anything that hinders communication.

Preoccupation with factors unrelated to the speaker's remarks is an example of communication *noise*.

7. speaking (SPEEK ing) **voice** (vois)—adjective + noun

Refers to the basic factors relating to speech.

The basic factors relating to *speaking voice* include **volume** (loudness, softness), **pitch** (highness, lowness), **inflections** (variations of pitch), **tempo** (speaking rate), **tone** (attitude toward a subject, such as humorous or serious), **diction** (choice and use of words), and **pronunciation.**

8. active (AK tiv) and **passive** (PAS iv) **voice** (vois)—adjectives + noun

A verb is in the active voice when the subject of the sentence does the action the verb describes:

Karen <u>washed</u> the car.

A verb is in the passive voice when it acts upon the subject:

The car <u>was</u> <u>washed</u> by Karen.

Generally, it is best to use the active voice for both writing and speaking because it produces more direct, powerful, and interesting communication.

9. enunciation (i NUN sē Ā shən)—noun

Refers to the correct and precise pronunciation of words.

In casual conversations, it's usually okay for us to mispronounce or slur certain words, such as saying "accidently" instead of "accidentally" and "wif" instead of "with," but in more formal speaking situations, we should make sure our *enunciation* of all words is appropriate.

10. impromptu speaking (im PROMP too SPEEK ing)—adjective + noun

Speaking done with little or no advance preparation.

Though always a challenge, *impromptu speaking* can be effective and rewarding if the speaker focuses upon one or two main ideas and then provides specific examples for clarification or support.

Copyright © by Houghton Mifflin Company. All rights reserved.

Name .... Section .... Date ....

EXERCISES FOR LESSON 33
Oral Communications

I. *Directions:* Match each definition to the word or words it defines.

_____ **1.** venue	**a.** transformation of a message into meaning
_____ **2.** context	**b.** when the subject of the sentence does the action the verb describes
_____ **3.** encoding	
_____ **4.** decoding	**c.** the environment in which communication takes place
_____ **5.** catalyst	
_____ **6.** noise	**d.** anything that hinders communication
_____ **7.** speaking voice	**e.** speaking done with little or no advance preparation
_____ **8.** active voice	
_____ **9.** passive voice	**f.** the place where communication takes place
_____ **10.** enunciation	
_____ **11.** impromptu speaking	**g.** the correct and precise pronunciation of words

h. anything that improves communication

i. transformation of a thought into a message

j. refers to the basic factors relating to speech

k. when the verb acts upon the subject

II. *Directions:* In each space, write the appropriate word or words from those listed below.

| venue | encoding | catalyst | speaking voice | passive | impromptu |
| context | decoding | noise | active | enunciation | |

1. "The meal was cooked by Jeff" is in the _____ voice, whereas "Jeff cooked the meal" is in the _____ voice.

2. My instructor gave me three minutes to prepare for a(n) _____ speech on my favorite movie.

3. My emotions and thoughts whirled around before _____ took place; then I was able to explain why *Sleepless in Seattle* was my favorite movie.

4. The _____ for Dr. Wallace's speech will be the convention room on the first floor of the Dickson Inn on Essex Street.

Copyright © by Houghton Mifflin Company. All rights reserved.

5. Good acoustics is a(n) _____ contributing to effective communication.

6. His _____ of some words was faulty as he said "incidently" instead of "incidentally" and "choclate" instead of "chocolate."

7. Today's class was devoted to _____ , so we discussed such matters as volume, tone, and tempo when we gave a speech.

8. The _____ of a complex message can be aided by listing the main ideas it contains and then writing a summary of the ideas in your own words.

9. The _____ , or environment, in which a speech takes place includes a number of physical, social, and psychological factors, such as the size of the room, the room's temperature, and the ages, backgrounds, and attitudes of the listeners.

10. In oral communications, the term _____ doesn't refer only to loud, disturbing sounds; it refers to anything hampering the effective interchange of information.

III. *Directions:* If the words opposite each other in Columns A and B are similar in meaning, write *Yes* in the blank; if they are unrelated, write *No.*

A	B
1. catalyst	_____ something that aids communication
2. content	_____ interpretation of a message
3. speaking voice	_____ oral commands
4. impromptu speaking	_____ talking on the spur of the moment
5. active and passive voices	_____ the loudness and softness of sound
6. decoding	_____ conversion of messages into meaning
7. venue	_____ location where a speech is given
8. noise	_____ sound effects used to aid communication
9. enunciation	_____ feedback provided by an audience
10. encoding	_____ conversion of thoughts into messages

IV. *Directions:* Write either an original sentence or a definition for each word or words that clearly demonstrates your mastery of their meaning as used in oral communications.

1. **venue** _____

_____

2. **context** _____

_____

3. **encoding** _____

Copyright © by Houghton Mifflin Company. All rights reserved.

4. decoding _____

_____

5. catalyst _____

_____

6. noise _____

_____

7. speaking voice _____

_____

8. active voice _____

_____

9. passive voice _____

_____

10. enunciation _____

_____

11. impromptu speaking _____

_____

Copyright © by Houghton Mifflin Company. All rights reserved.

Oral Communications

1. **transitions** (tran ZISH əns)—noun

   Words and phrases a speaker uses to move from one major point to another.

   Examples of *transitions* often used by speakers include these: **to add information**—and, also, in addition, furthermore, moreover, besides; **to compare**—similarly, likewise, by the same token, in the same vein; **to contrast**—but, on the other hand, yet, however, although, in contrast, on the contrary, nevertheless; **to relate time**—then, when, afterward, meanwhile, during, thereafter; **to clarify**—for example, for instance, specifically; **to emphasize**—more important, to be sure, indeed, as long as, provided that, unless; **to show cause and effect**—as a result, because, therefore, thus, then, since, hence; **to summarize**—therefore, in summary, consequently, as a result.

2. **kinesics** (kə NĒS iks)—noun

   Refers to body movements or body language.

   Communication is influenced by *kinesics,* or body movements, which include gestures, posture, facial expressions, and eye behavior.

3. **rapport** (ra POR)—noun

   A harmonious or sympathetic connection between a speaker and his or her audience.

   To communicate effectively, speakers must establish *rapport* with their audience; humor is often used for this purpose.

4. **premise** (PREM is)—noun

   An assertion made by a speaker that serves as a basis for an argument or for a conclusion.

   The speaker's *premise* was that students should not have to pay to attend any athletic or musical events on campus because they already pay an activity fee each semester.

Copyright © by Houghton Mifflin Company. All rights reserved.

5. **fallacies** (FAL ə sēs)—noun

Mistakes in reasoning.

Among the common *fallacies* speakers sometimes commit are these: **Hasty Generalization**—basing a conclusion on too little evidence; for example, saying "Connecticut drivers are reckless" based on seeing only two Connecticut motorists driving in this manner. **Either–Or**—stating there are only two alternatives when there are more than that; for example, saying "To avoid a vitamin C deficiency, a person must drink either orange or grape juice every day" when in truth there are numerous other sources of vitamin C. **Ad Hominem**—attacking the person personally rather than the person's argument; for example, saying "Lawrence argues he's the best candidate for the school board, but I know for a fact he wasn't popular in high school, and besides, he's divorced." **Prestige Jargon**—using impressive language in an attempt to gain importance or acceptance of an argument; for example, saying "A student should faithfully attend his or her classes as there is a plethora of research connoting a positive correlation between a student's class attendance and his or her overall scholastic performance," instead of simply saying, "Students should attend their classes because good attendance is related to good grades."

6. **nonsexist language** (NON SEKS ist LANG gwij)—adjective + noun

Communication reflecting gender fairness.

To avoid stereotyping, insensitivity, and unfairness, speakers should use *nonsexist language.* For example, speakers should say police officers, **not** policemen or policewomen; mail carriers, **not** mailmen or mailwomen; sales representatives, **not** salesmen or salesladies; humankind, **not** mankind.

7. **objective** (əb JEK tiv)—adjective
   subjective (səb JEK tiv)—adjective

When speakers are objective, personal feelings or biases do not influence their remarks; however, when speakers are subjective, their personal feelings or biases do influence their remarks.

It is appropriate for speakers to be objective when they state the facts involved in an experience, event, or outcome; on the other hand, it is appropriate for speakers to be *subjective* when they remark about their reactions regarding the experience, event, or outcome.

8. **critique** (kri TEEK)—noun

A careful, in-depth review of something, such as a movie, book, piece of artwork, organization, or product.

The speaker gave a *critique* of the student support programs currently existing on campus. For the most part, she was complimentary of the programs and the people responsible for them; however, she felt the financial aid office was significantly understaffed.

Copyright © by Houghton Mifflin Company. All rights reserved.

9. **deduction** (dē DUK shən)—noun
   induction (in DUK shən)—noun

   Deduction is reasoning that starts with an accepted principle and leads to specific instances that support the accepted principle.

   Induction is the drawing of a conclusion after gathering appropriate information.

   A speaker can often use *deduction* and/or *induction* to justify his or her opinions, assumptions, conclusions, and suggestions, as in these examples: **Deduction**—At the study skills seminar, the speaker urged us to devote the majority of our studying time on the information our instructors emphasize in class; he said numerous studies conducted over the years indicate that most college students who follow this principle achieve high grades. **Induction**—The speaker also said the data he has collected during the past eight semesters reveal that students who study at the same time and at the same place usually achieve higher grades than students who study at various times and at various places; therefore, he has concluded that studying at a specific time and at a specific place is another principle college students would be wise to follow.

10. **multimedia presentation** (MUL ti MĒ dē ə PREZ ən TĀY shən)—adjective + noun

    A talk or similar event that uses several forms of communication, such as slides, videos, and films.

    The speaker's *multimedia presentation* was impressive as she used a computer to display various charts, photographs, and video clips on a large screen.

Copyright © by Houghton Mifflin Company. All rights reserved.

Name .... Section .... Date ....

EXERCISES FOR LESSON 34
Oral Communications

I. *Directions:* Match each definition to the word it defines.

_____ **1.** transitions
_____ **2.** kinesics
_____ **3.** rapport
_____ **4.** premise
_____ **5.** fallacies
_____ **6.** nonsexist language
_____ **7.** objective
_____ **8.** subjective
_____ **9.** critique
_____ **10.** deduction
_____ **11.** induction
_____ **12.** multimedia presentation

a. mistakes in reasoning
b. a talk that uses a variety of sources, such as graphs and slides
c. communication reflecting gender fairness
d. reasoning that draws a conclusion after making observations
e. reflecting personal feelings or biases
f. reasoning that begins with an accepted principle
g. harmonious connection between speaker and audience
h. connections between words and phrases
i. assertion that serves as a basis for an argument
j. body movements
k. lacking personal feelings or biases
l. in-depth review of a product, organization, or event

II. *Directions:* In each space, write the appropriate word or words from those listed below.

transitions   kinesics   rapport   premise   fallacies   nonsexist language
objective   subjective   critique   deduction   induction   multimedia

1. Our instructor's use of _____ , especially his gestures and facial expressions, effectively convey his sense of humor as well as the main points he wishes to stress during class discussions.

2. The speaker's basic assumption was that all college students enjoy team sports, and since we were college students, we all enjoyed team sports; however, his _____ was faulty from the beginning because a number of my friends and I don't care about team sports at all.

Copyright © by Houghton Mifflin Company. All rights reserved.

3. The speaker also used _____ as he said he had observed over the years that students gain an average of ten pounds during their first year of college, so he has concluded that we will too; but I sure hope he's wrong, at least in my case.

4. I appreciate Professor Libby's use of _____ , such as "for example" or "for instance," when she explains difficult concepts.

5. She has excellent _____ with us as she calls on us by name and obviously appreciates what we have to say.

6. Although jury members may not like the looks of the defendant, they should remain _____ and base their verdict on the evidence presented during the trial.

7. Today's history class was particularly interesting because of Dr. Hewitt's _____ presentation, which included newspaper articles, photos, and film clips about World War II.

8. "Flight attendant" instead of "stewardess" is an example of _____.

9. Attacking a person personally instead of his or her argument and making a hasty generalization are examples of _____ .

10. Although Todd and Bridget's love for that part of the city obviously influenced their decision about which apartment to rent, I think it was okay for them to be _____ in this instance, don't you agree?

11. My _____ is that it's important to feel "at home" where you live, even if where you live causes some minor inconveniences.

12. In communications class today, Jarrett gave an impressive _____ of last weekend's rock concert. Although he praised the band's musicianship and choice of numbers, he said the lead singer overpowered the other singers and that the band's sound system was inadequate, at least for Hudson Hall, the place where the concert was held.

III. *Directions:* If the words opposite each other in Columns A and B are similar in meaning, write *Yes* in the blank; if they are unrelated, write *No*.

A	B
1. subjective	_____ insulting
2. rapport	_____ harmony
3. fallacies	_____ jokes
4. transitions	_____ connecting words
5. objective	_____ agreeable
6. multimedia presentation	_____ talk using various audio and visual aids
7. induction	_____ drawing a conclusion after gathering evidence
8. premise	_____ obligation

Copyright © by Houghton Mifflin Company. All rights reserved.

9. nonsexist language   _____ stereotyping talk
10. critique   _____ careful evaluation
11. deduction   _____ brief speech
12. kinesics   _____ body language

IV. *Directions:* Write either an original sentence or a definition for each word or words that clearly demonstrates your mastery of their meaning as used in oral communications.

1. **transitions** _____

_____

2. **kinesics** _____

_____

3. **rapport** _____

_____

4. **premise** _____

_____

5. **fallacies** _____

_____

6. **nonsexist language** _____

_____

7. **objective** _____

_____

8. **subjective** _____

_____

9. **critique** _____

_____

10. **deduction** _____

_____

11. **induction** _____

_____

12. **multimedia presentation** _____

_____

Copyright © by Houghton Mifflin Company. All rights reserved.

Psychology

Psychology is devoted to the systematic study of behavior as well as to the motives for that behavior. Mastery of the psychological terms contained in this and the following two lessons can contribute to your understanding of this interesting subject.

1. **behavior** (bi HĀV yər)—noun

   Any activity of a human or other organism.
   Thinking, though unobservable, is part of a person's *behavior.*

2. **cognitive** (KOG nə tiv)—adjective

   Relating to knowing, understanding, thinking.
   A major stage in a child's *cognitive* development is reached when he or she becomes capable of abstract reasoning.

3. **variable** (VAR ē ə bəl)—noun

   In an experiment, the condition or factor that can be changed or manipulated.
   The brand of tires was the only *variable* involved in the testing of the car's gas-mileage performances.

4. **empirical** (em PIR ə kəl)—adjective

   Relating to what has been precisely experienced or observed in experiments.
   The *empirical* facts were recorded so that the experiment could be evaluated.

5. **control group** (kən TRŌL GRŌOP)—adjective + noun

   A group of subjects exposed to all the features of a particular experiment except for the variable being studied. The characteristics of the control group are always matched as closely as possible to those of the experimental group.
   The experimental group, which was given the vaccine, had significantly fewer colds and other viruses during the twelve weeks of the investigation than did the *control group,* which was not administered the vaccine.

Copyright © by Houghton Mifflin Company. All rights reserved.

6. **experimental group** (ik SPER ə MEN təl GROOP)—adjective + noun

A group of subjects, which could consist of people or other organisms, exposed to the variable being investigated in an experiment. The researcher is attempting to discover the effects of the variable.

Both groups were on the same diet; however, only the *experimental group* was led in exercises for fifteen minutes a day. The goal was to determine whether exercises of that duration would contribute to additional weight loss.

7. **motor skills** (MŌ tər SKILS)—adjective + noun

Coordinated physical movements, such as those required to walk or swim.
Gymnastics requires advanced development of many *motor skills.*

8. **organism** (OR gə niz əm)—noun

Any living animal or plant.
A monkey was injected with the bacterial *organism* for the experiment.

9. **sibling** (SIB ling)—noun

One of two or more individuals having one common parent; a brother or a sister.
Jack, my oldest *sibling,* is studying law at a university in Texas.

10. **theory** (THĒR ē)—noun

An association of ideas that attempts to provide a reasonable explanation for events observed or to predict what will be observed under a given set of circumstances.
One *theory* is that the moon was once part of the earth.

Copyright © by Houghton Mifflin Company. All rights reserved.

EXERCISES FOR LESSON 35
Psychology

I. *Directions:* Match each definition with the word it defines.

_____ **1.** organism
_____ **2.** motor skills
_____ **3.** theory
_____ **4.** cognitive
_____ **5.** behavior
_____ **6.** variable
_____ **7.** empirical
_____ **8.** experimental group
_____ **9.** control group
_____ **10.** sibling

a. based upon observable facts or experiences
b. relating to knowing and thinking
c. a brother or sister
d. condition manipulated in an experiment
e. a living creature
f. those in an experiment exposed to the treatment condition
g. reasonable explanation
h. any activity of an organism
i. physical abilities that involve movement
j. those in an experiment not exposed to the treatment condition

II. *Directions:* In each space, write the appropriate word or words from those listed below.

behavior   empirical   motor skills   theory
cognitive   control group   organism
variable   experimental group sibling

1. Bradley believes he has the necessary _____ to do a somersault on skis.

2. Dr. Skolberg's _____ is that vitamin C's ability to prevent colds and other viral infections has been greatly exaggerated.

3. Marguerite was a member of the _____ , so she received vitamin C.

4. Kristen was a member of the _____ , so she did not receive vitamin C.

5. Thus, vitamin C was the _____ manipulated in this experiment.

Copyright © by Houghton Mifflin Company. All rights reserved.

6. Based upon the _____ evidence, Dr. Clarke concluded that vitamin C is somewhat helpful in the prevention of colds and other viral infections.

7. Do you know if Todd's oldest _____ is a brother or a sister?

8. A guinea pig was the subject, or _____, used by the fourth-grade class in its nutritional study.

9. The psychological definition of _____ includes all activities, both physical and mental, done by a person or other organism.

10. As a person matures, his or her _____ skills become more developed, so he or she is capable of solving more complex problems.

III. *Directions:* If the words opposite each other in Columns A and B are similar in meaning, write *Yes* in the blank; if they are unrelated, write *No.*

A	B
1. organism	_____ living creature
2. motor skills	_____ physical abilities
3. theory	_____ truth
4. cognitive	_____ classification
5. behavior	_____ all activities
6. variable	_____ disagreement
7. empirical	_____ costly
8. experimental group	_____ those exposed to the factor manipulated in an experiment
9. control group	_____ those not included in an experiment
10. sibling	_____ mother or father

IV. *Directions:* Write either an original sentence or a definition for each word or words that clearly demonstrates your mastery of their meaning as used in psychology.

1. **behavior** _____

_____

2. **cognitive** _____

_____

3. **variable** _____

_____

4. **empirical** _____

_____

Copyright © by Houghton Mifflin Company. All rights reserved.

5. control group _____

_____

6. experimental group _____

_____

7. motor skills _____

_____

8. organism _____

_____

9. sibling _____

_____

10. theory _____

_____

Copyright © by Houghton Mifflin Company. All rights reserved.

Psychology

1. **intrin<u>sic</u> motiva<u>tion</u>** (in TRIN sik mō tə VĀ shən)—adjective + noun

   A reason or desire for action that comes from within the individual.

   Carolyn wants to prove to herself that she can get better grades, so her additional studying is the result of *intrinsic motivation.*

2. **<u>extrinsic</u> motiva<u>tion</u>** (eks TRIN sik mō tə VĀ shən)—noun

   A reason or desire for action that comes from outside the individual.

   Matthew's increased studying this semester results from *extrinsic motivation* as his parents promised to give him $500 if he improves all his grades.

3. **defense mechan<u>isms</u>** (də FENS MEK ə NIZ əms)—adjective + noun

   Unconscious strategies for protecting ourselves against unpleasant emotions. Defense mechanisms are also used to protect our self-images.

   Repression (selective forgetting) and rationalization (excuse making) are common *defense mechanisms.*

4. **therapeut<u>ic</u>** (ther ə PŪ tik)—adjective

   Relating to the treatment of disease, especially describing something intended to bring about healing.

   Kara says playing her clarinet has a *therapeutic* effect on her when she is emotionally upset.

5. **hypothesis** (hī POTH ə sis)—noun

   A logical explanation that needs further investigation before it can be said to be true.

   The *hypothesis* that poliomyelitis was caused by a virus proved to be true when the virus was identified in the 1950s.

6. **<u>introspection</u>** (in trə SPEK shən)—noun

   The observation of one's own mental and emotional condition.

   After weeks of *introspection,* Aiden realized he'd be happier if he quit his job and returned to school.

Copyright © by Houghton Mifflin Company. All rights reserved.

239

7. **autism** (AW tiz əm)—noun

Abnormal self-absorption; extreme withdrawal into fantasy.

Autism is a severe mental illness generally beginning in early childhood and characterized by isolation, fantasy, and defective thinking and language abilities.

8. **neurosis** (nyoo RŌ sis)—noun

An emotional disorder characterized by anxiety or other symptoms. A neurosis is not due to physical disease, and the sufferer of a neurosis does not lose contact with reality. A neurosis is not as severe a disorder as a *psychosis* (see below).

A person suffering from a *neurosis* may experience disabling anxiety.

9. **psychosis** (sī KŌ sis)—noun

Severe mental disorder involving personality disorganization and lack of contact with reality.

A person suffering from a *psychosis* is considered insane.

10. **ego** (Ē gō)—noun

id (ID)—noun

superego (SOO pər Ē gō)—noun

The ego, id, and superego are terms associated with Sigmund Freud (1856–1939), the founder of psychoanalysis. The **ego** is the conscious part of the personality and is responsible for logical thinking.

The **id** is the instinctive part of the personality, including the sexual and aggressive instincts, that seeks immediate gratification. Freud maintained that the id is the first system to develop within a person because it is most closely related to the biological realm. The id is the "home" of all psychological energy, or libido (Latin for "lust").

The **superego** is the moralistic part of the personality, including beliefs about what conduct is right or wrong.

The *ego* has to resolve the conflicting demands of the *id, superego,* and external reality. The *id* is the pleasure-loving, selfish side of a person's personality that seeks immediate gratification regardless of consequences. The *superego,* or conscience, is largely a product of parental and societal influences.

Copyright © by Houghton Mifflin Company. All rights reserved.

Copyright © by Houghton Mifflin Company. All rights reserved.

Name .... Section .... Date ....

EXERCISES FOR LESSON 36
Psychology

I. *Directions:* Match each definition with the word it defines.

_____ **1.** superego	**a.** stimulation coming from outside a person
_____ **2.** therapeutic	
_____ **3.** defense mechanisms	**b.** emotional disorder causing anxiety or other distress; person does not lose contact with reality
_____ **4.** introspection	
_____ **5.** ego	
_____ **6.** autism	**c.** unconscious devices used to reduce anxiety
_____ **7.** intrinsic motivation	
_____ **8.** id	**d.** stimulation coming from within a person
_____ **9.** hypothesis	
_____ **10.** psychosis	**e.** conscience; part of the personality concerned with right and wrong
_____ **11.** extrinsic motivation	
_____ **12.** neurosis	**f.** descriptive term used for the treatment of illness

g. a reasonable assumption; a theory

h. the primitive, instinctive side of the personality

i. severe mental illness characterized by isolation and fantasy; often first displayed in childhood

j. examination of one's own thoughts

k. the conscious part of the personality, responsible for logical thinking

l. severe mental disorder in which person loses contact with reality; insanity

II. *Directions:* In each space, write the appropriate word or words from those listed below.

intrinsic	therapeutic	autism	ego
extrinsic	hypothesis	neurosis	id
defense mechanisms	introspection	psychosis	superego

1. An individual who lacks contact with reality and has a major personality disorder is suffering from a(n) _____ .

2. The _____ seeks immediate gratification regardless of consequences, while the _____ strives to maintain moral standards; the _____ attempts to reconcile the difference between the two.

3. The medical school was given a substantial grant to conduct research on _____ , a mental illness characterized by fantasy and isolation.

4. Although my business partner is often plagued with anxiety, he is able to meet his responsibilities; nevertheless, he's wisely decided to seek the help of a psychologist in an effort to overcome his _____ .

5. After months of soul-searching and intense _____ , Bill has decided to quit his job to fulfill his lifelong dream of becoming a commercial pilot.

6. The scientist is confident his explanation for that particular outcome is the correct one, but until he has proof, his explanation remains a(n) _____ .

7. Olivia is practicing the piano for two hours each day because of _____ motivation as her parents promised her a Florida vacation if she practiced every day for the next three months.

8. To free my mind from everyday stress, I find regular exercise to be _____ .

9. If a person performs some behavior because of personal reasons, he or she is prompted by _____ motivation.

10. After someone else was given the promotion he had also requested, Ted said that was okay with him because the salary raise wasn't much, and besides, he didn't think he would like the people he'd have to work with anyway. Ted's statement represents the possible use of _____ .

III. *Directions:* If the words opposite each other in Columns A and B are similar in meaning, write *Yes* in the blank; if they are unrelated, write *No.*

A	B
1. defense mechanisms	_____ motivational strategies
2. intrinsic motivation	_____ comes from within
3. extrinsic motivation	_____ comes from outside
4. therapeutic	_____ helpful to healing
5. introspection	_____ refusal to examine one's own thoughts and emotions
6. neurosis	_____ instinctive side of one's personality
7. superego	_____ honesty and morality side of a person's personality
8. psychosis	_____ abnormal fear
9. id	_____ unnatural behavior

Copyright © by Houghton Mifflin Company. All rights reserved.

10. ego   _____ logical, conscious side of a person's personality

11. hypothesis   _____ factual statement

12. autism   _____ harsh criticism

IV. *Directions:* Write either an original sentence or a definition for each word or words that clearly demonstrates your mastery of their meaning as used in psychology.

1. intrinsic motivation _____

_____

2. extrinsic motivation _____

_____

3. defense mechanisms _____

_____

4. therapeutic _____

_____

5. hypothesis _____

_____

6. introspection _____

_____

7. autism _____

_____

8. neurosis _____

_____

9. psychosis _____

_____

10. ego _____

_____

11. id _____

_____

12. superego _____

_____

Copyright © by Houghton Mifflin Company. All rights reserved.

Sociology

Sociology is concerned with the systematic study of human society, including the social interactions among nations, communities, and families. Mastery of the terms in this lesson and the following lesson can give you insight into this valuable social science.

1. **acculturation** (ə kul chə RĀ shən)—noun

   Modification of a culture as a result of contact with another culture.

   The *acculturation* of the Japanese to many aspects of Western culture began after World War II.

2. **agrarian** (ə GRAR ē ən)—adjective

   Relates to rural life, agricultural groups, and farm ownership.

   The United States has moved from a predominantly *agrarian* to an urban society.

3. **culture** (KUL chər)—noun

   The patterns of life shared by the members of a society and transmitted from one generation to another.

   Eating three meals a day is part of our *culture.*

4. **demography** (di MOG rə fē)—noun

   The statistical study of human populations, such as information about the number of births, deaths, and marriages.

   A study of *demography* reveals that one of the highest birthrates in the United States occurred in the late 1940s.

5. **mores** (MŌR āz)—noun

   Social norms that reflect the moral standards of a society.

   Marrying a close relative is opposed by the *mores* of most societies.

6. **peer group** (PĒR GRŌŌP)—noun + noun

   A grouping of individuals of the same general age and social position.

   As a child becomes older, his or her *peer group* has more influence.

Copyright © by Houghton Mifflin Company. All rights reserved.

245

7. social norms (SŌ shəl NORMZ)—adjective + noun

Standards that guide people in what they should or should not do in any particular social situation.

Laws are serious and formal *social norms*.

8. stereotype (STER ē ə tīp)—noun

A standardized image applied to individuals who are identified with a particular group.

The *stereotype* of the cowboy of the Old West is that of a fearless, rugged, independent man.

9. urbanism (UR bə niz əm)—noun

Patterns of life characteristic of cities.

Some of the benefits of *urbanism* include access to outstanding museums, theaters, and restaurants.

10. values (VAL yōoz)—noun

Ideas about what is good, proper, wise, and worthwhile.

Achieving success in work is one of society's *values*.

Copyright © by Houghton Mifflin Company. All rights reserved.

EXERCISES FOR LESSON 37
Sociology

I. *Directions:* Match each definition with the word or words it defines.

_____ **1.** social norms   **a.** adopting new patterns of life

_____ **2.** mores   **b.** a fixed view of individuals

_____ **3.** values   **c.** customs and values shared by a

_____ **4.** culture   society

_____ **5.** peer group   **d.** standards for social behavior

_____ **6.** stereotype   **e.** refers to country life and farming

_____ **7.** demography   **f.** guides that provide moral standards

_____ **8.** acculturation   **g.** study of population figures

_____ **9.** urbanism   **h.** ideas about what is beneficial

_____ **10.** agrarian   **i.** refers to cities

         j. individuals of similar backgrounds

II. *Directions:* In each space, write the appropriate word or words from those listed below.

acculturation	demography	social norms	values
agrarian	mores	stereotype	
culture	peer group	urbanism	

1. A word referring to city life is _____ .

2. Guides that help us to decide how we should behave when in public are _____ .

3. Because friends are important to all of us, we wish to be accepted by our _____ .

4. Human population figures have to do with the subject of _____ .

5. Strict guides concerned with society's important moral standards are called _____ .

6. Getting a good education is one of the _____ of our society because of education's personal and vocational benefits.

7. A person who is overly aggressive, loud, and deceptive is the _____ many people have of a used-car salesman.

Copyright © by Houghton Mifflin Company. All rights reserved.

8. Iowa and Nebraska are considered _____ states because of the importance of agriculture to their economy.

9. Laws, religion, and manners are part of our _____ .

10. A United States citizen who moves to the Philippines undergoes a(n) _____ process because of the necessity to acquire new ways of functioning in a different society.

III. *Directions:* If the words opposite each other in Columns A and B are similar in meaning, write *Yes* in the blank; if they are unrelated, write *No.*

A	B
1. social norms	_____ behavior guides
2. mores	_____ moral guidelines
3. values	_____ ideals
4. culture	_____ advanced civilization
5. peer group	_____ those of the upper class
6. stereotype	_____ common image
7. demography	_____ study of land
8. acculturation	_____ universal praise
9. urbanism	_____ relates to cities
10. agrarian	_____ rural

IV. *Directions:* Write either an original sentence or a definition for each word or words that clearly demonstrates your mastery of their meaning as used in sociology.

1. acculturation _____

_____

2. agrarian _____

_____

3. culture _____

_____

4. demography _____

_____

5. mores _____

_____

Copyright © by Houghton Mifflin Company. All rights reserved.

6. **peer group** _____

_____

7. **social norms** _____

_____

8. **stereotype** _____

_____

9. **urbanism** _____

_____

10. **values** _____

_____

Copyright © by Houghton Mifflin Company. All rights reserved.

Sociology

1. **bureaucracy** (bū ROK rə sē)—noun

   Government structure operated by numerous offices and officials, with clearly defined responsibilities; often characterized by the following of inflexible rules and the creation of endless red tape.

   The Duncans did not let the irritating *bureaucracy* discourage them from attempting to adopt a child.

2. **ethnic group** (ETH nik GROOP)—adjective + noun

   A group within a society that shares the same traits, such as race, nationality, religion, language, and customs.

   Immigrants from Germany were an *ethnic group* that helped to settle Cincinnati, Ohio.

3. **ethnocentrism** (eth nō SEN triz əm)—noun

   The attitude that one's own race, nation, or culture is superior to all others.

   When people are initially exposed to a different culture, they may fall victim to *ethnocentrism,* a feeling that the new culture is inferior to the one to which they are accustomed.

4. **folkways** (FŌK wāz)—noun

   Social customs approved by society; unlike mores (see Lesson 37), folkways are not considered morally significant, so they are not strictly enforced.

   One of the *folkways* in our society is that a person should dress at least fairly formally when attending church, but it is not considered a serious offense if someone shows up wearing jeans.

5. **Malthusian theory** (mal THOO zē ən THĒ ə rē)—adjective + noun

   Thomas R. Malthus's (1766–1834) theory that if population is not controlled, the result will be famine, war, and other tragedies.

   The *Malthusian theory* was one of the first theories to predict that world hunger would result if population growth got out of control.

Copyright © by Houghton Mifflin Company. All rights reserved.

6. matriarchal family (mā trē AR kəl FAM ə lē)—adjective + noun

A family headed by the mother.

Because my father was frequently absent on business trips, ours was a *matriarchal family;* mother was dominant and made the major family decisions.

7. patriarchal family (pā trē AR kəl FAM ə lē)—adjective + noun

A family headed by the father.

A *patriarchal family* is most often portrayed in American literature, that is, a family dominated by the father's influence.

8. sanction (SANK shən)—noun

A mechanism of social control for enforcing a society's standards.

Because of the recent disturbances involving young people, the city council has enacted a 10:00 P.M. curfew for all teenagers; this *sanction* will be in effect for the remainder of the summer.

9. status (STĀ təs)—noun

A person's social standing in society.

Doctors enjoy a high social *status* in most communities.

10. utopia (ū TŌ pē ə)—noun

An imaginary place where everything is perfect.

Some young people yearn to go to Hollywood because they think this city must be *utopia.*

Copyright © by Houghton Mifflin Company. All rights reserved.

Name .... Section .... Date ....

EXERCISES FOR LESSON 38
Sociology

I. *Directions:* Match each definition with the word or words it defines.

_____ **1.** matriarchal family	**a.** perfect community
_____ **2.** patriarchal family	**b.** customs that are not strictly
_____ **3.** bureaucracy	enforced
_____ **4.** utopia	**c.** mother dominant
_____ **5.** ethnocentrism	**d.** punishment or approval
_____ **6.** Malthusian theory	**e.** organization with rigid rules
_____ **7.** folkways	**f.** people sharing certain characteristics
_____ **8.** sanction	**g.** father dominant
_____ **9.** status	**h.** belief that one's own culture is
_____ **10.** ethnic group	the best
	i. the idea that uncontrolled population
	leads to serious problems
	j. one's position in society

II. *Directions:* In each space, write the appropriate word or words from those listed below.

bureaucracy	folkways	patriarchal family	utopia
ethnic group	Malthusian theory	sanction	
ethnocentrism	matriarchal family	status	

1. Marybeth was accused of _____ after stating that England's culture is superior to the culture of any other country.

2. People who are of French descent have been a significant _____ in Maine's history.

3. The newspaper's editor blamed the state _____ for the endless paperwork involved in the proposed construction of a new city bridge.

4. According to the _____, controlled population growth is essential to avoid serious societal problems.

5. Because his father died when Wallis was only two years old, he was raised in a(n) _____ .

6. My Aunt Dolores was a part of a(n) _____ : her father dominated all family matters.

Copyright © by Houghton Mifflin Company. All rights reserved.

7. Among the _____ in our society is the expectation that store clerks will be courteous to customers.

8. An example of a _____ in the military is demotion to a lower rank.

9. Mr. Porter, a popular coach and biology teacher, enjoys a respected _____ in the community.

10. Maura's idea of _____ is Arizona because of its warm, dry climate and its opportunities for geological exploration.

III. *Directions:* If the words opposite each other in Columns A and B are similar in meaning, write *Yes* in the blank; if they are unrelated, write *No.*

A	B
1. matriarchal family	_____ family headed by mother
2. patriarchal family	_____ family headed by father
3. bureaucracy	_____ structure with numerous regulations
4. utopia	_____ heaven on earth
5. ethnocentrism	_____ dictator in power
6. Malthusian theory	_____ belief that earth formed 10 thousand years ago
7. folkways	_____ traditions expected to be observed
8. sanction	_____ something that tends to reinforce or discourage certain actions
9. status	_____ penalty for misbehavior
10. ethnic group	_____ individuals in local power

IV. *Directions:* Write either an original sentence or a definition for each word or words that clearly demonstrates your mastery of their meaning as used in sociology.

1. **bureaucracy** _____

_____

2. **ethnic group** _____

_____

3. **ethnocentrism** _____

_____

4. **folkways** _____

_____

Copyright © by Houghton Mifflin Company. All rights reserved.

5. **Malthusian theory** _____

_____

6. **matriarchal family** _____

_____

7. **patriarchal family** _____

_____

8. **sanction** _____

_____

9. **status** _____

_____

10. **utopia** _____

_____

Copyright © by Houghton Mifflin Company. All rights reserved.

United States History and Political Science

The United States is a republic, which means that the citizens exercise the powers of government through representatives. To meet this responsibility, citizens need to understand the country's heritage and political system; this is the overriding reason students are required to study history and government. In this regard, knowledge of the terms in this and the following two lessons is useful for the study of history and political science.

1. **amendment** (ə MEND mənt)—noun

   A change or addition to the Constitution, the basic document establishing the framework of the federal government. There are currently twenty-six amendments to the Constitution.

   The Thirteenth *Amendment* to the United States Constitution forbids slavery.

2. **Bill of Rights**—noun + preposition + noun

   Adopted in 1791 soon after the Constitution went into effect, the first ten amendments to the Constitution are known as the Bill of Rights. It is concerned with such important freedoms as religion and speech.

   Trial by jury is one of the important provisions in the *Bill of Rights.*

3. **boycott** (BOI kot)—noun or verb

   An economic means of influencing another nation or business by refusing to purchase its products.

   After the British government enacted the Stamp Act, colonial merchants decided to *boycott* English goods, especially tea.

4. **branches of governments**—noun + preposition + noun

   The United States federal government comprises three branches:

legislative (LEJ is lā tiv)—adjective, noun	Congress, made up of the House of Representatives and the Senate, which makes the laws

Copyright © by Houghton Mifflin Company. All rights reserved.

| **executive** (ig ZEK yə tiv)—adjective, noun | the president, who enforces the laws |
| **judiciary** (joo DISH ē ər ē)—adjective, noun | the Supreme Court, which interprets the laws |

5. checks and balances (CHEKS, BAL əns əs)—noun + conjunction + noun

Rights and procedures in the Constitution that reserve certain privileges to each of the three branches of government and that enable each branch to check, or limit, the powers of the other two.

Among the *checks and balances* existing in our government are the following: Congress (legislative) has the power to remove from office the president and Supreme Court justices; the president (executive) can refuse to sign bills passed by Congress and has the power to appoint Supreme Court justices when vacancies occur; the Supreme Court (judiciary) can declare bills approved by Congress and signed into law by the president unconstitutional.

6. eminent domain (EM ə nənt dō MĀN)—adjective + noun

The power of the government to acquire private property for public purposes.

The state government's power of *eminent domain* forced the O'Connors to sell a section of their farm so the highway could be altered.

7. laissez-faire (les ā FĀR)—adjective

Characterized by an economic policy that opposes government interference in business affairs.

Both presidential candidates stated they favor the *laissez-faire* doctrine, or government noninterference, when it came to such economic concerns as wages and prices.

8. lobbyist (LOB bē ist)—noun

A person who represents a special interest group that seeks to influence either the passage or defeat of certain bills.

The *lobbyist* for the oil company appeared before the committee to argue for the bill that would allow new offshore oil drilling.

9. ratification (rat ə fə KĀ shən)—noun

A power held by a legislative body to approve proposed agreements and amendments.

The Senate's *ratification* is necessary before the treaty becomes official.

10. veto (VĒ tō)—noun or verb

The president's refusal or act of refusing to sign a bill into law.

The president said he would *veto* the education bill passed by Congress.

Copyright © by Houghton Mifflin Company. All rights reserved.

EXERCISES FOR LESSON 39
United States History and Political Science

I. *Directions:* Match each definition with the word or words it defines.

_____ **1.** branches of government	**a.** legislative power to approve certain government actions
_____ **2.** amendment	**b.** first ten amendments to the Constitution
_____ **3.** Bill of Rights	
_____ **4.** checks and balances	**c.** noninterference
_____ **5.** veto	**d.** legislative, executive, judicial
_____ **6.** ratification	**e.** president's refusal to sign a bill
_____ **7.** boycott	**f.** representative for a special concern
_____ **8.** laissez-faire	**g.** change in the Constitution
_____ **9.** eminent domain	**h.** ways government branches can limit one another
_____ **10.** lobbyist	**i.** refusal to buy
	j. government's right to secure private property

II. *Directions:* In each space, write the appropriate word or words from those listed below.

amendment	branches of government	laissez-faire	veto
Bill of Rights	checks and balances	lobbyist	
boycott	eminent domain	ratification	

1. The _____ guarantees numerous personal freedoms.

2. Believing in as few restrictions on business as possible, the president is encouraging Congress to follow his _____ philosophy.

3. The striking workers are urging people to _____ the company's products.

4. Some historians believe a(n) _____ to the Constitution should be adopted to simplify presidential elections.

5. The president remains confident that the Senate's _____ of the treaty will occur in two or three days.

6. The governor has suggested that the legislature exercise its right of _____ to enlarge the state park near the coast.

Copyright © by Houghton Mifflin Company. All rights reserved.

7. The three _____ are the legislative, the executive, and the judicial.

8. The president warned that he would _____ any bills requiring an increase in taxes.

9. Mr. Tapley is a(n) _____ for an environmental organization.

10. The _____ contained in the Constitution are designed to prohibit any branch of government from exceeding its powers.

III. *Directions:* If the words opposite each other in Columns A and B are similar in meaning, write *Yes* in the blank; if they are unrelated, write *No.*

A   **B**

1. branches of government   _____ legislative, executive, treasury
2. amendment   _____ addition to or change in the Constitution
3. Bill of Rights   _____ first twelve amendments
4. checks and balances   _____ economic safeguards
5. veto   _____ president's disapproval of a bill
6. ratification   _____ presidential appointment
7. boycott   _____ refusal to buy
8. laissez-faire   _____ economic controls
9. eminent domain   _____ power to declare war
10. lobbyist   _____ representative for a special group

IV. *Directions:* Write either an original sentence or a definition for each word or words that clearly demonstrates your mastery of their meaning as used in United States history and political science.

1. **amendment** _____

_____

2. **Bill of Rights** _____

_____

3. **boycott** _____

_____

4. **branches of government** _____

_____

5. **checks and balances** _____

_____

Copyright © by Houghton Mifflin Company. All rights reserved.

6. eminent domain _____

_____

7. laissez-faire _____

_____

8. lobbyist _____

_____

9. ratification _____

_____

10. veto _____

_____

Copyright © by Houghton Mifflin Company. All rights reserved.

United States History and Political Science

1. filibuster (FIL ə bus tər)—noun

A technique by which a minority of senators attempts to block the passage of a bill through continuous talk, thus delaying the vote.

The *filibuster* in the Senate has lasted six hours so far, so the controversial bill has never come to a vote.

2. impeachment (im PĒCH mənt)—noun

The constitutional procedure for removing the president and other high federal officials from office for illegal activities.

Andrew Johnson, who served as president from 1865 to 1869 after the assassination of Abraham Lincoln, and William Clinton, who served as president from 1993 to 2000, are the only presidents to have faced *impeachment*; both were acquitted by the Senate.

3. lame duck (LĀM DUK)—adjective + noun

An elected official whose influence is weakened because he or she is soon to leave office, as a result of either an election defeat or a law that prohibits another term.

The senator, a *lame duck* as a result of losing the fall election, announced he would be joining a Washington, D.C., law firm after his senate term expires.

4. red herring (RED HER ing)—adjective + noun

An irrelevant topic that diverts attention from the main issue.

The candidate running against the senator angrily claims that the senator's remarks about her divorce years ago is a *red herring* to draw attention away from his poor record regarding such important matters as education, universal medical coverage, and the national debt.

Copyright © by Houghton Mifflin Company. All rights reserved.

5. **appropriation** (ə PRŌ prē Ā shən)—noun

A grant of money to finance a government program.
Congress has approved an *appropriation* to improve the interstate highway system.

6. **entitlement** (en TĪ təl mənt)—noun

A law requiring the government to pay money to people who meet specific eligibility requirements.
Workers who have social security payments deducted from their salaries are eligible for an *entitlement* when they retire.

7. **patronage** (PĀ trə nij)—noun

The power given to political leaders to make appointments to government positions and to award contracts and favors to friends and supporters.
Patronage can lead to abuses, but it can also lead to benefits if political leaders appoint only well-qualified people to government positions.

8. **referendum** (REF ə REN dəm)—noun

An electoral device by which voters can either approve or disapprove of an action taken by their state legislature.
The *referendum* indicated overwhelming approval of the proposed dam project.

9. **gerrymandering** (JER ē MAN dər ing)—noun or verb

Establishment of a voting district in such a way as to give an advantage to one political party.
The Democrats accused the Republicans of *gerrymandering* the boundaries of the metropolitan area to obtain a voting advantage during elections.

10. **sedition** (sə DISH ən)—noun

Actions causing public disorder or rebellion against the government.
An illegal attempt to overthrow the government is called *sedition*.

Copyright © by Houghton Mifflin Company. All rights reserved.

Name .... Section .... Date ....

EXERCISES FOR LESSON 40
United States History and Political Science

I. *Directions:* Match each definition with the word it defines.

_____ **1.** referendum

_____ **2.** red herring

_____ **3.** appropriation

_____ **4.** filibuster

_____ **5.** patronage

_____ **6.** lame duck

_____ **7.** impeachment

_____ **8.** gerrymandering

_____ **9.** entitlement

_____ **10.** sedition

a. officerholder whose term is almost over

b. power to make appointments and grant favors to supporters

c. redrawing voting boundaries to gain an election advantage

d. public disorder against the government

e. enables citizens of a state to vote on action taken by its legislature

f. continuous talk designed to stop a bill from coming to a vote

g. something that distracts from the chief issue

h. method of removing high government officials from office

i. money budgeted for a government program

j. requires the government to pay money to qualified people

II. *Directions:* In each space, write the appropriate word or words from those listed below.

filibuster   appropriation   referendum
impeachment   entitlement   gerrymandering
lame duck   patronage   sedition
red herring

1. When Grover Cleveland became president, he exercised his power of _____ by appointing thousands of Democrats to postal positions.

2. A(n) _____ is a financial obligation the government has to people meeting specific criteria.

3. Congress's _____ for space research has been increased for next year.

Copyright © by Houghton Mifflin Company. All rights reserved.

4. Attempts to overthrow the government through sabotage are considered
_____ .

5. A state _____ to be held this fall will enable the voters of
this state to express their feelings regarding the controversial environmental
law.

6. _____ is a term dating back to 1812 when Elbridge Gerry,
the governor of Massachusetts, had the boundaries of voting districts redrawn
to gain an election advantage.

7. The newspaper editorial maintains that the crime issue is a(n)
_____ that blurs the city's major problem, which, in the editor's opinion, is skyrocketing property taxes.

8. The mayor, now a(n) _____, said she will resume her teaching career after her present term expires.

9. Many historians believe President Nixon would have faced certain
_____ if he hadn't resigned after the Watergate scandal.

10. The senator's _____ lasted nine hours in an effort to delay
the vote on the bill.

III. *Directions:* If the words opposite each other in Columns A and B are similar in
meaning, write *Yes* in the blank; if they are unrelated, write *No.*

A	B
1. red herring	_____ smokescreen that keeps attention away from the main issue
2. impeachment	_____ presidential inauguration
3. lame duck	_____ officerholder found guilty of a crime
4. filibuster	_____ stalling talk
5. patronage	_____ rebellion against the government
6. referendum	_____ voters approve or reject an action of the state legislature
7. sedition	_____ a bill that has been enacted into law
8. entitlement	_____ officerholder's authority to appoint supporters to political jobs
9. gerrymandering	_____ political bribery
10. appropriation	_____ the seizing of illegal goods crossing state lines

Copyright © by Houghton Mifflin Company. All rights reserved.

IV. *Directions:* Write either an original sentence or a definition for each word or words that clearly demonstrates your master of their meaning as used in United States history and political science.

1. **filibuster** _____

_____

2. **impeachment** _____

_____

3. **lame duck** _____

_____

4. **red herring** _____

_____

5. **appropriation** _____

_____

6. **entitlement** _____

_____

7. **patronage** _____

_____

8. **referendum** _____

_____

9. **gerrymandering** _____

_____

10. **sedition** _____

_____

Copyright © by Houghton Mifflin Company. All rights reserved.

Biology

Biology and its many subdivisions contribute to our understanding of all forms of life. The terms in this and the next two lessons are among those we need to know to establish a solid foundation in this important science.

1. **chromosomes** (KRŌ mə sōms)—noun

   Threadlike bodies in the nucleus of a cell that determine the particular characteristics of an organism; each cell in a human body has forty-six chromosomes.
   The majority of animal and plant species have between ten and fifty *chromosomes*.

2. **dormant** (DOR mənt)—adjective

   Describes an organism that is at rest and not developing.
   Seeds will remain *dormant* until the temperature and other environmental conditions are suitable for sprouting.

3. **genes** (JĒNZ)—noun

   Elements in chromosomes that control the development of hereditary characteristics.
   The color of a dog's coat is determined by *genes*.

4. **habitat** (HAB ə tat)—noun

   The natural physical area where an animal or a plant lives and thrives.
   The *habitat* for seals is the seashore and the sea.

5. **hybrid** (HĪ brid)—noun, adjective

   The offspring of two animals or plants of different species that are crossbred.
   The mating of a horse and a donkey results in a mule, which is a *hybrid*.

6. **Mendel, Gregor Johann** (1822–1884)

   Austrian priest whose systematic study of pea plants led him to discover basic principles that govern heredity. Mendel's discoveries are ranked among the greatest in biology.

Copyright © by Houghton Mifflin Company. All rights reserved.

Mendel's discovery of the principles of heredity led to the accurate predicting of offspring characteristics.

7. **muta<u>tion</u>** (mū TĀ shən)—noun

A change in the genes of an organism that is transmitted to the offspring, resulting in offspring differing in some significant way from the parents.

Professor Bailey said the effects of a *mutation* on the offspring can sometimes be beneficial, but generally a *mutation* results in harmful abnormalities.

8. **natural sele<u>ction</u>** (NACH ər əl si LEK shən)—adjective + noun

The belief that in the struggle for existence, the animals and plants of a particular species that survive are those possessing unique adaptive characteristics. This struggle is often called *survival of the fittest.*

Natural selection, often called survival of the fittest, serves as the foundation for the *theory of evolution* developed by English naturalist Charles Darwin (1809–1882).

9. **pro<u>lif</u>ic** (prō LIF ik)—adjective

Producing offspring in abundance.

As a result of their frequent litters, rabbits are well known for being *prolific* breeders.

10. **transpira<u>tion</u>** (tran spə RĀ shən)—noun

Evaporation of water from plants that occurs mainly through the small holes (stomata) in the leaves of plants.

Transpiration benefits plants because it increases the amount of water passing up their stem.

Copyright © by Houghton Mifflin Company. All rights reserved.

EXERCISES FOR LESSON 41
Biology

I. *Directions:* Match each definition with the word or words it defines.

_____ **1.** chromosomes
_____ **2.** dormant
_____ **3.** genes
_____ **4.** habitat
_____ **5.** hybrid
_____ **6.** Mendel
_____ **7.** mutation
_____ **8.** natural selection
_____ **9.** prolific
_____ **10.** transpiration

a. describes inactivity
b. discovered laws of heredity
c. survival of the fittest
d. elements in chromosomes responsible for eye color and other characteristics
e. producing a large number of offspring
f. abnormality caused by a change in a parent's genes
g. result when two plants or animals of different species breed
h. bodies in cells responsible for hereditary characteristics
i. loss of water vapor by plants
j. place where an organism lives and thrives

II. *Directions:* In each space, write the appropriate word or words from those listed below.

chromosomes	habitat	mutation	transpiration
dormant	hybrid	natural selection	
genes	Mendel	prolific	

1. Much of the feeder corn that is raised in the Midwestern states is a(n) _____ developed by crossbreeding varieties of corn.

2. Evaporation of water from plants is called _____, a process occurring mainly through the leaves.

3. The effects of a sudden alteration of an organism's genes, which is called a(n) _____, are unpredictable and usually detrimental.

4. Fish are considered _____ because they produce thousands of eggs.

Copyright © by Houghton Mifflin Company. All rights reserved.

5. Flower bulbs are _____ in the winter, but they develop shoots in the spring.

6. The hereditary factors that lie within the chromosomes of organisms are called _____ .

7. _____ maintains that organisms that survive a changing environment while others perish do so because of unique features they possess.

8. Surprisingly, glacial ice is the _____ of some types of bacteria.

9. The experiments of _____ were a great breakthrough for understanding certain laws of heredity.

10. _____ contain genes, or hereditary units.

III. *Directions:* If the words opposite each other in Columns A and B are similar in meaning, write *Yes* in the blank; if they are unrelated, write *No.*

A	**B**
1. chromosomes	_____ precious vitamins
2. dormant	_____ active
3. genes	_____ hereditary units
4. habitat	_____ home
5. hybrid	_____ offspring of two different species
6. Mendel	_____ developed theory of evolution
7. mutation	_____ maturity
8. natural selection	_____ freedom of choice
9. prolific	_____ intelligent
10. transpiration	_____ loss of water vapor by plants

IV. *Directions:* Write either an original sentence or a definition for each word or words that clearly demonstrates your mastery of their meaning as used in biology.

1. **chromosomes** _____

_____

2. **dormant** _____

_____

3. **genes** _____

_____

Copyright © by Houghton Mifflin Company. All rights reserved.

4. habitat _____

_____

5. hybrid _____

_____

6. Mendel _____

_____

7. mutation _____

_____

8. natural selection _____

_____

9. prolific _____

_____

10. transpiration _____

Copyright © by Houghton Mifflin Company. All rights reserved.

Biology

1. <u>**amphibians**</u> (am FIB ē əns)—noun

   Vertebrate animals with moist, smooth skin whose offspring are hatched from eggs; amphibians live partly on land and partly in water.
   Toads and frogs are *amphibians.*

2. **arthro<u>pods</u>** (AR thrə pods)—noun

   Invertebrates with a hard outer covering and jointed legs, such as insects.
   Crabs and lobsters are *arthropods* that live in water.

3. **carni<u>vorous</u>** (kar NIV ə rəs),
   herbi<u>vorous</u> (hur BIV ə rəs),
   omni<u>vorous</u> (om NIV ə rəs)—adjectives

   Herbivorous animals eat primarily plants; carnivorous animals eat primarily meat; omnivorous animals eat both plants and meat.
   Cows are *herbivorous;* wolves are *carnivorous;* humans, because we eat both plants and animals, are *omnivorous.*

4. **fauna, flora** (FON ə, FLŌR ə)—nouns

   Fauna are the animals and flora the plants of a particular region or period.
   Some citizens are protesting the planned draining of the swamp because they fear the draining will destroy the *fauna* and *flora,* the animals and plants native to the swamp region.

5. **hominids** (HOM ə nids)—noun

   The human family and their ancestors, including extinct humanlike types.
   Prehistoric humans are considered *hominids.*

6. **mammals** (MAM əls)—noun

   Vertebrate animals, including humans, whose skins are all, or practically all, covered with hair and whose young are born alive and are fed from mammary glands.
   Humans, horses, monkeys, and whales are *mammals.*

Copyright © by Houghton Mifflin Company. All rights reserved.

275

7. **plankton** (PLANK tən)—noun

The microscopic plants and animals floating near the surface in almost all bodies of water.

Important food sources for most fish are the tiny animals and plants, known as *plankton,* drifting in the water.

8. **reptiles** (REP tīls)—noun

Vertebrate animals with horny skins whose offspring are hatched from eggs; all reptiles breathe oxygen, but some live on land and some in water.

Turtles, crocodiles, lizards, and snakes are *reptiles.*

9. **taxonomy** (tak SON ə mē)—noun

The science concerned with the describing, naming, and classifying of animals and plants.

Taxonomy places organisms with similar structures in the same category.

10. **vertebrates, _in_vertebrates** (VUR tə brātes, in VUR tə brātes)—nouns

Animals with backbones are vertebrates; animals without backbones are invertebrates.

Dogs are classified as *vertebrates* because they have a spinal column; worms are classified as *invertebrates* because they have no backbone.

Copyright © by Houghton Mifflin Company. All rights reserved.

EXERCISES FOR LESSON 42
Biology

I. *Directions:* Match each definition with the word it defines.

_____ **1.** plankton	**a.** eating plants
_____ **2.** flora	**b.** animals with backbones
_____ **3.** fauna	**c.** animals with smooth skin that hatch
_____ **4.** taxonomy	eggs and are at home on land and in
_____ **5.** vertebrates	water
_____ **6.** invertebrates	**d.** eating both plants and animals
_____ **7.** arthropods	**e.** animals of a specific area or period
_____ **8.** reptiles	**f.** animals with horny skins that
_____ **9.** amphibians	hatch eggs
_____ **10.** mammals	**g.** eating mainly meat
_____ **11.** hominids	**h.** plants of a specific area or period
_____ **12.** herbivorous	**i.** animals with hard external cover-
_____ **13.** carnivorous	ing and jointed legs
_____ **14.** omnivorous	**j.** involves the classification of plants

and animals
k. animals that lack backbones
l. extremely small animals and plants
that live near the surface of water
m. animals with skin covered with hair
and whose young are born alive
n. humans and their ancestors

II. *Directions:* In each space, write the appropriate word from those listed below.

amphibians	omnivorous	mammals	vertebrates
arthropods	fauna	plankton	invertebrates
carnivorous	flora	reptiles	
herbivorous	hominids	taxonomy	

1. It surprises many people to learn that whales are _____ , as
their young are born alive.

2. Snakes are invertebrate animals classified as _____ .

3. The classification of organisms based on similar features is the concern of
_____ .

Copyright © by Houghton Mifflin Company. All rights reserved.

4. The terms _____ and _____ are used for the plants and animals of a particular region.

5. The primitive Java man is classified with _____ since he is considered a human ancestor.

6. Tiny animals and plants drifting in water are _____ .

7. _____ animals are those that eat both meat and plants; _____ animals are those that eat mainly meat; and _____ animals are those that eat plants.

8. Since they have backbones, birds are _____ ; spiders, lacking backbones, are _____ .

9. Frogs are _____ as their natural habitat is both land and water.

10. Centipedes, which have a hard, protective covering and jointed legs, are classified as _____ .

III. *Directions:* If the words opposite each other in Columns A and B are similar in meaning, write *Yes* in the blank; if they are unrelated, write *No.*

A	**B**
1. plankton	_____ tiny water plants and animals
2. flora	_____ region's native animals
3. fauna	_____ region's native plants
4. taxonomy	_____ dissection of animals
5. vertebrates	_____ animals with backbones
6. invertebrates	_____ animals with no spinal columns
7. arthropods	_____ any four-legged animal
8. reptiles	_____ invertebrates living in water only
9. amphibians	_____ vertebrates living on both land and water
10. mammals	_____ vertebrates whose offspring are born alive
11. hominids	_____ water organisms
12. herbivorous	_____ plant eating primarily
13. carnivorous	_____ eating both plants and animals
14. omnivorous	_____ meat eating primarily

IV. *Directions:* Write either an original sentence or a definition for each word that clearly demonstrates your mastery of its meaning as used in biology.

1. amphibians _____

_____

Copyright © by Houghton Mifflin Company. All rights reserved.

2. arthropods _____

_____

3. carnivorous _____

_____

4. herbivorous _____

_____

5. omnivorous _____

_____

6. fauna _____

_____

7. flora _____

_____

8. hominids _____

_____

9. mammals _____

_____

10. plankton _____

_____

11. reptiles _____

_____

12. taxonomy _____

_____

13. vertebrates _____

_____

14. invertebrates _____

_____

Copyright © by Houghton Mifflin Company. All rights reserved.

Biology

1. **The body's systems**   The seven major systems of the body are as follows:

digestive (dī JES tiv)—adjective

Involved in the absorption and elimination of food; includes the mouth, esophagus (tube connecting the mouth to the stomach), stomach, large and small intestines.

The study indicates that eating the day's largest meal in the morning rather than in the evening results in a more efficient *digestive* system.

respiratory (RES pər ə tōr ē)—adjective

Involved in breathing; includes nose, mouth, trachea (windpipe), and lungs.

The patient was having a difficult time breathing because of a *respiratory* infection.

reproductive (rē prō DUK tiv)—adjective

Involved in the producing of offspring; includes the ovaries of the female and the testes of the male as well as the other sexual organs.

Typically, a female's *reproductive* system reaches maturity at an earlier age than does a male's.

urinary (YOOR ə ner ē)—adjective

Involved in the elimination of liquid waste; includes the kidneys, bladder, and tubes called ureter and urethra.

Kidney stones can become lodged in a person's *urinary* tract, resulting in severe pain.

circulatory (SUR kə lə tor ē)—adjective

Involved in the transportation of blood throughout the body; includes the heart and blood vessels, such as arteries (carry blood away from the heart), veins (carry blood back to the heart), and capillaries (connect the arteries and veins).

A low-fat diet, along with regular exercise, contributes to a healthy *circulatory* system.

skeletal (SKEL ə təl)—adjective

Involved in the structure and physical functioning of the body; includes the body's 206 bones and 650 muscles, as well as tendons, which are tough cords that attach muscles to bones and to other muscles.

The marrow inside the bones that make up the skeletal system is involved in the production of blood cells.

Copyright © by Houghton Mifflin Company. All rights reserved.

nervous (NUR vəs)—adjective

Involved in the regulation of all the other systems' activities; includes the brain, spinal cord, and nerves.

Neurologists, doctors specializing in the *nervous* system, undergo many years of rigorous training.

2. **cardiac** (KAR dē ak)—adjective

Refers to the heart.

Regular exercise strengthens the *cardiac* muscles.

3. **The three major parts of the brain are as follows:**

cerebrum (sə RĒ brəm)—noun

Front part of the brain and the largest part; involved in the body's voluntary movements, certain mental actions, stimuli, and impulses.

The *cerebrum,* consisting of billions of cells, is associated with thinking, speaking, and voluntary muscle movements.

medulla oblongata (mə DUL ə ob long GA tə)—noun

Lower part of the brain that connects with the spinal cord; involved in the senses of hearing, tasting, and touching, as well as heart and breathing actions.

The rhythms of our breathing and heartbeat are among the important functions controlled by the *medulla oblongata.*

cerebellum (ser ə BEL əm)—noun

Back of the brain; involved in muscle coordination and balance.

The *cerebellum,* which accounts for only one-eighth of the brain weight, is responsible for our equilibrium, or balance.

4. <u>**congenital**</u> (kən JEN ə təl)—adjective

Inborn or existing since birth.

Jeremy says that he has never been able to distinguish certain colors very well. Is color blindness a *congenital* condition?

5. **dorsal, ventral** (DOR səl, VEN trəl)—adjectives

Dorsal pertains to the back; *ventral* pertains to the abdomen or the belly.

The *dorsal* region of the body is more rigid than the *ventral* section.

6. **enzymes** (EN zīms)—noun

Chemicals produced by living cells that participate in many of the body's processes.

Enzymes in saliva help to break down food in the digestive process.

Copyright © by Houghton Mifflin Company. All rights reserved.

7. **homeostasis** (hō̄mē ō STĀ sis)—*noun*

   The body's tendency to maintain its internal systems in a normal, stable condition.

   Professor Baxter said that *homeostasis* occurs when we, in an effort to maintain a normal oxygen level, automatically breathe deeply after running.

8. **metabolism** (mə TAB ə liz əm)—*noun*

   The total chemical and physical processes in the body, including the process by which energy is produced.

   Digestion and respiration activities are involved in *metabolism.*

9. **ossification** (os ə fə KĀ shən)—*noun*

   Formation and hardening of the bones.

   As people mature, their bones harden, a process called *ossification.*

10. **protoplasm** (PRŌ tə plaz əm)—*noun*

    A chemically complex, colorless, semifluid substance considered the physical basis of life.

    Scientists believe that *protoplasm* is the building block of all animal life.

Copyright © by Houghton Mifflin Company. All rights reserved.

EXERCISES FOR LESSON 43
Biology

I. *Directions:* Match each definition with the word or words it defines.

_____ **1.** homeostasis
_____ **2.** congenital
_____ **3.** protoplasm
_____ **4.** metabolism
_____ **5.** enzymes
_____ **6.** ossification
_____ **7.** body's systems
_____ **8.** cardiac
_____ **9.** cerebrum
_____ **10.** medulla oblongata
_____ **11.** cerebellum
_____ **12.** dorsal
_____ **13.** ventral

a. front and largest part of the brain
b. chemical substances produced by cells
c. refers to the back
d. hardening of the bones
e. part of the brain connected with spinal cord
f. semifluid substance that is the basis of life
g. existing since birth
h. refers to the abdomen
i. the sum of the body's chemical and physical actions
j. maintenance of the body's balance internally
k. seven of them, including digestive and circulatory
l. part of the brain involved in coordination and balance
m. pertains to the heart

II. *Directions:* In each space, write the appropriate word or words from those listed below.

body's systems	congenital	homeostasis
cardiac	dorsal	metabolism
cerebrum	ventral	ossification
medulla oblongata	enzymes	protoplasm
cerebellum		

1. The _____ , connected to the spinal cord, is essential for certain heart and respiration functions, as well as for some sense perceptions.

2. The word _____ pertains to the abdomen.

3. The hardening of the bones is called _____ .

Copyright © by Houghton Mifflin Company. All rights reserved.

4. A colorless substance, _____, is the physical basis for life.

5. The total chemical and physical operations of the body, including the production of energy, are involved in _____.

6. _____ is a term referring to the heart.

7. The skeletal and nervous systems of the body are both included in the _____.

8. The _____, located in the front part of the skull, is the largest part of the brain.

9. A word that refers to the back is _____.

10. _____ is the word used to describe the body's tendency to keep the internal systems in a stable condition.

11. _____ are produced by cells, and they are crucial to many of the body's functions.

12. The _____ is the part of the brain involved in muscle coordination and equilibrium.

13. My veterinarian said my dog has always had a defective heart valve, an unusual _____ condition.

III. *Directions:* If the words opposite each other in Columns A and B are similar in meaning, write *Yes* in the blank, if they are unrelated, write *No*.

A	**B**
1. homeostasis	_____ common infection
2. congenital	_____ inborn
3. protoplasm	_____ hormones
4. metabolism	_____ sum of body's operations
5. enzymes	_____ reflexes
6. ossification	_____ hardening of bones
7. body's systems	_____ skeletal, circulatory, glandular
8. cardiac	_____ refers to heart
9. cerebrum	_____ back of brain
10. medulla oblongata	_____ appendix
11. cerebellum	_____ front of brain
12. dorsal	_____ back region
13. ventral	_____ abdominal area

Copyright © by Houghton Mifflin Company. All rights reserved.

IV. *Directions:* Write either an original sentence or a definition for each word or words that clearly demonstrates your mastery of their meaning as used in biology.

1. **the body's systems** _____

   _____

2. **cardiac** _____

   _____

3. **cerebrum** _____

   _____

4. **medulla oblongata** _____

   _____

5. **cerebellum** _____

   _____

6. **congenital** _____

   _____

7. **dorsal** _____

   _____

8. **ventral** _____

   _____

9. **enzymes** _____

   _____

10. **homeostasis** _____

    _____

11. **metabolism** _____

    _____

12. **ossification** _____

    _____

13. **protoplasm** _____

    _____

Copyright © by Houghton Mifflin Company. All rights reserved.

Physical Science

Physical science can refer to general or earth science courses or courses focused primarily upon physics, chemistry, astronomy, and other such science specialties. Physical science courses contribute to our understanding of the hows and whys relating to our world and universe.

Developments in the various subdivisions of physical science have led to advances in agriculture, industry, engineering, medicine, and a host of other fields.

This lesson and the two that follow will familiarize you with many of the key terms used in basic physical science courses.

1. **Major eras of earth's geological (physical) history:**

   Precambrian (prē KAM brē ən)—adjective
   This era was 4.6 billion years ago, which amounts to 85% of geological time. The earth's primitive crust was formed, some mountain building occurred, and the first seas appeared.

   Paleozoic (pā lē ə ZŌ ik)—adjective
   This era was 225–600 million years ago, which is 10% of geological time. Fossils (remains or imprints of ancient animals or plants) indicate that marine (sea) life, insects, and reptiles developed and flourished during this era.

   Mesozoic (mez ə ZŌ ik)—adjective
   This era was 65–225 million years ago, which is 4% of geological time. Flowering plants appeared, and dinosaurs appeared then disappeared. A supercontinent, Pangaea, began to break up during this period, and certain terrestrial mammals became isolated in such widely separated regions as Antarctica, South America, Africa, and Australia. There has been a drifting of the continents since this era.

   Cenozoic (sen ə ZŌ ik)—adjective
   This era embraces 65 million years ago to the present, which is 1.5% of geological time. This period reflects a continuing rise in the number of mammals, and several of the world's greatest mountain chains (including the Rockies in North America, the Andes in South America, the Alps in Europe, and the Himalayas in northern India) uplifted. The last 2.5 to 3 million years of the Cenozoic Era is often referred to as the *Age of Man* because *homo sapiens* (humankind) appeared for the first time during this period.

Copyright © by Houghton Mifflin Company. All rights reserved.

2. paleontology (pā lē ən TOL ə je)—noun

The study of ancient life that concentrates on fossil remains of plants and animals.
Lesley has been interested in fossils since her grade school days, so it's not surprising she's majoring in *paleontology* at the state university.

3. topography (tə POG rə fē)—noun

The detailed mapping or description of the surface features of a region.
New Hampshire's *topography* includes lakes, mountains, and valleys.

4. sediment (SED ə ment)—noun

Small pieces of a solid, such as a mineral, that settle to the bottom of water;
includes the disintegration of pre-existing rocks and organic matter.
Rock is changed physically and chemically by environmental factors to produce
sediment.

5. delta (DEL tə)—noun

The sedimentary deposit formed at the mouth of a river because of the loss of
stream speed when the river enters the sea.
The prominent landforms near where the Mississippi River enters the Gulf of
Mexico are called *deltas.*

6. sedimentary rocks (sed ə MEN tə rē ROKS)—adjective + noun

Rocks formed from the deposits of sediment.
Sedimentary rocks, formed over time from such sediment as sand, are generally
soft rocks, so they are easily weathered.

7. metamorphic rocks (met ə MOR fik ROKS)—adjective + noun

Rocks formed from sedimentary rocks that have been subjected to great pressure
and heat beneath the earth's surface; the most common rocks in the earth's crust.
Metamorphic rocks are hard; marble, for example, is a *metamorphic rock.*

8. magma (MAG mə)—noun

The hot liquid of rock formed by tremendously high temperatures and great pressures within the earth; sometimes referred to as molten rock.
Magma is usually brought to the earth's surface by volcanic action.

9. igneous rocks (IG nē əs ROKS)—adjective + noun

Rocks formed from cooled magma.
Granite and basalt are *igneous rocks.*

Copyright © by Houghton Mifflin Company. All rights reserved.

10. strata (STRAT ə)—noun

Distinct layers of material; often refers to layers of sedimentary rock.

Layers of sedimentary rock are called either *strata* or beds.

11. stalactites (stə LAK tīts)—noun

Icicle-shaped rocky deposits hanging from the roofs of caves.

Stalactites are formed on the roofs of caves from the drippings of water containing certain minerals.

12. stalagmites (stə LAG mīts)—noun

Rocky deposits that build up on the floors of caves.

Stalagmites, formed by the drippings of water containing certain minerals, resemble upside-down stalactites.

Copyright © by Houghton Mifflin Company. All rights reserved.

Name .... Section .... Date ....

EXERCISES FOR LESSON 44
Physical Science

I. *Directions:* Match each definition to the word it defines.

_____ **1.** delta	**a.** geological age in which dinosaurs
_____ **2.** topography	appeared and a supercontinent
_____ **3.** Mesozoic	broke up
_____ **4.** paleontology	**b.** rocky deposits hanging from cave
_____ **5.** sediment	roofs
_____ **6.** Precambrian	**c.** hot liquid rock
_____ **7.** Cenozoic	**d.** geological age of 225–600 million
_____ **8.** stalagmites	years ago
_____ **9.** Paleozoic	**e.** rocks most common in the earth's
_____ **10.** stalactites	crust
_____ **11.** igneous	**f.** rocky deposits built up on cave floors
_____ **12.** strata	**g.** oldest geological period
_____ **13.** metamorphic	**h.** rocks formed from cooled magma
_____ **14.** magma	**i.** rocks formed from deposits of
_____ **15.** sedimentary	sediment

j. *homo sapiens* appeared during this geological era

k. landform built up at the mouth of a river

l. small pieces of solid material that settle on the bottom of water

m. study of fossil remains

n. layers of rock or soil

o. concerned with a region's surface features

II. *Directions:* In each space, write the appropriate word from those listed below.

Precambrian	topography	metamorphic	stalactites
Mesozoic	sediment	magma	stalagmites
Cenozoic	deltas	igneous	Paleozoic
paleontology	sedimentary	strata	

1. _____ of sedimentary rocks are visible in many of the bluffs along the Missouri River.

2. Granite, used to create buildings, stairs, and other structures, is a(n) _____ rock.

Copyright © by Houghton Mifflin Company. All rights reserved.

3. Oddly shaped _____ could be seen hanging from the cave's roof while large _____ had built up on the cave's floor.

4. Dinosaurs appeared during the _____ era.

5. _____ includes the study of geography, geology, chemistry, and cartography (mapmaking) because these subjects contribute to the understanding of an area's surface features.

6. Through the ages, numerous _____ have formed where the Nile River in Egypt empties into the Mediterranean Sea.

7. After the ice melted, _____ settled in the bottom of the lake.

8. The _____ Era, the period during which the earth's crust was formed, embraces the most geological years.

9. _____ is a rock that liquefies as the result of tremendous heat and pressure.

10. _____ rocks are soft rocks formed from sediment.

11. _____ rocks, formed from another class of rocks, are the most common rocks in the earth's crust.

12. _____ involves the study of fossilized animals and plants.

13. Many of the world's most impressive mountain ranges, including the Rockies and the Alps, uplifted during the _____ Era.

14. Fossils in the _____ Era indicate that abundant sea life developed and flourished during this period.

III. *Directions:* If the words opposite each other in Columns A and B are similar in meaning, write *Yes* in the blank; if they are unrelated, write *No.*

A	B
1. topography	_____ mapping of a region's surface features
2. paleontology	_____ study of oceans
3. Cenozoic	_____ world's largest volcano
4. sediment	_____ filtered water
5. Precambrian	_____ age of the dinosaurs
6. sedimentary rocks	_____ formed from lava
7. Mesozoic	_____ 65–225 million years ago
8. stalagmites	_____ brittle deposits on cave walls
9. metamorphic rocks	_____ formed from igneous rocks
10. stalactites	_____ rocky deposits on cave roofs
11. magma	_____ liquid rock
12. strata	_____ layers
13. igneous rocks	_____ soft rocks
14. Paleozoic	_____ second major geologic era
15. delta	_____ landform deposit at the mouth of a river

Copyright © by Houghton Mifflin Company. All rights reserved.

IV. *Directions:* Write either an original sentence or a definition for each word or words that clearly demonstrates your mastery of their meaning as used in physical science.

1. **Precambrian** _____

_____

2. **Paleozoic** _____

_____

3. **Mesozoic** _____

_____

4. **Cenozoic** _____

_____

5. **paleontology** _____

_____

6. **topography** _____

_____

7. **sediment** _____

_____

8. **delta** _____

_____

9. **sedimentary rocks** _____

_____

10. **metamorphic rocks** _____

_____

11. **magma** _____

_____

12. **igneous rocks** _____

_____

13. **strata** _____

_____

14. **stalactites** _____

_____

15. **stalagmites** _____

_____

Copyright © by Houghton Mifflin Company. All rights reserved.

Physical Science

1. **centrifugal, centripetal** (sen TRIF ə gəl, sen TRIP ə təl) adjectives

   Centrifugal refers to the force that propels an object outward from the center of rotation; *centripetal* refers to the force that tends to draw an object inward toward the center of rotation.

   When a rock is swung at the end of a string, the rock exerts an outward force on the string as it seeks to fly off in space; this is *centrifugal* force at work. On the other hand, the string pulls inwardly on the moving rock to keep it in its circular path; this is *centripetal* force at work.

2. **energy** (EN ər jē)—noun

   The ability to do work.

   Electricity and heat can be used to do work, so they are forms of *energy.*

3. **force** (FŌRS)—noun

   A push or pull.

   Water is a common *force.*

4. **hydraulic** (hī DROL ik)—adjective

   Describes the use of water or other liquid.

   Many machines are operated by *hydraulic,* or liquid, pressure.

5. **inertia** (in UR shə)—noun

   The characteristic of an object to resist any change in its motion, that is, the tendency of an object to maintain its condition of rest or movement.

   A force is required to alter an object's *inertia.*

6. **kinetic energy, potential energy** (kə NET ik EN ər jē, pə TEN shəl EN ər jē)— adjectives + nouns

   Kinetic energy is energy in motion; potential energy is stored energy.

   A swinging hammer displays *kinetic energy;* a resting hammer has *potential energy.*

Copyright © by Houghton Mifflin Company. All rights reserved.

7. **malleable** (MAL ē ə bəl)—adjective

Describes objects that can be hammered or shaped without breaking.
Metals are *malleable;* that is, they can be processed into desired shapes.

8. **mass** (MAS)—noun

The measure of the amount or quantity of a material.
Any material possesses *mass.*

9. **oscillate** (OS ə lāt)—verb

To swing to and fro, vibrate, or fluctuate to make a wavelike motion.
The pendulum will *oscillate* when it is released.

10. **work** (WURK)—noun

The result of a *force* moving an object.
In the language of science, something must be moved before it can be said that
work has occurred.

Copyright © by Houghton Mifflin Company. All rights reserved.

EXERCISES FOR LESSON 45
Physical Science

I. *Directions:* Match each definition with the word or words it defines.

_____ **1.** mass	**a.** to sway in a wavelike motion
_____ **2.** potential energy	**b.** outward force
_____ **3.** work	**c.** using liquid
_____ **4.** energy	**d.** quantity of matter
_____ **5.** kinetic energy	**e.** pliable, capable of being shaped
_____ **6.** force	**f.** push or pull
_____ **7.** inertia	**g.** ability to do work
_____ **8.** centrifugal	**h.** inward force
_____ **9.** centripetal	**i.** force that moves an object
_____ **10.** hydraulic	**j.** energy in motion
_____ **11.** oscillate	**k.** energy that is stored
_____ **12.** malleable	**l.** resistance to any change in motion

II. *Directions:* In each space, write the appropriate word from those listed below.

centrifugal	force	kinetic	mass
centripetal	hydraulic	potential	oscillate
energy	inertia	malleable	work

1. The book on the desk will not move on its own accord because of _____ .

2. _____ is the ability to do work.

3. Did the lines on the screen _____ ? That is, did the lines wave back and forth?

4. The amount of material is defined scientifically as the matter's _____ .

5. When an object is rotating, the outward force on the object is called _____ ; the inward force is called _____ .

6. Force must cause movement before it can be said that any _____ has been done.

7. _____ is defined simply as a push or a pull.

Copyright © by Houghton Mifflin Company. All rights reserved.

8. Because steel can be hammered into desired shapes, it is said to be _____ .

9. Water that is held in reserve behind a dam is a good example of _____ energy.

10. Water cascading over a dam is an example of _____ energy.

11. The lifts used most frequently in garages to elevate cars are operated in part by _____ power.

III. *Directions:* If the words opposite each other in Columns A and B are similar in meaning, write *Yes* in the blank; if they are unrelated, write *No.*

A	B
1. mass	_____ diameter
2. force	_____ pull or push
3. work	_____ force that results in movement
4. energy	_____ action
5. kinetic energy	_____ energy in motion
6. potential energy	_____ sun energy
7. inertia	_____ pull toward the earth
8. centrifugal force	_____ outward force
9. centripetal force	_____ inward force
10. hydraulic	_____ automatic
11. oscillate	_____ vibrate
12. malleable	_____ expensive

IV. *Directions:* Write either an original sentence or a definition for each word or words that clearly demonstrates your mastery of their meaning as used in physical science.

1. centrifugal force _____

_____

2. centripetal force _____

_____

3. energy _____

_____

4. force _____

_____

5. hydraulic _____

_____

Copyright © by Houghton Mifflin Company. All rights reserved.

6. inertia _____

_____

7. kinetic energy _____

_____

8. potential energy _____

_____

9. malleable _____

_____

10. mass _____

_____

11. oscillate _____

_____

12. work _____

_____

Copyright © by Houghton Mifflin Company. All rights reserved.

Physical Science

1. **atom** (AT əm)—noun

   The smallest particle of an element that still has all the chemical properties of the element.

   One oxygen *atom* combines with two hydrogen atoms to form water.

2. **catalyst** (KAT ə list)—noun

   A substance that initiates or accelerates a chemical reaction without itself undergoing any permanent change.

   Chlorophyll, a specific protein, has been identified as the *catalyst* responsible for the increased rate at which food is manufactured in plants.

3. **compound** (KOM pound)—noun

   A pure substance composed of two or more elements chemically united in a specific proportion; thus it can be broken down into two or more other pure substances by a chemical change.

   Water is a *compound* whose molecules contain two atoms of hydrogen and one atom of oxygen (H_2O).

4. **element** (EL ə mənt)—noun

   A fundamental substance that cannot be separated into other substances by chemical means; there are more than one hundred elements.

   Hydrogen is classified as an *element* because it cannot be broken down into other substances.

5. **molecule** (MOL ə kūl)—noun

   Smallest particle of any material capable of existing independently; it contains all the chemical properties of the material.

   A *molecule* is formed from atoms with balancing attractive forces.

6. **nucleus** (NOO klē əs)—noun

   The central part of an atom containing protons and neutrons.

   The *nucleus* of an atom has a positive charge because of its protons.

Copyright © by Houghton Mifflin Company. All rights reserved.

7. **organic, inorganic chemistry** (or GAN ik, in or GAN ik)—adjectives + nouns

Organic chemistry is concerned with basic substances and matter containing carbon, which include all organisms. Inorganic chemistry is concerned with basic substances and matter except for those containing carbon.

The compounds of plants and animals, which contain carbon, are among the topics studied in *organic chemistry.*

Acids and minerals containing no carbon are studied in *inorganic chemistry.*

8. **proton, electron, neutron** (PRŌ ton, i LEK tron, NOO tron)—nouns

A proton is a very small particle in all atoms; it has a positive electric charge. An electron is a very small particle in all atoms; it has a negative electric charge. A neutron is a very small particle in all atoms except hydrogen; it has no electric charge.

Atoms contain minute particles called *protons, electrons,* and *neutrons.*

9. **solute** (SOL ūt)—noun

Any gas or solid that will dissolve or disappear when water or other liquid is added.

Salt is a *solute;* when added to water, the salt dissolves.

10. **synthesis** (SIN thə sis)—noun

The process of combining elements to form a compound or of combining simple compounds to form a complex compound.

The *synthesis* involved in various chemical processes led to the development of manufactured material such as nylon.

Copyright © by Houghton Mifflin Company. All rights reserved.

Name .... Section .... Date ....

EXERCISES FOR LESSON 46
Physical Science

I. *Directions:* Match each definition with the word or words it defines.

_____ **1.** catalyst
_____ **2.** element
_____ **3.** atom
_____ **4.** proton
_____ **5.** nucleus
_____ **6.** compound
_____ **7.** molecule
_____ **8.** organic chemistry
_____ **9.** synthesis
_____ **10.** solute
_____ **11.** electron
_____ **12.** inorganic chemistry
_____ **13.** neutron

a. a pure substance containing two or more elements

b. atom's central part

c. increases rate of chemical action

d. a fundamental substance that cannot be broken down into other substances

e. a solid or gas that dissolves when liquid is added

f. study of materials containing carbon

g. atomic particle with negative charge

h. atomic particle with no electric charge

i. atomic particle with positive electric charge

j. smallest particle of a material that can exist independently and still retain all chemical properties of the material

k. smallest particle of an element

l. combining process

m. study of noncarbon materials

II. *Directions:* In each space, write the appropriate word from those listed below.

atom	element	organic	electron	solute
catalyst	molecule	inorganic	neutron	synthesis
compound	nucleus	proton		

1. The process of combining elements or compounds is called _____ .

2. A substance that increases a chemical reaction rate is known as a(n) _____ .

3. The study of noncarbon material is included in _____ chemistry.

Copyright © by Houghton Mifflin Company. All rights reserved.

4. The smallest particle of an element is a(n) _____ .

5. Formed from atoms, the smallest particle of a material that can exist independently is a(n) _____ .

6. A(n) _____ is a basic substance that cannot be separated into other substances.

7. A(n) _____ is a pure substance composed of united elements.

8. A(n) _____ dissolves when a liquid is added to it.

9. A(n) _____ has no electric charge; a(n) _____ has a positive electric charge; a(n) _____ has a negative electric charge.

10. The study of materials that contain carbon is called _____ chemistry.

11. The _____ is located in the center of an atom.

III. *Directions:* If the words opposite each other in Columns A and B are similar in meaning, write *Yes* in the blank; if they are unrelated, write *No.*

A	B
1. catalyst	_____ something that speeds chemical reaction rate
2. element	_____ basic substance
3. atom	_____ separating process
4. proton	_____ positive electric charge
5. electron	_____ negative electric charge
6. neutron	_____ no electric charge
7. nucleus	_____ atom's center
8. compound	_____ substance containing two or more elements
9. molecule	_____ measuring device
10. organic	_____ contains oxygen
11. inorganic	_____ contains no oxygen
12. synthesis	_____ combining process
13. solute	_____ any liquid

IV. *Directions:* Write either an original sentence or a definition for each word or words that clearly demonstrates your mastery of their meaning as used in physical science.

1. **atom** _____

_____

2. **catalyst** _____

_____

3. **compound** _____

_____

4. **element** _____

_____

5. **molecule** _____

_____

6. **nucleus** _____

_____

7. **organic chemistry** _____

_____

8. **inorganic chemistry** _____

_____

9. **proton** _____

_____

10. **electron** _____

_____

11. **neutron** _____

_____

12. **solute** _____

_____

13. **synthesis** _____

_____

Copyright © by Houghton Mifflin Company. All rights reserved.

Computer Science

Computer science is changing so rapidly that keeping up with its technological innovations and ever-expanding vocabulary is a major challenge. However, the terms that are featured in this and the next lesson remain at the heart of computer language.

1. **terminal** (TUR mə nəl)—noun

   Consists of a keyboard that enters information into the computer and a screen that displays the computer's responses.

   A computer *terminal* combines the features of a typewriter and a television screen.

2. **monitor** (MON ə tər)—noun

   The screen displaying computer information. A monitor is also known as a CRT (cathode ray tube).

   This *monitor* displays tables and graphs in vivid colors.

3. **peripheral** (pə RIF ər əl)—noun

   An extra device, such as a printer or a data storage component, that is added to the computer.

   A *peripheral* you should consider adding to your computer is a letter-quality printer.

4. **port** (PORT)—noun

   A connector on the back of a computer where a peripheral is attached.

   The printer cable must be attached to the correct *port*.

5. **cursor, mouse** (KUR sor, MOWSE)—nouns

   A cursor is a movable pointer on a computer screen that indicates where an insertion, deletion, or other operation can take place.

   The *cursor* moves automatically to the next space after you type. You can also move the *cursor* up, down, backward, or forward.

Copyright © by Houghton Mifflin Company. All rights reserved.

A mouse is a hand-held device for moving a cursor and entering simple commands and information.

After selecting the symbol you want, press the button on the *mouse.*

6. icons (Ī kons)—noun

Small pictures representing the various options available to the user of that particular computer program. Icons are displayed on the monitor, or computer screen.

You can get rid of your old e-mail by clicking your mouse on the wastepaper basket *icon.*

7. fonts (FONTS)—noun

The various type sizes, styles, and symbols a computer is capable of producing, such as italics, script, and boldface.

A special set of *fonts* will give you the ability to change the type size and style.

8. modem (MŌ dem)—noun

A device used to link a computer to a telephone network, permitting information to be transmitted from one computer system to another. A fax/modem allows data to be transmitted to a fax (facsimile) machine, which prints the data out on paper.

The college has a local computer bulletin board accessible by a *modem.*

9. memory (MEM ə rē), RAM (Random Access Memory), ROM (Read Only Memory)—nouns

Memory refers to the computer's capacity for storing information. Today, most memory is stored on a hard disk (as opposed to a floppy disk or diskette) permanently installed inside the computer. <u>RAM</u> is the part of the computer's memory that can be added to or deleted from; because RAM can be changed, it is also called read/write memory. <u>ROM</u> is the computer's preprogrammed memory; it cannot be added to or deleted from.

RAM is the computer's electronic *memory*; it contains instructions and data a specific computer program can execute.

ROM is the preprogrammed *memory* that loads the computer's operating system.

10. <u>bi</u>nary, bit, byte (BĪ nə rē, BIT, BĪ T)—nouns

Binary refers to two digits: 0 and 1. Computer operations are based on a *binary* number system.

A *bit* is a single binary digit. A *bit* is the smallest piece of information stored in a computer.

Byte is the unit of data or memory now universally taken to mean eight bits. The size of a computer's memory is described in terms of *bytes.*

Copyright © by Houghton Mifflin Company. All rights reserved.

EXERCISES FOR LESSON 47
Computer Science

I. *Directions:* Match each definition with the word it defines.

A

_____ **1.** peripheral

_____ **2.** binary

_____ **3.** ROM

_____ **4.** monitor

_____ **5.** icons

_____ **6.** RAM

_____ **7.** mouse

a. computer screen

b. memory that can be added to or deleted from

c. accessory added to a computer

d. based on 0 and 1

e. computer's preprogrammed memory

f. hand-held device used for entering commands

g. small pictures representing various computer options

B

_____ **1.** bit

_____ **2.** terminal

_____ **3.** fonts

_____ **4.** cursor

_____ **5.** modem

_____ **6.** byte

_____ **7.** port

a. consists of eight bits

b. various typefaces, such as italics

c. connector on the back of a computer

d. a single binary digit

e. computer keyboard and screen

f. movable screen pointer

g. permits computers to communicate over telephone wires

II. *Directions:* In each space, write the appropriate word from those listed below.

terminal	port	icon	RAM	bits
monitor	cursor	fonts	ROM	byte
peripheral	mouse	modem	binary	

1. A _____ is a device used to link a computer to a telephone network.

2. A computer uses a _____ number system, that is, of two digits, 0 and 1.

3. A _____, controlled by one hand, is used to enter commands into the computer.

Copyright © by Houghton Mifflin Company. All rights reserved.

4. This set of _____ contains a number of decorative type-faces.

5. A _____ is a unit of data or memory consisting of eight _____ .

6. Reggie moved the _____ on the screen and clicked on "Edit."

7. You'll have to connect the printer cable to a _____ on the back of the computer.

8. My roommate bought a new _____ , or computer screen, that is one of the largest I've seen, but it is less than two inches thick.

9. _____ is the computer's preprogrammed memory, so it can't be changed; on the other hand, _____ is memory that can be added to or deleted from.

10. Because a keyboard is a necessity, it is not considered a _____ .

11. The _____ I clicked on the most is the one showing a tiny picture of an envelope, which gets me to my e-mail.

12. The keyboard and screen of a laptop or notebook computer are significantly smaller than the _____ of a desktop computer.

III. *Directions:* If the words opposite each other in Columns A and B are similar in meaning, write *Yes* in the blank; if they are unrelated, write *No.*

A	B
1. fonts	_____ keyboard's assortment of typefaces
2. ROM	_____ Read Only Memory
3. bit	_____ a computer timing device
4. port	_____ popular Internet website
5. peripheral	_____ computer accessory, such as a printer
6. mouse	_____ computer screen saver
7. cursor	_____ a computer error
8. RAM	_____ one of the most popular computer models
9. monitor	_____ computer screen
10. terminal	_____ an outdated computer program
11. binary	_____ movable pointer
12. byte	_____ a unit of information consisting of eight bits
13. icons	_____ small pictorial representations representing
14. modem	options
	_____ memory-saving part of the computer

Copyright © by Houghton Mifflin Company. All rights reserved.

IV. *Directions:* Write either an original sentence or a definition for each word that clearly demonstrates your mastery of its meaning as used in computer science.

1. **terminal** _____

   _____

2. **monitor** _____

   _____

3. **peripheral** _____

   _____

4. **port** _____

   _____

5. **cursor** _____

   _____

6. **mouse** _____

   _____

7. **icons** _____

   _____

8. **fonts** _____

   _____

9. **modem** _____

   _____

10. **memory** _____

    _____

11. **RAM** _____

    _____

12. **ROM** _____

    _____

13. **binary** _____

    _____

14. **bit** _____

    _____

15. **byte** _____

    _____

Copyright © by Houghton Mifflin Company. All rights reserved.

Computer Science

1. hardware, software (HARD WAR, SOFT WAR)—nouns

<u>Hardware</u> refers to the physical parts of the computer system, such as the terminal and monitor. <u>Software</u> refers to computer programs written to perform specific tasks.

The insurance company is spending thousands of dollars to update its computer *hardware* and *software*.

2. file (FĪL)—noun

A collection of related information stored on a disk. A file can contain a professionally prepared program or a user-created document.

A *file* must be given a specific title, such as "Rough Draft," and steps must be taken to save it on the computer's hard disk or the *file* will be lost when the computer is shut off.

3. database (DĀ tə bāys)—noun

A computer program used to manage large collections of information related to a particular subject or purpose.

Mailing lists, phone numbers, and payroll information are examples of information often contained in *databases*.

4. spreadsheet (SPRED shēt)—noun

A computer program that organizes numerical data into rows and columns.

The accountant entered the numbers on the *spreadsheet* program, which then presented the data in rows and columns on the screen.

5. hacker (HAK ər)—noun

A person who "hacks" or breaks into other people's computer files to look at, copy, change, or destroy their data. A hacker is able to do this by figuring out the password being used to protect such data; this is called "cracking" the password.

Hackers are electronic outlaws because they illegally tamper with other people's computer files.

Copyright © by Houghton Mifflin Company. All rights reserved.

315

6. **virus** (VĪ rəs)—noun

A computer virus is a program that attaches itself to other programs and then reproduces itself, damaging the data in the other programs.

Most computer *viruses* are deliberately written by *hackers* who either want to destroy data or want to frustrate other computer users.

7. **download** (DOWN lohd)—verb

To copy a file onto one's computer.

Susan is *downloading* an antivirus program onto her computer.

8. <u>Internet</u> (IN tər net)—noun

A computer network is a group of computers connected together so they can communicate with one another; the Internet connects thousands of such computer networks. The Internet, then, is actually a network of networks.

Computer networks of governments, libraries, business, universities, and other organizations throughout the nation and the world make up the *Internet.*

9. **World Wide Web** (WURLD WĪD WEB)—noun

The World Wide Web (WWW), or Web, is the powerful Internet facility that permits access to information from hundreds of sources and from all parts of the world. Web "pages" feature <u>hypertext,</u> which is a system that highlights key words, when you "click" your mouse on a key word, the screen provides more in-depth information relating to your topic. <u>Hypermedia</u> is similar, but it displays pictures and other types of illustrations as well.

The *World Wide Web* provided me with numerous sources about Monticello, Thomas Jefferson's home. Then by clicking my mouse on a number of hypertext and hypermedia words, I was able to secure the information and illustrations I needed to complete my research project.

10. **search engine** (surch EN jin)—adjective + noun

A search engine is a web site used to locate other web sites that will lead you to the specific information you desire.

After an appropriate word or phrase is typed at the top of its web page, a *search engine,* such as Google, will list the most promising sites for the information being sought.

Copyright © by Houghton Mifflin Company. All rights reserved.

EXERCISES FOR LESSON 48
Computer Science

I. *Directions:* Match each definition with the word or words it defines.

_____	**1.** database	**a.** a computer's physical equipment
_____	**2.** spreadsheet	**b.** network of networks
	3. World Wide Web	**c.** damages other programs by reproducing itself
_____	**4.** hacker	
_____	**5.** hardware	**d.** information stored on a disk
_____	**6.** Internet	**e.** programs written to perform specific tasks
_____	**7.** download	
_____	**8.** search engine	**f.** program used to manage large data collections
_____	**9.** virus	
_____	**10.** software	**g.** web site used to locate information available on the Internet
_____	**11.** file	

h. breaks into other computer users' programs

i. to copy a file onto a computer

j. Internet facility providing world wide information

k. organizes numerical data into rows and columns

II. *Directions:* In each space, write the appropriate word or words from those listed below.

hardware	database	virus	World Wide Web
software	spreadsheet	downloading	search engine
file	hacker	Internet	

1. This _____ contains the names, addresses, phone numbers, and e-mail addresses of hundreds of the college's alumni.

2. I went to the popular _____ known as Google to find information about the community college I'm interested in attending.

3. Chris is _____ a program of games onto his computer.

4. To save the document you've been working on, click "_____" on the top of your screen, then "Save."

5. The _____ displayed my data in neat rows and columns.

Copyright © by Houghton Mifflin Company. All rights reserved.

6. The _____ responsible for the _____ that destroyed hundreds of other peoples' files will be prosecuted this month by the state's attorney general.

7. The _____, a network of networks, can provide access to information for almost any topic imaginable.

8. The _____ "pages" feature hypertext, a system highlighting key words, and hypermedia, a system displaying illustrations.

9. Do you think a computer's _____, or physical equipment, changes as often as its _____, or the programs it's capable of running?

III. *Directions:* If the words opposite each other in Columns A and B are similar in meaning, write *Yes* in the blank; if they are unrelated, write *No.*

A		B
1. virus	_____	program that improves other programs
2. Internet	_____	The network of computer networks
3. WWW	_____	World Wide Web
4. file	_____	document saved on a disk
5. database	_____	fax machine
6. search engine	_____	a computer's waste basket
7. hardware	_____	computer slang for a popular web site
8. software	_____	computer slang for an out-of-date web site
9. spreadsheet	_____	program that protects against invasion of privacy
10. hacker	_____	a computer beginner
11. download	_____	to duplicate a file or program onto another computer

IV. *Directions:* Write either an original sentence or a definition for each word or words that clearly demonstrates your mastery of their meaning as used in computer science.

1. hardware _____

_____

2. software _____

_____

3. file _____

_____

Copyright © by Houghton Mifflin Company. All rights reserved.

4. database _____

_____

5. spreadsheet _____

_____

6. hacker _____

_____

7. virus _____

_____

8. download _____

_____

9. Internet _____

_____

10. World Wide Web _____

_____

11. search engine _____

_____

Copyright © by Houghton Mifflin Company. All rights reserved.

Business and Economics

A degree in business is the goal of thousands of college students; in addition, thousands of others elect, or are advised to take, a business or economics course so they can gain insight into the nation's economic system. Learning the terms included in this and the following lesson will help you grasp the concepts dealt with in business and economics.

1. **commodities** (kə MOD i tēs)—noun

   Products bought, sold, or traded.
   Food, clothes, metals, and cars are among the country's chief *commodities*.

2. **GNP** (gross national product)—noun

   The total value of goods and services produced by a nation's business during a specific period, usually a year.
   GNP is the official measure of a nation's economic output.

3. **balance of trade** (BAL əns uv TRĀD)—noun + preposition + noun

   The relationship between a nation's exports (what it sells to other countries) and its imports (what it buys from other countries).
   The *balance of trade* for the United States in the past four months indicates that more goods were bought from other countries than were sold abroad.

4. **reciprocity** (RES ə PROS i tē)—noun

   A mutual exchange policy in which each part grants the other corresponding privileges. (Informally, this policy is sometimes referred to as "If you'll scratch my back, I'll scratch yours.")
   The two nations have a policy of *reciprocity* as they have removed the tariff on certain goods coming from each other's country.

5. **assets** (AS ets)—noun

   All items of value owned by a person or persons.
   The building, equipment, land, and patents are among the company's *assets*.

Copyright © by Houghton Mifflin Company. All rights reserved.

6. **liabilities** (LĪ ə BIL ə tēs)—noun

Debts owed to other firms or persons.

The store owner declared bankruptcy after his *liabilities* continued to exceed his assets.

7. **solvency** (SOL vən sē)—noun

The ability to meet one's financial obligations.

The firm's *solvency* enabled the board of directors to pay off all debts and to modernize the plant's equipment.

8. **fiscal** (FIS kəl)—adjective

Pertaining to financial matters.

The company's *fiscal* year begins on July 1.

9. **inflationary** (in FLĀ shə NER ē)—adjective

Describes a substantial rise in prices caused by an excessive expansion of paper money or bank credit.

The union representative argued that the company's salary offer did not match the rise in the cost of living caused by an extensive *inflationary* period.

10. **recession** (ri SESH ən)—noun

A prolonged economic period in which business is poor and unemployment is high. (Depression is used to describe a severe recession.)

A number of leading economists had predicted a *recession* during the second half of the year, but business and the employment rate continued to be good.

11. **bear market, bull market** (BĀR MAR kit, BUL MAR kit)—nouns

The stock market is the business of buying, selling, and trading of stocks, bonds, and other financial investments. A bear market refers to a falling stock market, that is, when such investments are declining in value. A bull market refers to a rising market, that is, when such investments are increasing in value.

Though my investments have continued to decline during the current *bear market,* my financial advisor said I shouldn't be discouraged because he was confident a *bull market* would occur before the year ended.

Copyright © by Houghton Mifflin Company. All rights reserved.

EXERCISES FOR LESSON 49
Business and Economics

I. *Directions:* Match each definition with the word or words it defines.

_____ **1.** liabilities	**a.** stocks show positive growth
_____ **2.** fiscal	**b.** showing a significant rise in prices
_____ **3.** GNP	**c.** period of poor business and high
_____ **4.** commodities	unemployment
_____ **5.** recession	**d.** ability to meet financial obligations
_____ **6.** bull market	**e.** cash, property, and all other things
_____ **7.** inflationary	of value
_____ **8.** reciprocity	**f.** mutual exchange policy
_____ **9.** bear market	**g.** comparison between what a country
_____ **10.** assets	sells and what it buys
_____ **11.** solvency	**h.** total value of goods and services of
_____ **12.** balance of trade	a nation
	i. debts
	j. products bought, sold, or traded
	k. refers to financial concerns
	l. stocks show a decrease in value

II. *Directions:* In each space write the appropriate word from those listed below.

commodities	balance of trade	assets	solvency	inflationary	bear
GNP	reciprocity	liabilities	fiscal	recession	bull

1. A(n) _____ period is especially hard on people with fixed incomes because an increase in their cost of living is not accompanied by a rise in their incomes.

2. Our company is one of the few I know of that uses a(n) _____ year of forty-eight weeks in order to have twelve months of four weeks each.

3. "In the black financially" is one way _____ could be defined.

4. _____ sold by this diversified organization include fruit juices, appliances, and plywood.

5. My investments increased dramatically in value during last year's _____ , but, unfortunately, they have decreased in value just as dramatically during this year's prolonged _____ .

Copyright © by Houghton Mifflin Company. All rights reserved.

6. As a whole, the country's economy has suffered this year, resulting in a decline in the nation's _____.

7. Because of the economic _____, car sales, property transactions, and factory production figures have been well below average.

8. One indicator of a country's economic health is its _____, that is, how its export sales and import purchases compare.

9. The corporation's financial picture is excellent as it possesses _____ worth over twelve billion dollars whereas its _____, or debts, total less than one billion.

10. "If you'll scratch my back, I'll scratch yours" is an informal definition of _____.

III. *Directions:* If the words opposite each other in Columns A and B are similar in meaning, write *Yes* in the blank; if they are unrelated, write *No.*

	A		B
1.	commodities	_____	worthless products
2.	GNP	_____	gross national product
3.	assets	_____	valuable possessions
4.	balance of trade	_____	ratio of imports to exports
5.	fiscal	_____	healthy financial condition
6.	inflationary	_____	downward plunge in prices
7.	liabilities	_____	debts
8.	recession	_____	booming economic period
9.	reciprocity	_____	exchange of rights and privileges
10.	solvency	_____	sound financial condition
11.	bull market	_____	investors are happy
12.	bear market	_____	investors are unhappy

IV. *Directions:* Write either an original sentence or a definition for each word or words that clearly demonstrates your mastery of their meaning as used in business and economics.

1. commodities _____

_____

2. GNP _____

_____

3. balance of trade _____

_____

Copyright © by Houghton Mifflin Company. All rights reserved.

4. reciprocity _____

_____

5. assets _____

_____

6. liabilities _____

_____

7. solvency _____

_____

8. fiscal _____

_____

9. inflationary _____

_____

10. recession _____

_____

11. bear market _____

_____

12. bull market _____

_____

Copyright © by Houghton Mifflin Company. All rights reserved.

Business and Economics

1. **portfolio** (port FŌ le Ō)—noun

   The collection of securities (stocks and bonds) held by a single investor.

   By carefully managing her *portfolio* over the years, my aunt was able to retire at age fifty-five.

2. **entrepreneur** (AN trə prə NUR)—noun

   A French term for an individual who develops an enterprise through innovation and risk taking.

   The *entrepreneur* risked a fortune in establishing her unique business, which is now showing an impressive profit.

3. **CEO** (chief executive officer)—noun

   The person ultimately responsible for all decisions affecting the management of an organization; generally reports to a board of directors.

   A. S. Robinson, the *CEO,* has successfully guided the company for the past seven years.

4. **franchise** (FRAN chīz)—noun

   A legal agreement granting an individual or group the right to sell a firm's products or services. Can also mean the businesses that operate under this agreement.

   After agreeing to the conditions stipulated in the contract, Mr. Sanchez was granted a *franchise* to operate one of the company's fast-food restaurants.

5. **capital** (KAP it ul)—noun

   Wealth in the form of money or property.

   Mr. Sanchez is also raising the necessary *capital* to secure a second franchise in a another part of the city.

Copyright © by Houghton Mifflin Company. All rights reserved.

6. conglomerate (kən GLOM ər it)—noun

A corporation comprising companies that conduct a variety of unrelated businesses.

The *conglomerate* includes branches concerned with computers, batteries, and plumbing fixtures.

7. appreciation, depreciation (ə PRĒ shē Ā shən, di PRĒ shē Ā shən)—nouns

Appreciation is the increase in value of an asset; depreciation is the decline in value of an asset.

The land I owned near the city limits has shown a remarkable growth in *appreciation* over the past five years.

Years of mismanagement resulted in a *depreciation* of the company's manufacturing facilities.

8. affirmative action (ə FUR mə tiv AK shən)—adjective + noun

Action designed to increase opportunities for females and minorities through recruitment, training, and promotion so that they are fairly represented in the work force.

The company has hired many more women and Hispanics this past decade as a result of its *affirmative action* program.

9. divestiture (dī VEST i chər)—noun

The loss or voluntary surrender of property, interest, right, or title.

Because the corporation had an unfair advantage over its competitors, the court ordered a *divestiture* of certain of its assets.

10. obsolescence (OB sə LES əns)—noun

Condition when certain products are no longer marketable because of scientific or technological advances.

Typewriters are on the verge of *obsolescence* because of computers.

11. audit (AH dit)—noun, verb

An examination of the financial records of a business (noun); to examine the financial records of a business (verb).

Company officials have hired an accounting firm to conduct an independent *audit* of the company's financial records and procedures.

12. golden parachute (GŌL dən PAR ə SHOOT)—adjective + noun

An exceedingly generous promise of pay and other benefits given to a top executive in case his or her company is taken over by another firm or he or she retires.

Copyright © by Houghton Mifflin Company. All rights reserved.

The CEO's *golden parachute,* which includes generous severance pay and other costly benefits, is being sharply criticized by the company's stockholders.

13. tariff (TAIR if)—noun

Taxes on imported goods.

To protect domestic car makers, the government has placed a *tariff* on cars imported to this country.

14. cartel (kər TEL)—noun

A group of businesses that have joined together to control some industry.

An international oil *cartel* is responsible for the dramatic rise in gasoline prices.

15. embargo (em BAR gō)—noun

Official prohibition of trade by one nation against another.

Many countries have an *embargo* against that nation because of its failure to stop the export of illegal drugs.

Copyright © by Houghton Mifflin Company. All rights reserved.

EXERCISES FOR LESSON 50
Business and Economics

I. *Directions:* Match each definition to the word it defines.

A

_____ **1.** divestiture	**a.** an increase in value
_____ **2.** franchise	**b.** banning of trade by one nation against another
_____ **3.** conglomerate	**c.** designed to promote fair career opportunities for females and minorities
_____ **4.** appreciation	
_____ **5.** cartel	**d.** legal right to sell a firm's products
_____ **6.** affirmative action	**e.** act of shedding property
_____ **7.** embargo	**f.** securities owned by an investor
_____ **8.** portfolio	**g.** organization formed to establish a business monopoly
	h. many companies owned by a corporation

B

_____ **1.** tariff	**a.** products no longer marketable
_____ **2.** entrepreneur	**b.** taxes on imported goods
_____ **3.** golden parachute	**c.** wealth in the form of money or property
_____ **4.** CEO	
_____ **5.** audit	**d.** a decline in value
_____ **6.** capital	**e.** chief executive officer of a business
_____ **7.** depreciation	**f.** a bold, daring business person
_____ **8.** obsolescence	**g.** inspection of financial records
	h. lavish severance pay and other benefits

II. *Directions:* In each space, write the appropriate word from those listed below.

A

portfolio	conglomerate	golden parachute	capital	audit
franchise	obsolescence	CEO	divestiture	

1. The corporation sold two of its overseas businesses; this voluntary _____ took its competitors by surprise.

Copyright © by Houghton Mifflin Company. All rights reserved.

2. Her _____ is diversified, ranging from oil and gas stocks to state and municipal bonds.

3. My brother is in an executive training program for a(n) _____ that has numerous businesses here and abroad.

4. Before he agreed to become _____ of the company, Mr. Andretti insisted on a(n) _____ in case he retired, was fired, or the company was sold.

5. Quartz watches led to the _____ of watches run by windup springs.

6. An independent _____ of the company's financial records uncovered only a few minor irregularities.

7. My cousin is trying to raise enough _____ to buy a _____ from a nationally known bagel company.

B

entrepreneur	depreciation	tariff	embargo
appreciation	affirmative action	cartel	

1. Protestors are urging the United States to impose a(n) _____ on that nation because of its widespread use of child labor.

2. A(n) _____ was formed by neighboring countries in an attempt to control the price for their iron ore.

3. Our sociology professor said that our country has benefited in many ways from _____, such as by the greater number of women now admitted to medical schools.

4. Major stockholders are concerned because the plant's equipment is fast becoming worn and outdated, resulting in a _____ of the plant's worth.

5. The dynamic _____ has earned the respect of the business world because her bold initiatives have helped to save what once was a failing company.

6. Lobbyists for the fruit-producing states are urging Congress to levy a _____ on all fruit, except for bananas, coming into this country.

7. The astounding _____ of real estate in this small community is due to the completion of a new highway, making possible a much easier commute to the city.

Copyright © by Houghton Mifflin Company. All rights reserved.

III. *Directions:* If the words opposite each other in Columns A and B are similar in meaning, write *Yes* in the blank; if they are unrelated, write *No.*

	A		B
1.	embargo	_____	government banning of trade with a specific country
2.	tariff	_____	tax on goods coming into a country
3.	capital	_____	money and other forms of wealth
4.	affirmative action	_____	steps recommended to increase profits
5.	cartel	_____	license to operate a private business overseas
6.	depreciation	_____	an increase in value
7.	entrepreneur	_____	cautious investor
8.	franchise	_____	tax on luxury goods
9.	audit	_____	financial inspection
10.	conglomerate	_____	government regulations businesses must observe
11.	divestiture	_____	surrender of property
12.	golden parachute	_____	an agreeable business merger
13.	CEO	_____	Congressional Economical Opportunities
14.	obsolescence	_____	passing out of use
15.	portfolio	_____	person's financial holdings
16.	appreciation	_____	decrease in value

IV. *Directions:* Write either an original sentence or a definition for each word or words that clearly demonstrates your mastery of their meaning.

1. portfolio _____

_____

2. entrepreneur _____

_____

3. CEO _____

_____

4. franchise _____

_____

5. capital _____

_____

6. conglomerate _____

_____

Copyright © by Houghton Mifflin Company. All rights reserved.

7. appreciation _____

_____

8. depreciation _____

_____

9. affirmative action _____

_____

10. divestiture _____

_____

11. obsolescence _____

_____

12. audit _____

_____

13. golden parachute _____

_____

14. tariff _____

_____

15. cartel _____

_____

16. embargo _____

_____

Copyright © by Houghton Mifflin Company. All rights reserved.

Legal Terms

The legal terms included in this and the following lesson are among those that must be understood to gain insight into the fundamental concepts presented in introductory paralegal, law enforcement, criminal justice, and other such courses.

1. acquittal (ə KWIT əl)—noun

The finding of the court or jury that the defendant is not guilty.
After the defendant's *acquittal* was announced, her family rushed to embrace her.

2. adjudicate (a JOO də kāt)—verb

To settle by legal decision as a judge or jury does; to judge.
A judge will *adjudicate* the divorce settlement, including custody of the children.

3. bail (BĀL)—noun

Security, usually in the form of money, used to release an accused person prior to a trial or hearing.
The defendant would forfeit a *bail* of $10,000 if he failed to appear at his hearing.

4. booking (BOOK ing)—noun

The process of entering the suspect's name, the offense with which the suspect is charged, and other pertinent information in the official arrest record.
An officer at the police station used a computer to complete the *booking;* he typed information about the suspect and the crime with which he was charged.

5. commute (kə MYOOT)—verb

To reduce a guilty person's sentence or punishment.
The judge *commuted* the prisoner's sentence from eight to five years.

6. culpability (kul pə BIL ə tē)—noun

Blameworthiness; guiltiness
The stockbroker admitted his *culpability* for the illegal business practices members of his firm had been following.

Copyright © by Houghton Mifflin Company. All rights reserved.

335

7. **indict** (in DĪT)—verb

To formally charge of a person with a criminal offense.

The grand jury is deliberating whether to *indict* the driver for vehicular manslaughter.

8. **perjury** (PUR jə rē)   noun

Lying under oath.

Because it was later established that the defense witness had lied, she was indicted for *perjury.*

9. **recidivism** (ri SID ə viz əm)—noun

Relapsing into a previous behavior pattern, especially criminal behavior.

Because of the state's high rate of repeat offenders during the past decade, a special governor's commission has recommended new prison reform and rehabilitation programs in an effort to reduce such *recidivism.*

10. **tort** (TORT) **law**—noun + noun

Law that is concerned with wrongful acts resulting in injury or damage for which people can seek legal satisfaction.

Tort law is a branch of civil law (as opposed to criminal or contract law) concerned with compensating individuals for personal injury, property damage, or other losses.

Copyright © by Houghton Mifflin Company. All rights reserved.

EXERCISES FOR LESSON 51
Legal Terms

I. *Directions:* Match each definition to the word it defines.

_____ **1.** culpability

_____ **2.** tort law

_____ **3.** recidivism

_____ **4.** booking

_____ **5.** indict

_____ **6.** adjudicate

_____ **7.** commute

_____ **8.** acquittal

_____ **9.** bail

_____ **10.** perjury

a. to reduce the severity of the punishment

b. process of entering suspect's name and other information in the official arrest record

c. lying under oath

d. to judge

e. a "not guilty" verdict

f. the deserving of fault or blame

g. backsliding to previous behavior

h. security posted to gain the release of the accused before the trial

i. to formally charge a person with a crime

j. branch of law specializing in personal injury and property damage cases

II. *Directions:* In each space, write the appropriate word or words from those listed below.

acquittal	bail	commuted	indict	recidivism
adjudicate	booking	culpability	perjury	tort law

1. The driver acknowledged his _____ for the accident as he confessed to running a red light.

2. Libel suits are among the concerns of _____ .

3. The grand jury decided not to _____ the suspect because of a lack of compelling evidence.

4. Researchers are constantly attempting to identify the causes of _____ so steps can be taken to help former criminals lead productive lives and stay out of prison.

5. Though she knew her testimony would prove damaging to her friend's defense, she resolved to tell the truth about the incident rather than commit _____ .

Copyright © by Houghton Mifflin Company. All rights reserved.

6. The _____ of the suspect took considerable time because he was most uncooperative, even refusing to give his name, address, and date of birth.

7. The suspect's family rushed to embrace him after his _____ .

8. Because his client has been a model prisoner, the lawyer is confident his client's sentence will be _____ from twenty to ten years.

9. The business partners couldn't reach an agreement, so they consulted an expert in contract law to _____ the matter.

10. The accused remained in jail after failing to raise the necessary money for his _____ .

III. *Directions:* If the words opposite each other in Columns A and B are similar in meaning, write *Yes* in the blank; if they are unrelated, write *No*.

A	B
1. indict	_____ charge with a crime
2. acquittal	_____ free from the accusation
3. perjury	_____ hung jury
4. adjudicate	_____ judge
5. tort law	_____ having to do with the legality of contracts
6. recidivism	_____ backsliding into crime
7. commute	_____ plead a case
8. bail	_____ flee before a trial
9. booking	_____ reduction of a sentence
10. culpability	_____ lying under oath

IV. *Directions:* Write an original sentence or a definition for each word or words that clearly demonstrates your mastery of their meaning as used in legal matters.

1. acquittal _____

_____

2. adjudicate _____

_____

3. bail _____

_____

4. booking _____

_____

Copyright © by Houghton Mifflin Company. All rights reserved.

5. commute _____

_____

6. culpability _____

_____

7. indict _____

_____

8. perjury _____

_____

9. recidivism _____

_____

10. tort law _____

_____

Copyright © by Houghton Mifflin Company. All rights reserved.

Legal Terms

1. **appeal** (ə PĒL)—noun

   The request for a new hearing of a case already tried.

   After the guilty verdict was announced, the defendant's lawyer immediately announced she would seek an *appeal*.

2. **change of venue** (CHĀNJ uv VEN yoo)—noun + preposition + noun

   A change in the place of the defendant's trial, generally from the country where the crime was committed to another judicial district.

   The judge agreed to the defense lawyer's request for a *change of venue* because of the widespread publicity about the crime.

3. **concurrent sentencing, consecutive sentencing** (kən KUR ənt, kən SEK yə tiv)—nouns

   <u>Concurrent</u> sentencing is when two or more sentences are handed out on the same occasion to be served during a common time period.

   <u>Consecutive</u> sentencing is when two or more sentences are handed out on the same occasion and the time to be served is to be equal to the sum of the sentences.

   The defendants, found guilty on all charges, hoped to receive *concurrent sentencing;* however, they received *consecutive sentencing,* so they must serve five years in prison for each crime they committed.

4. **extradite** (EK strə dīt)—verb

   To transfer an accused person to the authorities with the legal jurisdiction to try the case.

   Texas officials agreed to *extradite* the suspect to Florida, where she had escaped from prison.

5. **felony** (FEL ə nē)—noun

   A major crime punishable by death or a long prison sentence.

   Kidnapping is a *felony* punishable by death in many states.

Copyright © by Houghton Mifflin Company. All rights reserved.

341

6. misdemeanor (mis də MĒ nər)—noun

A crime punishable by a fine and/or imprisonment, usually for less than a year; a misdemeanor is a less serious crime than a felony.

The protestors were warned they would be charged with a *misdemeanor* unless they stopped blocking the entrance to the building.

7. subpoena (sə PĒ nə)—noun

A legal order requiring a person to appear in court to give testimony.

The *subpoena* requires the supervisor to testify in court regarding the safety procedures being followed on the day the accident occurred.

8. habeas corpus (HĀ bē əs KOR pəs)—noun. Latin term meaning "you have the body."

A legal order commanding a person being held in custody to be produced before a court to determine the lawfulness of the person's confinement.

A request for *habeas corpus* was granted by the judge to determine whether the lawyer's client should be released until his scheduled deportation hearing.

9. injunction (in JUNGK shən)—noun

A legal order directing a person to refrain from doing some activity. An injunction is a preventive measure to guard against future injuries; it does not provide a remedy for past injuries.

An *injunction* prohibits the former employee from coming within three blocks of the business establishment where he once worked.

10. jurisprudence (JUR is PROOD ns)—noun

The science of law. Jurisprudence is also used as a synonym (word having the same meaning) for law.

Law courses are challenging because the study of *jurisprudence* encompasses all matters relating to our legal system.

11. litigation (lit ə GĀ shən)—noun

A legal suit in a court of law.

Unfortunately, *litigation* was necessary to settle our boundary dispute with our once-friendly neighbors.

Copyright © by Houghton Mifflin Company. All rights reserved.

12. **plaintiff** (PLAYN tif)—noun

defendant (də FEN dənt)—noun

litigants (LIT ə gənts)—noun

The <u>plaintiff</u> is the one who legally complains and initiates court action against someone; the <u>defendant</u> is the one being sued or, in a criminal case, the one being accused. The plaintiff and defendant are known as the <u>litigants,</u> that is, the parties involved in a lawsuit.

The *litigants* in the lawsuit are Mr. Dawson and Mr. Burnell. Mr. Dawson, the *plaintiff,* says he was never paid in full for building Mr. Burnell's house. Mr. Burnell, the *defendant,* contends Mr. Dawson was not paid in full because he had failed to fulfill all the terms of their contract.

Copyright © by Houghton Mifflin Company. All rights reserved.

EXERCISES FOR LESSON 52
Legal Terms

I. *Directions:* Match each definition to the word it defines.

A

_____ **1.** felony
_____ **2.** habeas corpus
_____ **3.** extradite
_____ **4.** misdemeanor
_____ **5.** defendant
_____ **6.** litigation
_____ **7.** concurrent
_____ **8.** jurisprudence

a. the science of law
b. legal suit in a court of law
c. major crime punishable by death or a severe prison sentence
d. to send a prisoner to authorities in another state
e. describes jail time served during the same time period
f. requires a person be brought before the court to determine whether he or she is being held legally
g. person being sued or accused of a crime
h. crime punishable by a fine and/or imprisonment

B

_____ **1.** subpoena
_____ **2.** appeal
_____ **3.** litigants
_____ **4.** consecutive
_____ **5.** change of venue
_____ **6.** plaintiff
_____ **7.** injunction

a. alteration of the location of a defendant's trial
b. legal order barring a person from doing some activity
c. person bringing court action against someone
d. legal order requiring a person to testify in court
e. describes sentences served one after the other
f. parties involved in a lawsuit
g. request for a new trial

Copyright © by Houghton Mifflin Company. All rights reserved.

II. *Directions:* In each space, write the appropriate word or words from those listed below.

A

appeal	consecutive	extradite	felony
subpoena	plaintiff	defendant	litigants

1. Nevada officials requested California authorities to _____ the suspect to Nevada.

2. The prisoner received _____ sentencing, so he will serve a total of twenty years as each sentence called for ten years in prison.

3. The _____ in the case are a fired chauffeur, the _____, who is suing his ex-boss, and the _____ , who is being sued for breach of contract.

4. Robbing a bank is a(n) _____ , so the judge will undoubtedly sentence the guilty person to a long prison term.

5. Because she was a close friend of the accused, my neighbor wasn't surprised when she was served with a(n) _____ requiring her to give testimony at his trial.

6. The defendant and her lawyer were stunned by the jury's verdict, and they made it clear they would file a(n) _____ as soon as possible.

B

change of venue	concurrent	misdemeanor	habeas corpus
injunction	jurisprudence	litigation	

1. The teenagers were charged with a(n) _____ after they were caught spray-painting the front of the community swimming pool.

2. She was given _____ sentencing, so she will serve a total of ten years in federal prison even though the two crimes she was found guilty of each carry a ten-year sentence.

3. The judge issued a(n) _____ prohibiting the young man from having any further contact with his ex-girlfriend.

4. The lawyer assured his clients that the judge would agree to issue an order of _____ , so they would either be brought to court and charged with a crime or they would be released.

5. The community's widespread hostility against the defendant resulted in a(n) _____ for the trial.

6. The former employee was threatened with _____ unless he returned the company car within two days.

7. To earn a degree in _____ generally takes three years of full-time study beyond the bachelor's degree.

Copyright © by Houghton Mifflin Company. All rights reserved.

III. *Directions:* If the words opposite each other in Columns A and B are similar in meaning, write *Yes* in the blank; if they are unrelated, write *No*.

A		B
1. extradite	_____	inconclusive evidence
2. litigation	_____	the taking of legal action leading to a court trial
3. appeal	_____	request for a different location for the trial
4. misdemeanor	_____	illegal arrest
5. felony	_____	major criminal offense
6. consecutive	_____	sentences served one after the other
7. concurrent	_____	sentences served at the same time
8. change of venue	_____	request for a new trial
9. plaintiff	_____	person suing
10. injunction	_____	requires a court appearance to give testimony
11. habeas corpus	_____	crime victim's body
12. defendant	_____	person being sued or accused of a crime
13. subpoena	_____	the formal study of law
14. litigants	_____	parties involved in a lawsuit
15. jurisprudence	_____	a case decided by a jury rather than a judge

IV. *Directions:* Write an original sentence or a definition for each word or words that clearly demonstrates your mastery of their meaning as used in legal matters.

1. appeal _____

_____

2. change of venue _____

_____

3. concurrent sentencing _____

_____

4. consecutive sentencing _____

_____

5. extradite _____

_____

6. felony _____

_____

7. misdemeanor _____

_____

Copyright © by Houghton Mifflin Company. All rights reserved.

8. subpoena _____

_____

9. habeas corpus _____

_____

10. injunction _____

_____

11. jurisprudence _____

_____

12. litigation _____

_____

13. plaintiff _____

_____

14. defendant _____

_____

15. litigants _____

_____

Copyright © by Houghton Mifflin Company. All rights reserved.

Medical Terms

Although knowledge of the word parts, specialties, and frequently used medical terms presented in this lesson should benefit most students, those of you planning to enter the medical profession in some capacity, such as in nursing, will find this knowledge particularly helpful.

Part One: Word Parts

Word Part	Example
1. algia—pain	*Neuralgia* is pain extending along a nerve or a group of nerves.
2. arteri—blood vessel	*Arteries* are blood vessels that carry blood away from the heart.
3. arthr—joint	*Arthritis* is inflammation of the joints.
4. cardi—heart	*Bradycardia* is a heart rate of less than 60 beats per minute in an adult; *tachycardia* is a heart rate exceeding 100 beats per minute in an adult.
5. derm—skin	*Dermatology* is the branch of medicine concerned with the skin.
6. gastr—stomach	*Gastrology* is the study of the stomach and its diseases.
7. hem—blood	*Hematology* is the study of blood and the blood-producing organs.
8. itis—inflammation	*Bronchitis* is inflammation of the membrane lining the bronchial tubes.
9. my—muscle	*Myalgia* is muscular pain.
10. neur—nerve	*Neuritis* is inflammation of a nerve (see also *neuralgia* above).
11. osteo—bone	*Osteoporosis* is a disease in which the bones become weak and brittle, often leading to curvature of the spine.

Copyright © by Houghton Mifflin Company. All rights reserved.

349

12. **phleb**—vein   *Phlebitis* is inflammation of a vein.

13. **psych**—mind   *Psychiatry* is the branch of medicine concerned with mental disorders.

14. **pulmo**—lung   *Pulmonary* refers to the lungs.

15. **tomy**—act of cutting   *Splenectomy* is removal of the spleen.

Review the preceding medical word parts until you are confident you know them well; then do Exercise I on page 353.

Part Two: Medical Specialties

Specialty	Concerned with . . .
1. **anesthesiology** (an is thē zē OL ə jē)	the use of drugs (anesthetics) for reducing pain and rendering surgical patients unconscious
2. **audiology** (ə dē OL ə jē)	hearing
3. **cardiology** (kar dē OL ə jē)	heart diseases
4. **dermatology** (dur mə TOL ə jē)	skin conditions
5. **gastrology** (ga STRAL ə jē)	diseases of the stomach and other digestive organs
6. **gerontology** (jer ən TOL ə jē)	the processes and problems of aging
7. **gynecology** (gī nə KOL ə jē)	the health care of women, especially the reproductive organs
8. **neonatology** (nē ō nā TOL ə jē)	young babies, usually from birth to ten days
9. **nephrology** (nə FROL ə jē)	diseases of the kidneys and related organs
10. **neurology** (noo ROL ə jē)	the brain and other parts of the nervous system
11. **obstetrics** (ob STET riks)	the care of women during pregnancy and during and following childbirth
12. **oncology** (on KOL ə jē)	cancer
13. **ophthalmology** (əf thəl MOL ə jē)	anatomy, functions, and treatment of the eye
14. **orthopedics** (or thə PĒ diks)	injuries or disorders of bones, muscles, joints, and ligaments
15. **otolaryngology** (ō tō lar ing GOL ə jē)	conditions of the ear, nose, and throat
16. **pathology** (pa THOL ə jē)	the scientific study of disease and its causes
17. **pediatrics** (pē dē AT riks)	the care and treatment of infants and children

Copyright © by Houghton Mifflin Company. All rights reserved.

18. **pulmonology** (pul mə NOL ə jē)   diseases of the respiratory (breathing) system

19. **radiology** (rā dē OL ə jē)   the use of radioactive substances in the diagnosis and treatment of disease

20. **urology** (yoo ROL ə jē)   problems of the urinary tract

Review the preceding medical specialties until you are confident that you know them well; then do Exercise II on page 354.

Part Three: Frequently Used Medical Terms

1. **acute** (ə KYOOT)—describes an illness or pain with a rapid onset and a short, severe course

2. **asymptomatic** (ā simp tə MAT ik)—not showing any symptoms of disease

3. **atrophy** (AT rə fē)—wasting away of muscles or a decrease in the size of a body part due to disease, injury, or lack of use

4. **benign** (bə NĪN)—harmless, not deadly

5. **chronic** (KRON ik)—describes an illness or pain of long duration

6. **coagulate** (kō AG yə lāt)—to thicken or clot (as of blood)

7. **cognition** (kog NISH ən)—intellectual faculties; ability to think, reason, and make judgments

8. **congenital** (kən JEN ə təl)—inborn or existing since birth

9. **cyanosis** (sī ə NŌ sis)—blue or gray discoloration of the skin because of reduced oxygen levels in the blood

10. **dementia** (dē MEN shə)—a progressive decline in cognitive (mental) abilities; also referred to as Alzheimer's disease

11. **edema** (ə DĒ mə)—the swelling of body tissues with fluid

12. **etiology** (ē tē OL ə jē)—the causes or origins of a disease; the study of these causes

13. **febrile** (FEB rəl)—having a fever

14. **hospice** (HOS pis)—type of care of the terminally ill founded on the concept of allowing individuals to die with dignity and surrounded by those who love them

15. **malignant** (mə LIG nənt)—threatening to life; deadly

16. **natal** (NĀ təl)—pertaining to birth

17. **palliative** (PAL ē ə tiv)—describing care that relieves the symptoms of a disease without effecting a cure

18. **prognosis** (prəg NŌ sis)—forecast of the probable course and outcome of a disease

Copyright © by Houghton Mifflin Company. All rights reserved.

19. **protocol** (PRĒ tə kəl)—series of standing orders or procedures that should be followed under specific conditions

20. **recumbent** (rə KUM bənt)—in a lying-down position

21. **remission** (rə MISH ən)—the lessening of a disease's symptoms

22. **rigor mortis** (RIG ər MOR tis)—stiffening of the body after death caused by the contractions of the muscles

23. **subcutaneous** (sub kyoo TĀ nē əs)—under the skin, such as a hypodermic injection

24. **vertigo** (VUR tə gō)—dizziness; sensation of the head spinning

Review the preceding frequently used medical terms until you are confident you know them well; then do Exercise III on page 355.

Copyright © by Houghton Mifflin Company. All rights reserved.

EXERCISES FOR LESSON 53
Medical Terms

I. *Directions:* Use your knowledge of the medical word parts presented in **Part One** (as well as the other underlined word parts) to do this matching exercise.

A

_____ 1. <u>osteogenesis</u>
_____ 2. <u>gastroscope</u>
_____ 3. <u>pulmonic</u>
_____ 4. <u>fibromyalgia</u>
_____ 5. <u>psychosomatic</u>
_____ 6. <u>cardiograph</u>
_____ 7. <u>bursitis</u>
_____ 8. <u>arteriography</u>

a. chronic pain in the muscles
b. relating to the lungs
c. inflammation of a saclike body cavity containing a lubricating fluid
d. the formation and development of bony tissue
e. examination of arteries using x-rays
f. instrument used to examine the interior of the stomach
g. instrument that records heart movements
h. concerned with the influence of the mind on the body

B

_____ 1. <u>phlebology</u>
_____ 2. <u>dermatosis</u>
_____ 3. <u>lobotomy</u>
_____ 4. <u>arthroscopy</u>
_____ 5. <u>neural</u>
_____ 6. <u>hemoglobin</u>
_____ 7. <u>myasthenia</u>

a. abnormal weakness of the muscles
b. examination of a joint using an instrument inserted through a small opening
c. study of veins and their diseases
d. iron pigment in the red blood cells
e. surgical incision in the front part of the brain
f. relating to a nerve or the nervous system
g. skin disease

Copyright © by Houghton Mifflin Company. All rights reserved.

II. *Directions:* Apply your knowledge of the medical specialties presented in **Part Two** to do this matching exercise.

A

DOCTOR	SPECIALTY

_____ **1.** nephrologist

_____ **2.** pulmonologist

_____ **3.** anesthesiologist

_____ **4.** ophthalmologist

_____ **5.** radiologist

_____ **6.** dermatologist

_____ **7.** gerontologist

_____ **8.** neurologist

_____ **9.** neonatologist

_____ **10.** pathologist

a. deals with x-rays

b. studies the causes of diseases by examining body organs and tissues

c. specializes in skin diseases

d. specialist in the kidneys and related organs

e. specialist in the nervous system

f. concerned with the lungs and its diseases

g. reduces patients' pain and puts them asleep for surgery

h. specialist dealing with newly born babies

i. specializes in the medical problems of the elderly

j. eye specialist

B

DOCTOR	SPECIALTY

_____ **1.** audiologist

_____ **2.** cardiologist

_____ **3.** gastrologist

_____ **4.** gynecologist

_____ **5.** oncologist

_____ **6.** urologist

_____ **7.** otolaryngologist

_____ **8.** pediatrician

_____ **9.** orthopedist

_____ **10.** obstetrician

a. specialist in diseases of the stomach and digestive organs

b. ear, nose, and throat specialist

c. specialist in the treatment of cancer

d. specialist in the care of women during pregnancy, childbirth, and following childbirth

e. heart specialist

f. specialist in treating disorders or injuries to bones, muscles, ligaments, and joints

g. specialist in the treatment of children's illnesses

h. hearing specialist

i. deals with problems of the urinary tract

j. specialist in the health care of women, especially the reproductive organs

354   Academic Terms   Lesson 53

Copyright © by Houghton Mifflin Company. All rights reserved.

III. *Directions:* Use your understanding of the frequently used medical terms presented in **Part Three** to do this matching exercise.

A

_____ **1.** recumbent
_____ **2.** coagulate
_____ **3.** edema
_____ **4.** asymptomatic
_____ **5.** subcutaneous
_____ **6.** palliative
_____ **7.** rigor mortis
_____ **8.** benign

a. not showing any symptoms of illness
b. harmless, not deadly
c. providing relief but not a cure
d. clot
e. the rigidness of a dead body
f. in a lying-down position
g. under the skin
h. swelling of body tissue with fluid

B

_____ **1.** cyanosis
_____ **2.** hospice
_____ **3.** vertigo
_____ **4.** cognition
_____ **5.** febrile
_____ **6.** malignant
_____ **7.** protocol
_____ **8.** acute

a. mental abilities
b. procedures to be followed under specific circumstances
c. short, severe, or suddenly painful
d. special care of dying patients emphasizing their dignity and the presence of those who love them
e. blue or gray discoloration of the skin due to a lack of oxygen in the blood
f. feverish
g. deadly, harmful
h. dizziness

C

_____ **1.** prognosis
_____ **2.** dementia
_____ **3.** atrophy
_____ **4.** etiology
_____ **5.** remission
_____ **6.** natal
_____ **7.** chronic
_____ **8.** congenital

a. wasting away of muscles or another part of the body
b. lasting a long time
c. pertaining to birth
d. forecast regarding the course and outcome of a disease or injury
e. Alzheimer's disease; progressive decline of mental abilities
f. existing since birth
g. the origins or causes of a disease
h. the subsiding of a disease's symptoms

Copyright © by Houghton Mifflin Company. All rights reserved.

Parts of Speech

1. Adjectives

An **adjective** describes or modifies a noun or pronoun.

Did you see that gray cat?

Two cars were parked in the driveway.

He is tall, dark, and handsome.

Specific suffixes are associated with adjectives, including -able, -ible, -al, -ful, -ous, -ive, and -y:

She is a capable worker.

This is a reversible coat.

We celebrated the national holiday in Alaska.

Martin is a careful driver.

They own a spacious ranch in Wyoming.

The plaintiff is suing for punitive damages as well.

Sharon is cleaning her messy room.

Demonstrative adjectives: these people, this office

Descriptive adjectives: lovely day, pale color

Interrogative adjectives: What program? Whose coat?

Limiting adjectives: three children, several cars

Possessive adjectives: our apartment, my uncle

Proper adjectives: American flag, Canadian imports

Copyright © by Houghton Mifflin Company. All rights reserved.

2. Adverbs

An **adverb** describes or modifies a verb, an adjective, or another adverb.

modifying a verb: Brittany walked quickly to the door.

modifying an adjective: She was extremely happy to get the news.

modifying another adverb: Time went by very slowly.

Adverbs often indicate when, where, how, and to what extent.

when: The Andersons will arrive tomorrow.

where: Steve, place the chair here.

how: The children sang loudly.

to what extent: We were completely bewildered by the news.

Adverbs often end in the suffix -ly, as a number of preceding examples illustrate.

3. Conjunctions

A **conjunction** is a word used to join words or groups of words. There are coordinating, subordinating, adverbial, and correlative conjunctions.

Coordinating conjunctions: and, but, for, nor, or, yet, so

Rain and fog made driving difficult.

We had the day off, but Sheila had to work.

My husband bought a ticket, for he loves that type of music.

Meredith couldn't answer the question, nor could I.

You can have ice cream or pudding for dessert.

Shane had his car repaired, yet it is still giving him trouble.

We were tired, so we didn't attend the ceremony.

Subordinating conjunctions: after, although, because, if, etc.

After they left, the party broke up.

Although it was cloudy, Sandy still got a sunburn.

He refused dessert because he is on a diet.

The game will be played next week if it has to be canceled today.

Adverbial conjunctions: consequently, however, therefore, etc.

Bob never heard from him again; consequently, he rented the apartment to someone else.

Copyright © by Houghton Mifflin Company. All rights reserved.

I knew that he had applied for that position; <u>however</u>, I was surprised that he got it.

Our plane leaves at 6:30 A.M.; <u>therefore</u>, we will have to get up early.

Correlative conjunctions: either-or, neither-nor, not only-but also

I think that <u>either</u> the cat <u>or</u> the dog broke the lamp.

It is clear that <u>neither</u> the owners <u>nor</u> the workers want the strike to continue.

We were <u>not only</u> surprised <u>but also</u> embarrassed by the news.

4. Interjections

An **interjection** is a word or phrase that expresses strong emotion.

<u>Ouch</u>! I've been stung by a bee.

<u>Look out</u>! There's ice on the sidewalk.

5. Nouns

A **noun** is a person, place, or thing.

person: Emily

place: Prince Edward Island

thing: wrench

Common nouns refer to general classes: woman, city, building

Proper nouns refer to particular people, places, or things: Anne, Detroit, Empire State Building

Collective nouns name groups: family, team, class

Concrete nouns name tangible things: rock, flower, table

Abstract nouns name intangible things: idea, bravery, democracy

6. Prepositions

A **preposition** is a word that combines with a noun or pronoun to form a phrase; prepositional phrases generally serve as adjectives or adverbs.

prepositional phrase

Laura mowed the grass [after lunch.]

preposition ↗ ↖ noun

prepositional phrase

We have full confidence [in him.]

preposition ↗ ↖ pronoun

Copyright © by Houghton Mifflin Company. All rights reserved.

These words often function as prepositions:

above	behind	during	from	of	to
before	by	for	in	over	with

7. Pronouns

A **pronoun** is a word used in place of a noun.

noun: <u>Paul</u> is coming home tomorrow.

pronoun: <u>He</u> is coming home tomorrow.

These words are among those that serve as pronouns:

I	he	it	they	themselves	which	these	anybody
you	she	we	myself	who	what	those	somebody

8. Verbs

A **verb** is a word or group of words expressing action or the state of being of a subject.

action verb: Yolanda <u>laughed</u>.

state of being verb: Our guests <u>are</u> here.

A **transitive verb** expresses action and has an object.

Janet <u>set</u> the <u>package</u> on the table.

Wayne <u>flipped</u> the <u>pages</u> of the telephone directory.

An **intransitive verb** does not have an object.

The boy <u>shivered</u>.

The ice and snow <u>melted</u>.

A **linking verb** connects the subject and a complement that renames or describes the subject.

Jamie <u>is</u> the captain.

The clothes <u>seemed</u> inexpensive.

Copyright © by Houghton Mifflin Company. All rights reserved.

An **auxiliary** or **helping verb** combines with other verbs to form phrases.

helping verb
↓
Katherine <u>can paint</u>.

helping verb
↓
The windows <u>were closed</u>.

These words function as auxiliary or helping verbs:

am	been	can	did	does	has	is	might	shall	was
are	being	could	do	had	have	may	must	should	were

Copyright © by Houghton Mifflin Company. All rights reserved.

Using the Dictionary

A dictionary is the best source for learning the precise meanings of words; moreover, it provides other valuable information about words, including their pronunciation, spelling, parts of speech, and origin.

Printed below is the entry for **exonerate** found in the fourth college edition of *The American Heritage Dictionary,* one of the most recommended dictionaries for college students. By becoming familiar with the key parts that have been identified and explained, you will be able to take better advantage of the information a college-level dictionary provides.

```
  A                B       C        D
  |                |       |       /\
ex • on • er • ate (ĭg-zŏn′ ə rāt′) tr.v.  -at • ed,  -at • ing, -ates.
To free from blame. [< Lat. exonerare, to free from a burden.]—ex on er a tion. —ex on er a tive adj.
  |                |                              |
  E                F                              G
```

A. The **entry word** is printed in boldface type and divided into syllables.

B. The **pronunciation** of the word is shown in parentheses, with the pronunciation indicated by specific letters, lines, and symbols. A guide to the pronunciation is generally found in the inside cover of the dictionary as well as at the bottom of every other page.

C. The **parts of speech** of a word are indicated by an abbreviation; parts of speech are commonly abbreviated in this manner:

adj.—adjective   prep.—preposition
adv.—adverb   pron.—pronoun
conj.—conjunction   v.—verb
interj.—interjection   intr. v. (or vi)—intransitive verb
n.—noun   tr.v. (or vt)—transitive verb

See Appendix A for a review of the parts of speech.

D. The **verb tenses** of *exonerate* are provided (exonerat<u>ed</u>, exonerat<u>ing</u>, exonerat<u>es</u>).

E. The word's **definition.** (Keep in mind that a word may have more than one definition, so it is sometimes necessary to select the definition appropriate to the context in which the word is being used.)

Copyright © by Houghton Mifflin Company. All rights reserved.

F. The **etymology** of the word is enclosed in brackets; etymology is concerned with the origin and history of words. In our example, it is disclosed that *exonerate* comes from the Latin word *exonerare,* which means "to free from a burden." The following are typical of the abbreviations used to indicate the language from which a word originated.

OE—Old English, the language spoken in England from the years 700 to 1100
ME—Middle English, the language spoken in England from 1100 to 1500
OF—Old French, the language spoken in France from 800 to 1200
F—French, the language spoken in France today
Lat.—Latin, spoken by the Romans approximately 2,000 years ago
GK—Ancient Greek, spoken in Greece approximately 2,500 years ago

G. **"Relatives"** of the word are indicated; in our example, the noun *exoneration* and the adjective *exonerative* are related to the verb *exonerate*.

Guide words are printed in boldface type at the top of each dictionary page; they indicate the first and last words printed on that particular page. Because words in a dictionary are listed in alphabetical order, the guide words reveal whether the word you are looking for can be found on that particular page. For example, the guide words *exodus* and *expectancy* in *The American Heritage Dictionary* indicate that *exonerate* can be found on that page.

Most college-level dictionaries also include numerous introductory and supplementary pages devoted to a variety of topics like the following:

- Directions for using the dictionary
- Pronunciation guide and other explanatory notes
- Directories and tables of useful information
- Basic manual on grammar, punctuation, and style
- Brief history of the English language
- Biographical entries

Copyright © Houghton Mifflin Company. All rights reserved.

Index for Word Parts

a, 33
able, 33
ac, 163
age, 149
al, 164
algia, 349
ambi, 71
amphi, 71
an, 33
ance, 149
ann, 97
ante, 46
anthrop, 110
anti, 58
arch, 135
arteri, 349
arthr, 349
aster, 123
astro, 123
aud, 84
auto, 45

be, 164
bell, 71
ben, 58
bi, 58
bio, 45
bon, 83
boun, 83

cap, 98
cardi, 349
cent, 136
chron, 34
cide, 136
circum, 150
claim, 164
clam, 164
co, 7
col, 7

com, 7
con, 7
contra, 109
contro, 109
cor, 7
counter, 109
cred, 123

de, 7
dem, 150
derm, 72, 349
dermis, 72
dia, 98
dic, 109
dis, 22
dys, 163

em, 123
en, 123
ence, 149
enn, 97
equ, 46
er, 8
err, 163
eu, 45
ex, 8
extra, 84

fid, 46
fin, 71
fore, 110
ful, 83

gastr, 349
gen, 124
geo, 71
gram, 97
graph, 97
greg, 164

hem, 72, 349
hetero, 98
homo, 98
hydr, 71
hydro, 71
hyper, 58
hypo, 83

ible, 33
ic, 164
il, 7
im, 7
in, 7
inter, 21
intra, 72
intro, 72
ir, 7
ish, 149
ism, 34
ist, 8
itis, 123, 349
ize, 164

leg, 136
less, 72
log, 34
logy, 22
ly, 149

macro, 124
magn, 124
mal, 57
man, 72
medi, 163
meter, 109
metr, 109
micro, 135
mis, 22
mono, 8
mor, 97

mort, 97
multi, 83
my, 349

neo, 83
ness, 98
neur, 349
non, 84

ob, 22
omni, 57
onym, 150
op, 22
or, 8
osteo, 349
ous, 83

pan, 46
path, 58
ped, 135
peri, 123
phil, 57
phleb, 350
phon, 97
photo, 150
pod, 135
polis, 149
poly, 33
port, 135
pos, 97
post, 34
poten, 136
pre, 8
pro, 21
pseud, 124
psych, 109, 350
pulmo, 350

re, 8
rect, 46

scrib, 135
scrip, 135
se, 110
semi, 109
ship, 149
sol, 149
spec, 57
sta, 7
sub, 21
super, 33
sym, 46
syn, 46

tele, 45
temp, 84
ten, 22
terr, 110
the, 124
therm, 110
tion, 22
tomy, 350
tract, 150
trans, 33

ultra, 84
un, 8
uni, 21
urb, 149

ven, 136
vent, 136
ver, 34
vid, 124
vis, 124
voc, 58
vok, 58

ward, 84

Copyright © by Houghton Mifflin Company. All rights reserved.

Index for Challenging Words

Copyright © by Houghton Mifflin Company. All rights reserved.

Index for Academic Terms

acculturation, 245
acquittal, 335
acute, 351
adjudicate, 335
affirmative action, 328
agrarian, 245
alliteration, 213
amendment, 257
amphibians, 275
analogy, 213
anesthesiology, 350
antagonist, 213
anthology, 214
appreciation, 328
appeal, 341
appropriation, 264
arthropods, 275
assets, 321
asymptomatic, 351
atom, 303
atrophy, 351
audiology, 350
audit, 328
autism, 240

bail, 335
balance of trade, 321
bear market, 322
behavior, 233
benign, 351
bibliography, 207
Bill of Rights, 257
binary, 310
bit, 310
body's systems, 281
booking, 335
boycott, 257
branches of
    government, 257
bull market, 322
bureaucracy, 251
byte, 310

canon, 214
capital, 327

cardiac, 282
cardiology, 350
carnivorous, 275
cartel, 329
catalyst, 219, 303
Cenozoic, 289
centrifugal, 297
centripetal, 297
CEO (chief executive
    officer), 327
cerebellum, 282
cerebrum, 282
change of venue, 341
checks and balances,
    258
chromosomes, 269
chronic, 351
circulatory, 281
coagulate, 351
congenital, 351
cognition, 351
cognitive, 233
commodities, 321
commute, 335
compound, 303
concurrent sentencing,
    341
congenital, 282
conglomerate, 328
cognitive, 233
connotation, 207
consecutive sentencing,
    341
context, 219
control group, 233
critique, 226
culpability, 335
culture, 245
cursor, 309
cyanosis, 351

database, 315
decoding, 219
deduction, 227

defendant, 343
deduction, 227
defense mechanisms,
    239
delta, 290
dementia, 351
demography, 245
denotation, 207
depreciation, 328
dermatology, 350
digestive, 281
divestiture, 328
dormant, 269
dorsal, 282
download, 316

edema, 351
ego, 240
electron, 304
element, 303
embargo, 329
eminent domain, 258
empirical, 233
encoding, 219
energy, 297
enunciation, 220
entitlement, 264
entrepreneur, 327
enzymes, 282
ethnic group, 251
ethnocentrism, 251
etiology, 351
executive, 258
experimental group, 234
extradite, 341
extrinsic motivation, 239

fallacies, 226
fauna, 275
febrile, 351
felony, 341
figures of speech, 207
file, 315
filibuster, 263

fiscal, 322
flashback, 214
flora, 275
folkways, 251
fonts, 310
force, 297
foreshadowing, 214
franchise, 327

gastrology, 350
genes, 269
genre, 207
gerontology, 350
gerrymandering, 264
GNP (gross national
    product), 321
golden parachute, 328
gynecology, 350

habeas corpus, 342
habitat, 269
hacker, 315
hardware, 315
herbivorous, 275
homeostasis, 283
hominids, 275
hospice, 351
hybrid, 269
hydraulic, 297
hyperbole, 213
hypothesis, 239

icons, 310
id, 240
igneous rocks, 290
impeachment, 263
impromptu speaking, 220
indict, 336
induction, 227
inertia, 297
inflationary, 322
injunction, 342
inorganic chemistry, 304
Internet, 316

Copyright © by Houghton Mifflin Company. All rights reserved.

intrinsic motivation, 239
introspection, 239
invertebrates, 276

judiciary, 258
jurisprudence, 342

kinesics, 225
kinetic energy, 297

laissez-faire, 258
lame duck, 263
legislative, 257
liabilities, 322
literal, 207
litigants, 343
litigation, 342
lobbyist, 258

magma, 290
malleable, 298
malignant, 351
Malthusian theory, 251
mammals, 275
mass, 298
matriarchal family, 252
medulla oblongata, 282
memory, RAM, ROM, 310
Mendel, Gregor Johann, 269
Mesozoic, 289
metabolism, 283
metamorphic rocks, 290
metaphor, 208
misdemeanor, 342
modem, 310
molecule, 303
monitor, 309
mores, 245
motor skills, 234
mouse, 309

multimedia presentation, 227
mutation, 270

natal, 351
natural selection, 270
neonatology, 350
nephrology, 350
nervous, 282
neurology, 350
neurosis, 240
neutron, 304
noise, 220
nonsexist language, 226
nucleus, 303

objective, 226
obsolescence, 328
obstetrics, 350
omnivorous, 275
oncology, 350
ophthalmology, 350
organic chemistry, 304
organism, 234
orthopedics, 350
oscillate, 298
ossification, 283
otolaryngology, 350

paleontology, 290
Paleozoic, 289
palliative, 351
pathology, 350
patriarchal family, 252
patronage, 264
pediatrics, 350
patronage, 264
peer group, 245
peripheral, 309
perjury, 336
personification, 208
plagiarism, 213
plaintiff, 343
plankton, 276

port, 309
portfolio, 327
potential energy, 297
Precambrian, 289
premise, 225
prognosis, 351
prolific, 270
prose, 208
protagonist, 213
protocol, 352
proton, 304
protoplasm, 283
psychosis, 240
pulmonology, 351

radiology, 351
rapport, 225
ratification, 258
recession, 322
recidivism, 336
reciprocity, 321
recumbent, 352
red herring, 263
referendum, 264
remission, 352
reproductive, 281
reptiles, 276
respiratory, 281
rigor mortis, 352

sanction, 252
satire, 213
search engine, 316
sediment, 290
sedimentary rocks, 290
sedition, 264
sibling, 234
simile, 208
skeletal, 281
social norms, 246
software, 315
solute, 304
solvency, 322
spreadsheet, 315

stalactites, 291
stalagmites, 291
status, 252
stereotype, 246
strata, 291
subcutaneous, 352
subjective, 226
subpoena, 342
superego, 240
synopsis, 214
synthesis, 304

tariff, 329
taxonomy, 276
terminal, 309
theory, 234
therapeutic, 239
topography, 290
tort law, 336
transitions, 225
transpiration, 270

urbanism, 246
urinary, 281
urology, 351
utopia, 252

values, 246
variable, 233
ventral, 282
venue, 219
vertebrates, 276
vertigo, 352
veto, 258
virus, 316
voice
    active, 220
    passive, 220
    speaking, 220

work, 298
World Wide Web, 316

Copyright © by Houghton Mifflin Company. All rights reserved.